Brand Machines, Sensory Media and Calculative Culture

Sven Brodmerkel • Nicholas Carah

Brand Machines, Sensory Media and Calculative Culture

Sven Brodmerkel
Faculty of Society & Design
Bond University
Robina, Queensland, Australia

Nicholas Carah
School of Communication and Arts
University of Queensland
Brisbane, Queensland, Australia

ISBN 978-1-137-49655-3   ISBN 978-1-137-49656-0   (eBook)
DOI 10.1057/978-1-137-49656-0

Library of Congress Control Number: 2016952146

Cover illustration © Jakub Krechowicz / Alamy Stock Photo

Printed on acid-free paper

This Palgrave Macmillan imprint is published by Springer Nature
The registered company is Macmillan Publishers Ltd. London
The registered company address is: The Campus, 4 Crinan Street, London, N1 9XW, United Kingdom

To my parents, in gratitude. (SB)
To Nicola and Felix. (NC)

Acknowledgements

Some of the material used in this book was published in part or in a different form in *Mobile Media and Communication* and *New Media and Society*. We wish to thank these journals for permission to use this work here. A portion of the case study material on XXXX Gold was collected as part of a study funded by the Foundation for Alcohol Research and Education (FARE). Many thanks to FARE for their support of the critical examination of media technologies, which is an important part of the public debate about alcohol. Parts of the fieldwork for this book, particularly travel and attendance at industry conferences, was funded by our institutions, the University of Queensland's Early Career Researcher scheme in the case of Nicholas, and Bond University's Faculty Research Grants in the case of Sven.

Nicholas wishes to thank the University of Queensland's Centre for Critical Cultural Studies and its former colleagues for their support and encouragement over the past years. I am grateful for the opportunity to spend time there and give a public lecture in 2014. This proved instrumental in developing central ideas for the book. Amy Dobson, Zala Volcic, Mark Andrejevic, Gay Hawkins, Fiona Nicoll, Tom O'Regan, Caroline Wilson-Barnao, Natalie Collie, Mallory Peak, Daniel Angus, Pradip Thomas, Eric Louw and Graeme Turner in particular have been wonderful colleagues, interlocutors, collaborators and mentors throughout my time at UQ. Thank you to Gavin Smith too for giving me the opportunity to present this work in a lecture at the Australian National University and Andy Bennett during a Symposium at Griffith University. Much love to Nicola and Felix who come along for the ride on these endeavours, how wonderful our life together is.

Sven is thankful for the encouragement he has received from his colleagues at Bond University's Faculty of Society and Design. He particularly appreciates the support from Dean Raoul Mortley, the intellectual stimulation (and motivation for gym workouts) provided by Jeffrey Brand, Susie Ting's commitment (and patience with a sometimes slightly distracted colleague), Mike Grenby's enthusiasm for all the things that make life enjoyable (and his steady supply of culinary treats), and the lively discussions about advertising and media technologies he had with students during courses and seminars. And, last but most certainly not least, a big hug, kiss and thanks to Karin for her careful management of a sometimes absent-minded and occasionally disgruntled writer, and for now almost 25 years of unwavering support.

INTRODUCTION

In the seventh and final season of *Mad Men*, the critically acclaimed TV series about the fictional advertising agency Sterling Cooper in the 1950s and 1960s, change comes in an unexpected and massive form. The agency acquires an IBM 360, a state-of-the-art mainframe computer the size of a room. While the agency management enthusiastically welcome the computer, the agency's art directors and copywriters are less impressed. In a tellingly symbolic move, the computer is installed in the lounge where the creatives used to meet for brainstorming sessions. Michael Ginsberg, one of the young copywriters, is particularly disturbed by the agency's new acquisition, fearing that this new technology is going to render the agency's creatives superfluous.

The leitmotif of this particular episode is that of technology as a source of symbolic, physical and psychological disruption in the advertising industry. The arrival of the IBM 360 symbolically represents the schism that has characterised the industry and its professional ideology since its early days. While the computer embodies a scientific, data-driven approach to promotional communication, advertising creatives are proponents of an artistic conceptualisation of advertising, based not so much on hard facts but on the their aesthetic sensibilities and tacit cultural knowledge. Ironically, if creatives working in the late 1960s were worried about the computerisation of their craft, their fears have proved to be mostly unwarranted. At that point in time, after a decade of disruption and innovation, the advertising industry was about to enter a period of relative stability in terms of its formation, conceptual definition and practice. Nowadays, however, such concerns are most definitely uppermost with current advertising practitioners. In an interview with the industry publication *Advertising Age*, *Mad Men* director Matthew Weiner said that at the time he conducted research for the premier season of the series (2007) 'there was almost this feeling, as I would write to people in the advertising business, that this show was an elegy to the end of their science, the end of their profession' (Bruell 2015). 'IBM never undermined the Mad Men of the world. But Google and Facebook did', writes the leading technology magazine *Wired* (2014). It points out that 'as advertising has shifted to the internet, more and more of it is being managed not by the Ginsbergs and the Don Drapers, but by techies—engineers, programmers, and others who understand the world of social media sites, real-time ad exchanges, online analytics, and ad targeting systems'. While algorithmic media platforms such as Facebook and Google are the most prominent examples, various additional audience tracking and targeting platforms are also part of the digital media ecosystem. This ecosystem ushers in a computational approach to advertising that carries the potential to render the artistic skills and tacit knowledge of advertising creatives largely obsolete. These platforms hold the promise of 'waste free' advertising—personalised promotional messages delivered in real-time based on extensive behavioural tracking, predictive analytics and machine learning. One example of this approach are M&C Saatchi's artificially intelligent posters. These digital outdoor posters, which hit the streets of London in mid-2015, feature cameras registering and measuring engagement levels of passers-by based on their emotional signals. A 'genetic algorithm' then tests different creative executions (layout, copy text, image, type-font and so on) and either reproduces or kills off ad executions, according to the nature of consumer response. This represents, as the industry magazine *Campaign Brief* writes, 'a Darwinian approach to advertising whereby only the strongest creative executions survive' (Campaign Brief 2015). Some of these 'genes' will 'mutate at random, meaning that the next generation has to naturally improve over time'. As David Cox, Chief Innovation Officer at M&C Saatchi explains:

> This innovation is breaking new ground in the industry because it's the first time a poster has been let loose to entirely write itself, based on what works, rather than just what a person thinks may work. (Campaign Brief 2015)

Although he does not fail to add that he is 'not suggesting a diminished role for creative', this campaign is likely to get advertising creatives worried.

But this is only one of multiple forces that are disrupting the formerly settled advertising landscape. In addition to data-driven advertising, the opportunities social media platforms afford audiences to participate and co-create content is said to have turned formerly passive consumers into active, empowered 'prosumers' (Zwick et al. 2008) who are no longer susceptible to traditional forms of advertising. Thus, the advertising industry appears to be fighting a battle on two fronts, being simultaneously threatened by the computational power of algorithmic media platforms and by a participative and supposedly 'unmanageable' active audience.

Critical accounts over the past decade have begun theorizing advertising and branding in the context of this interactive and computational media system. These accounts tend to focus on either end of the spectrum. On the one side are approaches that understand and theorise brands as lived cultural practices, representing open-ended social relations (Banet-Weiser 2012; Moor 2003; Lury 2009; Arvidsson 2005; Holt 2002). These accounts pay close attention to the ways brands turn the creative capacities of audiences into a valuable resource for their own ends. Participating audiences who share and co-create content enable brands to embed themselves more deeply into the lived cultural practices of consumers and their (online) network of friends. Contrary to earlier critical accounts working exclusively in the tradition of structuralist semiotics and Marxist ideology critique (Barthes 1977; Williamson 1978; Wernick 1991; Goldman 1992), these approaches recognise that letting consumers 'run free' in their meaning making activities and appropriation of cultural texts increases, rather than diminishes, brand value.

At the other end of the spectrum are accounts that critically analyse how digital media platforms and brands utilise the data processing capacities of this media system to collect consumer intelligence, segment audiences and to target consumers with personalised promotional messages (Zwick and Knott 2009; Turow 2012; Couldry and Turow 2014; Andrejevic 2013). The increasingly algorithmic nature of today's media system affords media organisations the opportunity to qualify audiences in ever more specific and fine-grained ways, and to select and deliver content based on these qualifications. Since consumers are often unaware of the criteria that lead to their being sorted into certain segments and being targeted with particular promotional messages (Couldry and Turow 2014; Cheney-Lippold

2011), these accounts draw attention to the power imbalances and the negative societal effects that could follow from the sorting of consumers according to their prospective status as either profitable 'targets' or commercially less valuable 'waste' (Turow 2012). Researchers have also begun to investigate the broader effects of the emerging 'algorithmic culture' (Striphas 2015; Andrejevic et al. 2015; Morris 2015) of a participatory media system. Shifting the focus away from the textual analysis of mass media products and towards the mechanics of automated forms of information processing, these accounts pay close attention to the way the 'work of culture'—the 'sorting, classifying and hierarchizing of people, places, objects and ideas'—is increasingly delegated to computational processes (Striphas 2015: 395). Media power in these accounts is first and foremost a matter of logistics, rather than representation, and therefore not so much ideological, but epistemological (Packer 2013). The impact of what Kittler (1990) identifies as the core functions of media—the collection, storage and processing of data—is likely to become increasingly pronounced in the evolving 'sensor society' (Andrejevic and Burdon 2015) of the so-called 'internet of things'. With ever more elements of the physical environment being turned into *sensory media*, the material background of life becomes an always-on data collector and transmitter.

While both these research fields on the consequences of the commercialised 'digital enclosure' (Andrejevic 2007b) move away from critiquing advertising solely from the perspective of symbolic meaning making, they differ in one fundamental aspect: While the 'culturalist' analysis builds on the active participation of audiences (and to a certain degree even on their advertising savviness and resistance), the 'computational' account implicitly presupposes a rather passive audience. Or, at least, it begins the analysis with the 'products' of participation, namely the data points, and, by extension,– displaces questions about the savvy, ambivalent or other qualities of audience participation. As a consequence, these accounts have so far developed more or less separately from each other.

The first impulse of this book is to bring these two perspectives into a productive dialogue. We argue that to understand advertising and branding in a participatory and data-oriented media system, audience participation and computational media logistics need to be analysed as interrelated phenomena. Audience participation unfolds in a responsive, algorithmic media infrastructure, and brands both shape and adapt to these logics. If brands want to operate successfully in this media system, one of the central requirements is to make consumers visible to calculative online platforms and their algorithms. Thus, they need to activate and coordinate the participatory, creative capacities of consumers in a way that channels them into platforms and makes them available for further activation and computation. This inherently cultural component has so far remained unaddressed in the 'computational' accounts. At the same time, 'culturalist' perspectives have paid little attention to the underlying infrastructure, processes and consequences of what we call *calculative culture*. By this we mean the algorithmic brokering of attention and processing of participation employed by media platforms for calculating, structuring and coordinating the active and—according to the more celebratory accounts—'empowered' consumer. Media platforms are here understood as the calculative architectures into which the data that is produced by consumers is channelled for further processing. Importantly, and central to the argument of this book, this data does not only encompass media texts such as status updates and images uploaded to platforms such as Facebook and Instagram, or the trail of behavioural data people leave behind while surfing the internet, but also the sensations and affects that media technologies can digitise.

As we explain in Chapters 4 and 5, in the developing sensor society (Andrejevic and Burdon 2015) consumers now perform the affective labour of tuning their bodily and social capacities into the computational logic of media platforms. Sensory media enable the harnessing of these affective capacities. In the broadest sense, affect can be understood as a relation where bodies and devices stimulate, move or alter mental and physiological states. In terms of sensory media this means that a sensor-equipped device is capable of detecting, processing and transmitting a spectrum of environmental impulses. This is the case for more conventional sensory media such as, for example, smoke detectors as well as for more sophisticated devices such as wearable fitness trackers. Sensory media are affected by certain stimuli and able to affect technologies connected to it, for example by prompting security alarms (in the case of a smoke detector) or triggering customised messages (as a possible response to data captured and transmitted by a wearable device). Important here is that more and more of these sensory media are tuned to interacting with the affective capacities of the human body. The human body is itself best understood as the ultimate 'sensory medium' (Latour 2004; Durham-Peters 2015b). As Latour (2004: 205; emphasis in original) argues, 'to have a body is *to learn to be affected*, meaning "effectuated", moved, put into motion by other entities, humans or non-humans'. In terms of the human body, affect takes the form of affective practices, which Whetherell (2012: 159) describes as 'the recruitment and often synchronous assembling of multi-modal resources, including, most crucially, body states'. Affective practices pull body capacities, social relations and combinations of narratives into new 'articulations' (Whetherell 2012; Latour 2004). This understanding of affect emphasises the multimodality of affective practices, involving the patterned interaction of bodily reactions to materialised and spatialised contexts as well as 'sedimented social and personal history' and semiotic modes of representing these experiences (Whetherell 2012: 89; 96).

In the argument we develop in this book, this conceptualisation of affect points towards two crucial aspects. First, it stresses that affective practices do not only include humans and their particular psychologies and histories, but also encompass objects, spaces and the built environments. Advertising must be understood not only as a form of abstract textual representation, but as a form of 'biotechnical engagement' (McStay 2013). We discuss this important aspect in greater detail in Chapter 3. Secondly, sensory media now allow for the harnessing of certain embodied components of these affective practices. As a result—as we will illustrate throughout the book—advertisers are beginning to question the industry's focus on the symbolic as the foundation of advertising practice. Instead, they attempt to modulate people's behaviour by means of objects and architectures that act as *affect switches*. We develop this term to conceptualise the material touchpoints between living bodies and computational media systems. Many of the devices advertisers are developing now act as such affect switches, stimulating and translating human action, judgement and affect into data for further modulation. In short, media are turning into body-machine infrastructure. We therefore suggest that in the contemporary media system brands are best conceptualised as *brand machines*. In this understanding, brands are techno-cultural processes—they need to simultaneously perform 'cultural' and 'computational' work by providing the stimuli that prompt required forms of audience participation, which, in turn, make consumers' cultural and affective practices available for subsequent calculation and modulation. Brand machines are therefore based on the production of branded and culturally relevant applications, interfaces and devices that act as, or connect to already existing, infrastructures for the management of attention and action in networks of human relationships. In this mode of branding, 'material assemblages' in form of 'useful' devices, sensor-enabled environments and calculating platforms are becoming increasingly important as the *computational infrastructure* enabling brand machines to perform their work.

In our account, the affective and symbolic co-exist. Symbols can work as affective devices, and affects can be narrated as symbols. The symbolic register emphasises the subject who makes sense of meanings. Symbols are the meeting point in the relationship between a subject and their efforts to make sense of objects or processes in the world. Affects are the transfer point between living bodies and stimuli of all kinds. In the case of branding, symbols comprise instructions that attempt to govern associations and 'calls to action'. Where we focus on brands operating in the affective register, we emphasise the capacity of digital devices to sense and stimulate our bodies' movements, physiology, and mood. Where a symbolic account is concerned with how a subject makes meaning, an affective account is located in the effort to examine how bodily capacities of all kinds are apprehended and modulated by both other humans and non-human devices. In an increasingly sensor-equipped environment, media no longer primarily mediate our senses; rather, they mediate 'sensibility itself' (Hansen 2012: 54).

As a consequence, brands no longer rely so much on consumers buying into fixed brand narratives, be they of the authoritative kind that dominated advertising up until the mid-1950s, or in form of postmodern reflexive irony, which has characterised much of the advertising since its so-called 'creative revolution' in the 1960s (Holt 2002; Vargo and Lusch 2004; Foster 2008; Turner 2010). The interactive media environment provides the infrastructure that allows brands to build immersive and reflexive activation platforms that implicate the participating consumer into marketing activities that rely less on symbolic or ideological forms of persuasion than on their capacity to assemble and modulate affects and social relations. Brands therefore now increasingly create 'affective events' based on cross-media activations that utilise data and predictive analytics.

Contemporary advertising works at the intersection between data, the cultural-symbolic and (media) materiality. Consequently, critical analyses of contemporary advertising and branding need to pay closer attention to the question of how advertising, consumer participation and technology are interrelated in creating and facilitating lived experiences that create value for brands. The central argument we develop and illustrate in this book is that contemporary advertising increasingly works by eliciting, structuring and calculating consumer engagement. Our account will take consumer participation and its interconnectedness with calculative media platforms as the fundamental aspect of contemporary advertising. This is the vantage point for an approach to critiquing advertising and branding that responds to the way brands shape and adapt to a participatory and algorithmic media system.

CHAPTER OUTLINE AND APPROACH

The book is broadly structured into two parts. The first three chapters analyse the production context of contemporary advertising, with a particular focus on the way the advertising industry discursively re-imagines its practice and the contemporary consumer in the face of 'digital disruption'. We follow McFall (2004) in her argument that understanding advertising as a promotional practice as well as a societal institution requires research that pays attention to the production context of the promotional material (in terms of institutional, organisational and legal possibilities and constraints), the technological affordances available, and the interrelation between the way advertising practitioners conceive of themselves and their practice and the promotional material they produce based on this professional ideology.

The second part of the book, Chapters 4, 5 and 6, firstly illustrate in detail how advertising has become a practice focused on the development and utilisation of material devices and media infrastructures and, secondly, contextualise these practices from the perspective of recent critical accounts of brands and branding.

In **Chapter** 1 we start with analysing the interdependent relationship between the advertising industry and a media system that is increasingly characterised by the incorporation of audience participation into its mode of operation. Advertising has always been embedded within and shaped formations of media technologies and cultural practices. What is distinctive about the contemporary media system is the increasing incorporation of interactive, mobile and social media technologies into the production and distribution of content. Audiences are encouraged to engage in simultaneous multi-screen media consumption, to actively participate in the development, mediation and distribution of media texts and to mediate everyday life activities via mobile and interactive technologies. These activities are all subject to surveillance and big data analytics, which allows for the further customisation of content and activation of audiences, often in real time. This chapter analyses how the advertising industry is responding to the challenges posed by the participatory media environment and the algorithmic logic imposed by Google, Facebook and other key players in this system.

In **Chapter 2** we trace how the advertising industry conceptualises its own practice. We investigate the professional ideology of advertising practitioners and associated industry rituals. We use a method of critical industrial research drawing on ethnographic observation at industry events and the analysis of relevant industry publications and online resources. This method is aided by a proliferation of industry resources and discourses online. Industry presentations, key notes and panels are often published on the websites of advertising agencies and circulated on online platforms such as YouTube or Slideshare. These resources offer a rich account of how the industry 'theorises' contemporary issues and practices. The guiding question examined is how the advertising industry strategises marketing communications in the context of the interactive media environment and in relation to an imagined savvy and knowing audience. We investigate how the participatory media environment has affected advertising practitioners' notions of creativity and consumer agency and how these conceptualisations fundamentally change the industry's working understanding of what 'advertising' is and how it works. Throughout the chapter we explain and illustrate the key components of this new conceptualisation, which we call the 'participation paradigm'.

Chapter 3 focuses on the advertising industry's discursive construction of a version of the 'empowered consumer' that conforms to the central premises of this participation paradigm. We argue that, by drawing on central arguments regarding the fundamental nature of the human mind proposed by the neuro-sciences and behavioural economics, advertisers construct the consumer as simultaneously empowered and cognitively impaired. While considered to be savvy with regard to symbolic advertising appeals, these cognitive biases open up opportunities for steering consumers on the behavioural level by means of prompts and 'nudges'. Echoing moral justifications promoted by 'libertarian paternalists', who in recent years have gained influence in policy-making circles in the UK, USA and elsewhere, advertisers use the notion of the psychological flawed human being for promoting their craft as a valuable tool for consumers' self-responsibilisation in a 'neoliberalism after markets' (Boeckler and Berndt 2012).

In **Chapter 4** we demonstrate why much contemporary advertising and branding should be understood as a 'field of attention, attraction and affect', something which is 'experienced in a lived and embodied place, time, field of movement and action' (McStay 2013: 4). The guiding question examined is how contemporary branding utilises advertising practices based on the synergy between material devices and real-world engagement. We develop the concept of the affect switch to conceptualise the relationship between consumers and these devices. We pay particular attention to advertisers' experimentation with these devices for two reasons. First, we argue that these innovations represent the early indicators of a possible future trajectory of advertising in an interactive media environment, envisaging a mode of operation focussed on harnessing and modulating consumer engagement in an open-ended fashion. Secondly, these experiments with bespoke devices are in our view rich and instructive examples that illustrate our conceptualisation of consumer engagement as *calculative participation*. Consumers' creative mediations of their lives address other humans, but at the same time also the algorithmic logic of media platforms.

In **Chapter 5** we continue our conceptualisation of audience activity as 'calculative participation' by discussing how this orchestration of consumer action generates brand value. We critically engage with and advance the relevant literature on branding and brand value creation (Holt 2002; Moor 2003; Lury 2004; Arvidsson 2005; 2006; McStay 2011; 2013). In particular, we extend the notion of audience labour (Smythe 1981) by illustrating how the emerging mode of branding we are describing harnesses audience activity beyond the 'work of watching' (Smythe 1981) and 'being watched' (Andrejevic 2002). The focus of this chapter is thus on investigating the various and specific ways brand machines utilise the participatory media environment for making the active consumer productive.

In **Chapter 6** we discuss the implications of this mode of branding with regard to the possibilities of resistance and regulation. While media and cultural studies have moved beyond a solely textual critique of advertising, especially in work on mediatisation, they remain influential in a variety of important settings. Popular and public discussions from both journalists and activists almost exclusively focus on the representational power of advertising. Popular news commentary still regularly invokes 'moral panics' about the ideas presented in advertising and their effect on vulnerable consumers. Activists often respond to advertising on the basis of the way it represents gender, sexuality or other aspects of our identities. And, importantly, regulatory codes and frameworks remain fundamentally grounded in a representational understanding of advertising.

We argue however that ideological-representational explanations of how advertising works in culture and creates value for brands are no longer fit for understanding much of the contemporary, digitally mediated advertising landscape. We illustrate this argument by analysing how alcohol brands activate and engage with consumers via experiential multi-media marketing. Alcohol brands are a particularly instructive example, since most regulatory and self-regulatory regimes prohibit the use of many of the commonly used 'semiotic seductions'. For instance, alcohol ads must not depict people under the age of 25 (which would be the main target audience for most alcohol brands) and they must not associate the consumption of alcohol with social or sexual success. Thus, a close analysis of alcohol brands' promotional activities provides an ideal area for developing an account of how specific representations alone don't account for how brands create value as cultural processes embedded deeply into the mediation of everyday life. Crucially, this chapter goes beyond accounts that think of consumer participation only in terms of the production of content. Using contemporary cases we examine how alcohol brands operate as brand machines, orchestrating consumer relationships and actions in the world as much as they produce content and data. The conceptualisation of advertising and branding developed in this book is thus not only relevant for advancing the critical scholarly debate on commercial communication and culture, but also significant in outlining the challenges a participatory and data-driven media and marketing system poses for the regulation of advertising and social life in general.

We **conclude** the book by drawing together the different cases and themes discussed in the book to reiterate our fundamental claims, that, in the contemporary participatory media environment, brands function as *techno-cultural* processes; and, that the construction of brand value in this digital enclosure depends less on getting the audience to 'believe' in certain representations, but on getting consumers to act and participate in brand-infiltrated mediations of everyday life.

CONTENTS

CHAPTER 1

Intrusions: Managing Disruption

One would be hard pressed to find an industry that appears to revel so enthusiastically and exhaustively in the possibility of its own demise as the advertising industry. A case in point is a short video called 'The Last Advertising Agency on Earth' produced by Saatchi & Saatchi Canada for the FITC Design & Technology Festival 2010. In this short pseudo-documentary the viewer is guided through the empty offices of a fictitious advertising agency that has been abandoned after a 'catastrophe' put it out of business. The 'catastrophe' the video's narrator is referring to is the rise of the active consumer, which caught advertisers off guard. Instead of adapting to the new realities, this agency (like so many others, we are led to assume) stuck to its routine of producing traditional mass media advertising and adhered to its stereotypical 'creative' workplace culture characterised by 'playing foosball', the consumption of speciality coffees and the overriding impulse to care more about winning advertising awards than solving the clients' business problems. In the end, the narrator explains, all agencies disappeared, owing to 'arrogance, ignorance, and because they chose to ignore the changes that were going on all around them'.

The widely shared and discussed (see, Burrowes 2010; Garfield 2010; Hoffman 2010) video is—like many of the industry's pronouncements of its impending demise or the death of particular media formats and advertising tactics—as much a reflection of real concerns as it is part of advertising agencies self-promotional discourse. The expected 'death' of the TV spot is a particular popular topic within the industry (Hoffman 2011). On the one hand, with videos like these, agencies attempt to position

© The Author(s) 2016
S. Brodmerkel, N. Carah, *Brand Machines, Sensory Media and Calculative Culture*, DOI 10.1057/978-1-137-49656-0_1

themselves as cutting edge and, most importantly, nurture the impression that only they possess privileged insights into the changing nature of the media and communication landscape. On the other hand, though, videos like these are an expression of the industry's increasing insecurity regarding its purpose and standing in the field of marketing and promotional communication.

An instructive example of this struggle to arrive at a common understanding of the function and role of advertising and the advertising industry in the 21st century was the MIXX conference held by the Interactive Advertising Bureau (IAB) in New York in September 2013. The conference theme asked industry thought leaders to redefine what the term 'advertising' stands for. According to IAB President and CEO Randall Rothenberg this 'very simple question' was now 'at the centre of an ideological war in our industry' (IAB 2013a). He then summarised the key themes over which this war was fought. Depending on who you asked, advertising was and had to be predominantly 'social', 'mobile', 'a utility', a 'liquid cross-media' experience, or something else altogether (IAB 2013a). The collection of answers provided by the high-profile conference attendees reflected and reinforced the rupture within the industry's self-identity that has characterised it almost from the very beginning—the battle between proponents of the view that advertising is 'art' and supporters of the view that advertising is 'science'. For example, for Brian King, Global Brand Officer of Marriott International, advertising was 'art that drives commerce', and for Colleen DeCourcy, Global Co-Executive Creative Director of the agency network Wieden + Kennedy, it was 'magic' (IAB 2013b). In contrast, Martin Sorrell, CEO of the world's largest advertising holding company WPP, responded to the conference theme by saying

> I hear you use the word advertising and that I don't like. [...] It's not advertising. It's not an art anymore. It's a science, and it's much broader than advertising. (Kapko 2013)

As Randall Rothenberg, president and CEO of the IAB writes in an article for *Adweek*, 'digital technologies have put the very definition of advertising and marketing up for grabs', so that 'the definition of advertising has never been more unclear' (Rothenberg 2013).

Leading advertising practitioners admit that the industry is undergoing fundamental change. For example, Martin Sorrell argues 'the web has changed our industry just as fundamentally as it has changed society at large' (Sorrell 2014a). John Gutteridge, CEO of JWT Australia & New

Zealand agrees: 'The digital revolution has disrupted the Ad industry over the last decade at a speed few would have predicted' (Rietbroek 2014). And Jeff Goodby from the iconic agency Goodby, Silverstein and Partners is nostalgic for a time when advertisers still did things that were 'big and famous' instead of having to adapt to digital 'content delivery systems' (Marshall and Vranica 2015). To him, the 2015 instalment of the Cannes Lions International Festival of Creativity (the advertising industry's most prestigious awards ceremony) appeared more like an 'industrial roofing convention' than the world's leading award show for advertising creativity (Marshall and Vranica 2015).

Media industries form a complex, interrelated ecosystem that is responsive to environmental changes. Like all the other actors in this ecosystem, advertising agencies need to adapt to changing socioeconomic circumstances, new regulatory regimes, cultural shifts and—most importantly—new media technologies (Noll 2006; Napoli 2011). When Randall Rothenberg writes that advertisers were never more uncertain about their profession, this implies not only that the industry is currently undergoing a considerable restructuring, but also that there was a time when the advertising industry was more assured about its purpose and position in the media environment. It is no coincidence that the critically acclaimed US TV show *Mad Men* tells the story of the fictitious advertising agency Sterling Cooper from the 1950s up to the early 1970s. Within the contemporary advertising industry, theses two decades are commonly regarded—even mythologised—as the 'Golden Era' of advertising. The reasons for this are twofold. First, at the end of the 1960s the media environment had achieved a state of mutual accommodation between the 'triumvirate' of corporate marketers, media companies and advertising agencies. Secondly, at around the same time the advertising industry underwent the so-called 'creative revolution'—a pivotal reconceptualisation of the way advertising was imagined to work on consumers. Thus, during these years the advertising industry developed a stable professional ideology and *raison d'être*. This stability is a thing of the past. The advertising industry is indeed undergoing a significant restructuring, which impacts on existing industry formations, the professional ideology of advertising practitioners, the conceptualisation of the nature and purpose of advertising as a marketing tool and, ultimately, on the practice of advertising itself.

The purpose of the first two chapters of this book is to outline these disruptions and the advertising industry's response to the disintermediating processes of an increasingly algorithmically driven media system. We do this by situating contemporary developments in advertising practice within

the trajectory of the integrated relationship between corporate marketers, media companies and advertising agencies. In this chapter we begin
our discussion by locating the current reconceptualisation of advertising
in the context of the shifting economic logic of the 'audience marketplace' in the digital media environment and the related move to redefine
marketing as 'value co-creation' between marketers and consumers. Both
these processes require 'engaged' consumers. But contrary to all the hype
surrounding the notion of 'consumer engagement', the participating and
(supposedly) 'empowered' consumer is neither a new phenomenon, nor
does it constitute a problem for the advertising industry. We argue that the
trope of the 'empowered consumer' is rather a discursive effect that tends
to be promulgated most intensively at critical junctures: when advertisers
are developing new means for managing the open-ended meaning-making
processes of consumer culture. Algorithms play a key role in this process.
As we will highlight in this chapter and throughout the book, advertisers are becoming skilful in deploying algorithms and bespoke devices as
part of the broader project of producing brands that operate as 'brand
machines' and, ultimately, for future proofing advertising as a business.

Reconfiguring Media Audiences

In the 1950s a fundamental shift took place in the way the business of
broadcasting was conducted. Until then marketers had bought airtime
by the hour and advertising agencies had produced the sponsored pro-
gramme. But after a rigged quiz show and a subsequent investigation by
the US Federal Communications Commission had brought the sponsorship model into disrepute, the broadcast networks began to supply the
programmes themselves and started selling TV or radio-spots to advertisers (Sinclair 1987, 2012). By 1970, schedule and spot advertising had
almost completely replaced the sponsorship model. This reorientation
of the broadcast business model fundamentally changed the relationship
between corporate marketers, media companies and advertising agencies
(Sinclair 2012). The switch to selling short advertising spots required a
much more sophisticated approach to audience measurement, since marketers needed to be ensured that their ads were reaching a sufficient size
and segment of the audience. At the same time it increased the importance
of strategically sound media planning and buying. And, last but not least,
it put additional emphasis on the creative execution of the TV and radio
advertisements.

In response, advertising agencies transformed themselves into so-called 'full-service' agencies, acting as the intermediary between media companies, marketers and consumers. The advertising agency's role as intermediary had several dimensions. First, agencies acted as intermediaries between marketers and media companies in that they offered marketers the most cost-efficient way of securing and buying the limited media time available in traditional broadcast media. Secondly, advertising agencies regarded themselves as intermediaries between advertisers and consumers by providing marketers with intelligence about audiences that went beyond the market research conducted by publishers and marketers themselves. And, thirdly, they provided what agencies always promoted as their core competency: translating marketing objectives into creative ideas for promotional communication. Thus, these traditional 'full-service agencies' featured an account management team responsible for managing client relationships and the day-to-day business of the agency, account- and brand planners for conducting and interpreting market and consumer research, media planners and buyers, and the creative department, mainly comprising designers and copywriters.

An additional important consequence of the move away from the sponsorship model was the way it stabilised the advertising industry's business model by preserving agencies' revenue basis. Since the early days of their existence, advertising agencies were in a peculiar position: they were working for marketers, but used to be paid by the media. The first advertising agencies were solely in the business of buying media space from publishers in bulk and selling it to marketers, for which they received a commission from the newspapers (which ranged between 10 % and 15 %). The shift towards spot advertising preserved this revenue model despite the fact that it had put advertising agencies in the ambiguous position of being the 'agent' for the marketers but being paid by the media. This also meant that agencies had no incentive to introduce remuneration models that would make marketers pay for the consumer research, strategic planning and the creative work agencies produced. In other words, agencies refrained from putting a price on what they claimed was their main contribution to the marketing process—the creative ideas that would (to use industry vernacular) 'build the client's brand', 'break through the clutter' and 'resonate with the target audience'. The commission system was institutionally connected to an accreditation system. In Australia, for instance, agencies were required to be formally accredited by the Media Council of Australia. Since the media only paid commissions to accredited agencies, they de facto controlled and protected the field for the agencies it approved (Sinclair 1987). This system, which remained in place until the 1980s, favoured larger agencies and contributed to the growing trend of agency mergers. In short, at the end of the 1960s corporate marketers, media and advertising agencies had established a comfortable equilibrium: the media produced content that would attract audiences to which they would sell access via agencies who would act as relatively unchallenged intermediaries.

Thus, in the pre-digital media environment, the 'attention economy' (Goldhaber 1997; Davenport and Beck 2001; Crogan and Kinsley 2012) was predicated on media companies striving to maximise the number of audience members being exposed to media content. Consequently, 'exposure' served as the main currency used in the audience marketplace and the key analytical orientation for configuring the 'institutionally effective audience' (Ettema and Whitney 1994)—the specific, discursively constructed definition of the audience that serves the needs of the media industry.

The interactive capacities of the new media environment, however, have disrupted the comfortable equilibrium between the media industry's central players. The key drivers of this disruption are audience fragmentation and audience autonomy (Napoli 2011). In the digital media environment an ever-increasing array of content is provided across a multiplying set of content distribution platforms, disintegrating 'mass' audiences into clusters of narrowly defined niche audiences. As a consequence, audiences gain autonomy with regard to the process of media consumption. This dynamic renders simple 'exposure' metrics unsuitable and unsustainable. Audience fragmentation makes traditional exposure metrics difficult to generate and unreliable. At the same time, the interactive capacities of the digital media environment allow for the systematic gathering, aggregation and analysis of information about previously concealed dimensions of audience behaviour, shifting the strategic goal of many marketing campaigns from achieving maximum reach for the promotional content to precision-targeting of only the desirable audience members. In the interactive media economy all players are drawn into an 'information war', as Omar Tawakol, CEO of the data broker BlueKai, observes (quoted in Suich 2014). Chris Babel, the former Chief Business Officer at Google agrees, arguing that media companies are engaged in a race to have the best data and to become the leading 'intelligence broker' (quoted in Suich 2014). Thus, in the engagement economy of the digital media environment it is not exposure and spectatorship that is of central importance to publishers as well as marketers, but the amount and nature of audience participation (Bucher 2012). This naturally changes the criteria for success for media content—be it journalistic articles or advertising campaigns.

The interrelated dynamics of audience fragmentation and audience autonomy lead to a post-exposure audience marketplace (Napoli 2011) in which traditional, exposure-based approaches to conceptualising audiences are inadequate. Instead, measures like content preferences, degrees of engagement, appreciation of content and other, even more granular, dimensions of feedback gain importance and often replace 'exposure' as the industry's currency. This for instance prompts continuing efforts to turn passive media channels into participatory platforms by means of QR codes, audio tagging or similar technologies. The aim is to engage audiences in multiscreen advertising experiences, mostly centred on second-screen apps featuring integrated consumer monitoring technologies. Similar to attempts by media publishers to provide technologies that direct and transfer audiences from 'traditional', analogue media to related digital spaces where viewers can socialise, advertisers now need to ensure that the attention consumers pay to promotional content is translated into forms of 'engagement' that allow for the capture of sentiment, affect and consumer creativity. Imperative here is the 'fanification' of audiences (Lee and Andrejevic 2014)—the cultivation of an ideal viewer who is emotionally engaged, socially networked and happy to amplify advertising messages. Paradigmatic for the commercial logic of the post-exposure audience marketplace are the efforts to quantify the effectiveness of advertisements running during the Super Bowl, the premier sports event in the USA. With a price tag of about US $4.5 million for a 30-second advertising slot, the need to justify such expense is high—hence the increasing scope of the annual ritual of post-game advertising performance analysis. Among other metrics, ads are now rated and ranked according to pre-viewing ad traffic (in cases where the ads were pre-released on social media platforms), the amount of social media activity they generated on the various social media platforms, the social media sentiment the ads elicited, the ads that were shared the most, the number of related online searches the spots generated and which ads caused DVR-using TV viewers to fast forward or rewind the recording. For example, in the 2015 Super Bowl Budweiser produced the most shared ad across Facebook, Twitter and blogs (Shields and Marshall 2015). The spot also garnered the most Twitter mentions and the hashtag with the most impressions. The 'Like a Girl' campaign by the P&G brand Always drove the highest positive sentiment across social media mentions, and the spot for the Lexus RC 350 generated a surge in online searches of more than 1,800 % (Shields and Marshall 2015). The 'With Dad' ad by Nissan saw the largest international reach with more than 55 % of its buzz coming from outside the USA, while Avocados of Mexico saw the highest social buzz growth compared to an average day with an increase of 3000 % (Perez 2015).

Another example of these new and finely grained forms of rationalising audience understanding (Napoli 2011) is Facebook's 'brand awareness optimisation'. By this Facebook refers to a data-driven post-exposure protocol providing marketers with information on people who spend 'quality time viewing a newsfeed, video or display promo' (Heine 2015). This 'quality time' is calculated by comparing users' viewing patterns of a specific content item with their previous engagement with similar items. Thus, Facebook does not only provide marketers with individual ad-recall predictors, but also allows marketers to target their ads to users with similar viewing patterns.

The comprehensive and integrated functionalities of platforms such as Facebook—acting simultaneously as audience information system (Napoli 2011), media publisher and advertising platform—constitute a serious challenge for advertising agencies. The more value marketers put on data and on one-on-one, real-time engagement with consumers, the higher the danger for advertising agencies to lose their role as intermediaries between marketers and media companies. Traditionally, advertising agencies have acted as consultants and middlemen not only between marketers and the so-called 'legacy media' such as TV networks or newspaper publishers, but also between marketers and data-rich digital media companies such as Facebook, Twitter and Google. However, the more elaborate and finely tuned the advertising solutions offered by social media companies and algorithmically driven programmatic buying platforms become, the more likely it is for marketers to bypass advertising agencies and deal with these technology providers directly. The term 'programmatic buying' refers to the automated, computer-led buying and placement of online advertising inventory (Kontrowitz 2015).

The technicalities of digital advertising open up specialised areas of business (the generation, placement, distribution, measurement and general management of online advertisements as well as research, analysis and trading in ad inventory), and various players are now competing to occupy central positions in the new digital space between the agencies and the Internet (Sinclair 2012: 62). This market is currently however highly concentrated. According to a report by the media buying agency Zenith Optimedia (which is part of the Publicis Group), the revenue of only five players—Google, Facebook, Baidu, Yahoo and Microsoft—represents 68 % of all digital advertising spending. As the report states: 'Power in the digital advertising market is concentrated in the hands of a few large platforms, and is becoming even more concentrated' (ZenithOptimedia 2015). Based on media revenues as a measurement, Google is the world's largest media owner, 136 % bigger than the second-placed Walt Disney Company (ZenithOptimedia 2015). This market dominance puts advertising agencies and their holding companies in the uncomfortable position of having to cooperate with their main competitors. For instance, WPP's Martin Sorrell frequently refers to Google as the industry's 'frenemy' (Sorrell 2014b). However, as Sinclair (2012: 62) comments, 'WPP needs Google much more than Google needs WPP'. The numbers are telling. The combined 2014 revenue of all US advertising agencies of US $43.6 billion (Johnson 2014) represents only two-thirds of the US $66 billion revenue Google reported for 2014 (Google 2015b).

Consequently, if advertising agencies want to stay competitive, they need to be able to navigate this technological and highly data-driven landscape. Therefore it is not surprising that Martin Sorrell wants WPP to be seen as a 'data company'. In 2013, at the Interactive Advertising Bureau's MIXX conference he explicitly stated:

> I don't like the word advertising. It suggests the legacy approach of media and art, not science. We want to be as aggressive in the science part of the business as we can possibly be. We've moved on from the days of Mad Men. (Marshall 2013)

Similarly, Maurice Levy, CEO of Publicis Group, the world's third largest advertising holding company, explained Publicis' strategic goal in 2014 by saying that 'we will be much more an internet company than an advertising group' (Campaign 2014). He emphasised Publicis' early and ongoing investment in technological solutions for marketing and the growing importance of 'including consulting, technology, data and algorithmic models in an alchemy that is powered by creativity' (Jewish Business News 2014).

Algorithms in particular are a double-edged sword for the industry: While on the one hand advertising agencies are forced to adapt to the algorithmic logic of media platforms such as Google and Facebook, on the other hand they provide the industry with ways for managing the open-ended nature of meaning making characterising the postmodern consumer culture. Technology, data and algorithms have indeed become an important means for addressing what advertisers perceive as the 'decline of symbolic efficiency'.

Symbolic Inefficiency

The second defining feature of advertising's 'Golden Era' was that during this time the so-called 'creative revolution' swept through Madison Avenue and beyond—a formative reconceptualisation of the role of advertising in the marketing process and in society, which gained dominance over competing models and still informs industry culture and practice today. Since its early days, the advertising industry had to legitimise itself and make a case for its relevance and positive contribution to the marketing process (Slater 2011; Cronin 2004a). In fact, advertising's legitimacy depended on arguing that it was not part of the 'normal' commercial practice of marketing, but worked by deploying knowledge unavailable to marketing practitioners (Slater 2011). Motivated and fuelled by an increasing social mobility of consumers in the growing middle class of the 1950s and the developing countercultural critique of mass society in the 1960s, advertisers increasingly argued that advertising's main contribution to marketing was cultural rather than commercial—by replacing market processes with psychological technologies. Advertising promised 'to achieve normal business goals (sales volume, price premiums, profit) but not through normal business means' (Slater 2011: 26). Instead, advertisers' claim of privileged access to psychological and cultural knowledge was increasingly used as a legitimisation strategy. By the end of the 1960s these claims had congealed into a conceptualisation of advertising that favoured artistically minded, creative, intuitive and sometimes even ironic and self-reflexive 'artwork' over technical, rational, benefit-focused sales messages. The predominant view was that effective advertising was about the management of symbols (Schwarzkopf 2009), constituting a 'technology of meanings and desires' (Slater 2011: 32).

This carefully curated professional ideology attracted the interest of cultural theorists who, following Bourdieu's (1984) seminal analysis of taste and consumption, argued that advertising professionals occupy a privileged position as mediators between the business imperatives of producers and the desires of consumers. In these accounts, advertising practitioners are regarded as 'cultural intermediaries', 'specialists in symbolic production' (Featherstone 1991: 35), who channel taste and consumption practices based on their expert knowledge of taste cultures and the symbolic meaning of products. As 'cultural intermediaries', advertising practitioners act as guides for consumers in their attempts to navigate the increasingly complex cultural landscape. They qualify goods and mediate taste and consumption practices by way of 'subtle techniques of domination'—the manipulation of consumers' needs through symbolic meaning making and 'slyly imperative advice' (Bourdieu 1984: 310) on appropriate lifestyles for them to emulate.

Advertiser's role as symbolic meaning makers was also the focal point of critical research into advertising. Inspired by Marxist ideology critique and structural semiotics—and fuelled by a concern about the industry's use of psychoanalytical concepts for discovering consumers' unacknowledged desires—these critical accounts regarded advertising as a critical force in the perpetuation of the capitalist system (Leymore 1975; Ewen 1976; Williamson 1978; Vestergaard and Schroeder 1985; Haug 1986; Wernick 1991; Goldman 1992; Goldman and Papson 1996). Advertising, according to the central attack of these critics, artificially created exchange value by associating commodities with 'mythic qualities' (Williamson 1978). In the view of Goldman (1992: 2), the meaning-transference from the pre-commercial lifeworld onto formerly meaningless, undifferentiated mass-produced commodities produces 'commodity signs' and thereby reproduces 'the material and ideological supremacy of commodity relations'. Advertising was therefore conceptualised as a process of symbolic manufacture that creates and perpetuates an ideological system of 'a commodity defined self-fetishization' (Ewen 1976: 47). Consequently, advertisers were portrayed as powerful 'Hidden Persuaders' (Packard 1957) and 'Captains of Consciousness' (Ewen 1976), so much so that the industry publication *Advertising Age* recommended 'advertising people should read Mr. Ewen's book, if only to discover how powerful, how elitist, how successful they really are'.[1]

Given the almost exclusive focus on advertising's representational practices, the history of advertising is commonly written as one of ever-increasing persuasive sophistication. This evolutionary process is seen as resulting from the ongoing battle against an ever-accelerating decline of symbolic efficiency caused by consumers becoming increasingly advertising-savvy (Leiss et al. 2005; Holt 2002; for a critique see McFall 2004; Schwarzkopf 2009). For instance, Holt (2002) proposes a dialectical theory of consumer culture and branding, suggesting that consumer culture and the strategies used by marketers to exploit consumers are characterised by dialectical tensions: marketers try to push marketing and branding paradigms to the limit, while consumers over time become more and more knowledgeable and reflexive regarding established promotional strategies. These contradictions between consumer culture and the branding paradigm impel, as Holt (2002) argues, institutional shifts in both. While the 'modern branding paradigm' (up to the 1960s) was based on the belief that marketers could engineer culture and prescribe consumer lifestyles, the birth of the postmodern consumer culture in the 1960s required a different approach. Instead of trying to dictate meaning, brands learned that the resistant, sceptical consumer of the counterculture was a valuable source for product innovation and brand differentiation if let 'run free'. Important for brands was only that consumers' meaning-making activities were channelled through brands. Bill Bernbach's 'creative revolution' is epitomised as the key moment in the history of modern advertising because it imagined consumers not as passive recipients of marketing messages, but as active, savvy and—at times—cynical and resistant. Advertising and branding worked not because consumers were duped by an all-embracing marketing complex, but because it structured the symbolic and cultural landscape of people's everyday lives. The main challenge for advertisers in dealing with the developing postmodern consumer culture was, as Holt (2002) argues, to appear authentic—a feat that advertisers tried to achieve by representing brands as being removed from commercial agendas and by co-opting subcultural values and emerging cultural contradictions. The symbolic means and rhetorical techniques advertisers turned to in their attempts to appeal to the savvy, postmodern consumer were irony, reflexivity and intertextuality (Holt 2002, 2004; Leiss et al. 2005). Irony and the reflexive acknowledgement of advertising's commercial intentions in particular became popular techniques to distance brands from the 'hard sell' of overt persuasion attempts. However, as Holt (2002) notes, by the end of the 1990s the postmodern branding paradigm had run into a dead end because consumers had become used to these authenticity appeals. What once worked to set brands apart had turned into clichéd advertising convention.

The widespread adoption of the Internet in general and social media in particular is being framed as an even more disruptive challenge. It has become a widely held and propagated conviction that the Internet is not only a facilitator of complete transparency, but also a tool for consumer empowerment vis-à-vis marketers. For instance, Stanford University economist

Itamar Simonson and marketing consultant Emanuel Rosen are among the latest proponents of the view that the World Wide Web in general and social media in particular bring about 'an age of nearly perfect information' (Simonson and Rosen 2014). For the first time in history, they argue, consumers have the tools to assess the absolute value of things instead of having to rely on relative evaluations such as brand images and advertising.

The advertising industry appears to have enthusiastically adopted these narratives. Saatchi & Saatchi's video epitaph is probably the most entertaining illustration of the advertising industry's eagerness to nurture and reinforce the idea that traditional advertising has run its course. Nowhere is this self-reflexive scepticism towards symbolic, representational forms of commercial communication more obvious than in the way the industry constructs Generations Y and Z as 'the inherently empowered human "products" of an interactive media environment' (Serazio 2015: 4). Young people are, as the industry discourse never tires to reiterate, 'increasingly savvy at deflecting disruptive advertising' (Razorfish 2015), 'much savvier than their parents were at their age', and confident that 'they have the capacity to help a brand succeed or fail' (Havas Worldwide 2014). And according to a widely shared survey result by the US marketing firm The McCarthy Group, almost 85 % of young people do not 'respond to traditional advertising strategies' any more (Doyle 2015). Arguing along similar lines, trade magazines such as *Adweek* provide advice for how to advertise to members of Generation Y who still like brands but hate advertising (Castillo 2015).

THE TROPE OF THE 'EMPOWERED CONSUMER'

Advertisers' claim that consumers are savvy and empowered is not a particularly new one (Hood 2005). For example, in the 'Golden Era' the advertising legend Leo Burnett argued that no one would do well in advertising who thought that people can be 'fooled or pushed around', and David Ogilvy famously stated that 'the consumer isn't a moron; she is your wife' (quoted in Hood 2005: 123). In part, these claims need to be understood as a defence of advertising vis-à-vis accusations of consumer manipulation, which were particularly forcefully made by Vance Packard in his bestseller *The Hidden Persuaders* (Packard 1957).

One could also argue, however, that these claims were not only instrumental, but honest in the sense that they reflected the key innovation of the 'creative revolution'—the construction of the savvy, sceptical consumer, using advertising and branding as cultural resources for creating individual lifestyles (Holt 2002). Consumers were 'empowered' in that they were imagined to be able to resist instrumental marketing appeals and to deliberately misappropriate and adapt meanings produced by advertisers. The 'knowing wink' to the savvy consumer characterising Bernbach's iconic VW campaign can therefore be understood as a paradigm shift for advertising (see Garfield 2009). It acknowledged, for the first time, the productive role consumers played in making and performing their cultural world and the valuable resource this creative unruliness constituted for brands. Thus, the view that the history of advertising is one of countering consumer savviness by ever more sophisticated persuasive appeals might be misleading. We would argue that it is more plausible to look at the history of advertising—at least since the creative revolution—as one that is characterised by advertisers trying to develop new approaches for managing the open-ended, creative nature of consumer culture and for harnessing consumers' productive capacities. Since the 1960s, advertisers have moved more and more towards devising innovative ways for controlling consumers by trying to govern the context of meaning making instead of attempting to directly prescribe meaning. Thus, frictions and disruptions in advertising are not so much a result of increasing consumer savviness and the dialectics of consumer culture (Holt 2002), but of advertisers finding new ways for enabling, channelling and appropriating the productive capacities of consumers. In other words, the 'savvy consumer' is not the cause for changing conceptualisations of advertising, but the discursive effect of the multiple regimes of mediation advertisers are embedded in and forced to manage (Cronin 2004a; 2004b). New conceptualisations of advertising arise—among others—out of the appropriation of new media technologies, clients' expectations and demands, personal aspirations of advertising practitioners to win advertising awards (see Rothenberg 1988), the competitive nature and business imperatives of the industry and the constraints imposed by regulatory regimes. Consequently, the trope of the 'empowered consumer' is invoked most insistently and persistently at exactly these junctures—when advertisers, owing to shifts in media technology, socioeconomic conditions or the cultural environment, are at the brink of devising new techniques for managing the open-ended productive capacities of the 'empowered' consumer.

The important question is therefore not simply whether or not consumers are 'empowered', but *to what exactly* consumers are imagined to be empowered. The creative revolution responded to the increasing mobility of consumers (Arvidsson 2004) and the counterculture by constructing consumers as empowered to ignore, adapt or create their own meanings. The current consumer is—as we all know since in 2006 *Time* magazine elevated 'You' to the 'Person of the Year'—an empowered 'prosumer' and 'co-producer'. These notions have become essential features of current marketing thinking with its focus on 'value co-creation' (Prahalad and Ramaswamy 2004), 'collaborative marketing' (Peppers and Rogers 2004, 2005) or the 'service-dominant logic of marketing' (Vargo and Lusch 2004). These concepts, which have been intensively popularised and discussed since being published in the early 2000s, understand consumers not only as discerning choosers, but more so as engaged and empowered co-producers. The effort to define the active role of consumers in the production of advertising and brands has led to a proliferation of neologisms—'prosumers', 'produsers', 'consum-actors' or 'post-consumers', to name a few (see Cova et al. 2011). Marketing is thus no longer imagined as a top-down provider of products, services and modes of life, but as an enabling co-performer (Beckett and Nayak 2008). This view is echoed in the celebratory accounts of an evolving 'convergence culture' according to which the emergence of digital technologies facilitates a mutually beneficial relationship between producers and consumers (Jenkins 2006; Bruns 2008). Most prominently, Jenkins (2006) argues that the digital era leads to a potential win-win feedback loop where audiences gain access to media properties and participate in the creation of a brand's or media property's immersive image-world, while brands and media companies gain the intelligence provided by their creative collaborators which—arguably—renders them more responsive to consumers' demands. The mentality of consumer participation thus serves double duty. It is not only presented as an innovative business strategy for value generation and extraction, but serves simultaneously as moral justification for marketing, since it provides a conceptual framework in which the 'sovereign needs of the consumer and the desires of the producer are reconciled' (Beckett and Nayak 2008: 302). The consumer has thus evolved: from being considered merely advertising savvy in terms of being familiar with typical promotional appeals, consumers are now constructed as empowered by means of active participation in collaborative relationships with companies and brands. As Jenkins argues in his influential account of the 'affective economics' characterising today's 'convergence culture', owing to participatory media consumers now have the capacity to 'form their own kind of collective bargaining structure that they can use to challenge corporate decisions' (Jenkins 2006: 63).

Thus, through participation on interactive media platforms consumers now have the opportunity to form brand communities who, according to Jenkins, have the power to influence media producers. These interactive participatory fan cultures represent, as Jenkins argues, a form of emotional capital created and controlled by consumers, which they can utilise as a bargaining resource to impose their preferences on corporations. In Jenkins' account participation therefore becomes a form of empowerment, rooted in consumption communities and expanding 'the scope and reach of consumer activities' (Jenkins 2006: 226).

In the context of the new commercial logic of the post-exposure audience marketplace and the interrelated ideological reconfiguration of marketing as value co-creation, the 'death of advertising' appears thus to be a logical discursive response. What has to die, according to the video by Saatchi & Saatchi and the general industry discourse, is the 'traditional' form of advertising relying on frame-based representational content distributed via legacy media. It has to make way for a new conceptualisation focused on eliciting and structuring consumer participation. The discursive construction of this 'participation paradigm' will be analysed in more detail in Chapter 2. We will conclude this chapter by looking at how advertisers use algorithms as a central device for managing the open-ended nature of meaning making in consumer culture. In recent years, the notion of the 'algorithmic turn' (Uricchio 2011; McKelvey 2014) has gained traction in cultural and media studies. Algorithmically driven recommendation systems—such as Amazon, Netflix and Spotify—in particular have attracted attention for the role they play in intermediating culture by shaping taste and enable or hinder the discovery and experience of cultural content (Morris 2015; Striphas 2015; Langlois 2014). Far less attention has been paid so far, though, to the ways in which advertisers employ algorithms and how these affect the status of advertisers as cultural intermediaries.

Algorithmic (Dis)-intermediations

Algorithms are both a consequence and a cause of the 'Big Data' phenomenon that dominates contemporary technology discourse (Napoli 2014). McKelvey (2014: 597) describes the 'algorithmic turn' as the increasing reliance of communication infrastructures to 'depend on computational routines to control the information they acquire, produce and diffuse'. In the digital media environment, a multitude of algorithms cooperate but also compete with each other when performing their key tasks: the selection of content deemed to be most relevant to individual audience members and the control of circulation of information and content within and across media platforms (McKelvey 2014). In the digital media environment, a significant amount of the work of culture has thus been delegated to algorithms. Hallinan and Striphas (2014: 3) use the term 'algorithmic culture' to describe 'the use of computational processes to sort, classify and hierarchise people, places, objects, and ideas, and also the habits of thought, conduct and expression that arise in relationship to those processes'. These computational processes thus enact power by way of logistics—they organise and orient, arrange people and property in time and space, they include and exclude (Morris 2015). Algorithms function as control technologies and possess 'material agency' or, in other words, the capacity for nonhuman entities to act in the absence of sustained human intervention. Following Katzenbach's (2011) argument to conceptualise media technologies as institutions, Napoli (2014) proposes also to regard algorithms as institutional actors, since they 'have the capacity to directly structure user behaviours, impact preference formation and impact content production decisions'—all of which is 'achieved through mechanisms that are technological in nature but that are developed and frequently refined and recalibrated within complex social processes' (Napoli 2014: 343). As such they 'in many ways epitomize the complex intermingling of human and non-human actors that is central to an actor-network theory perspective on institutions' (Napoli 2014: 344).

Echoing the algorithmic turn are recent re-evaluations of the concept of cultural intermediaries that call for more nuanced applications and more empirical research into the contexts in which cultural intermediaries do their work. For example, Smith Maguire and Matthews (2012) suggest conceptualising cultural intermediaries as 'contextualized market actors' who find themselves in a density of contextualising conditions that enable and constrain their expert roles in value formation processes. Similarly, drawing on Latour's Actor-Network Theory and Callon's work in the field of the so-called 'new economic sociology', Moor (2012) suggests that cultural intermediaries do not only employ their dispositions and competencies when performing their mediating role, but need to recognise, utilise and adapt to material and non-human actors. She suggests conceiving of mediators, intermediaries and devices 'as combinations of human and non-human actors whose role in developing programmes of action may extend from merely transporting meaning to actively shaping outcomes, and in some cases modifying or even transforming them' (Moor 2012: 573). As Smith Maguire and Matthews (2012: 555) argue, 'framing as a material practice must be situated in terms of its location in particular networks of human and non-human actors, in order to understand the specific devices and constraints negotiated by cultural intermediaries in their attempts to influence how goods are perceived and practiced'. Following this line of argument, the following sections will illustrate how advertising practitioners utilise computational forms of power for managing the open-ended meaning-making processes of popular culture. We specifically look at two key competencies advertising agencies regard as central to their professional ideology: the detection of 'cool' and the development of creative, meaningful content.

Algorithmic Coolhunting

The invention of the 'Pepsi Generation' is regarded as one of the more important moments in the history of advertising. This branding initiative, conceived in 1963, is credited to have been the first true lifestyle campaign. Targeting the generation of young consumers born shortly after the Second World War, the original campaign invited consumers to think of themselves as people who see 'the young view of things' (Goodson 2012). In essence, instead of talking about the product and comparing itself to its main rival Coke, Pepsi presented itself as the choice of the 'next generation'—a brand image Pepsi has tried to maintain ever since (most famously with the 'Choice of a New Generation' campaign of 1984, featuring Michael Jackson as a celebrity endorser).

As the trade journal *Adweek* writes, 'by mingling the notions of young and young at heart, Pepsi had found a way to let anyone be part of the hip crowd' (Klara 2011). Positioning a brand as the 'next generation' brand for the hip and young at heart is not an easy task, however, since it requires an in-depth knowledge of cultural trends and carries the risk of associating the brand with fads instead of 'authentic' (sub)cultural interests and values. Goodson (2012) summarises this challenge succinctly:

> The next gen brand asks important questions about culture. They look for cultural connections that appeal to a next generation brand consumer. They look at values, at semiotics, at visual style, and insights that align with the subtle culture nuances that nicely connect the kinda-new, kinda-now with the savvy, visually-cued next gen global consumer.

The invention of lifestyle campaigns is thus closely connected to adver-tising practitioners' claim to being cultural intermediaries with an intuitive understanding of cultural trends—or, at least, access to the trendsetters and cultural vanguards that provide them with the necessary insights of how to connect lifestyle brands with cultural meanings. With lifestyle cam-paigns such as 'Pepsi Generation' advertisers had begun, in the words of Frank (1997), the 'conquest of cool'. In the view of some critics they have been exceptionally successful. For example, Taylor (2009) argues that in the early 21st century advertisers were not satisfied any more with their role as cultural intermediaries and began to consider themselves not just as trendspotters, but also as trendsetters. He writes: 'The new petite bour-geoisie in the advertising industry today is increasingly able to promulgate its own tastes on everyone else through its heightened involvement in the production of popular culture' (Taylor 2009: 418). The advertising indus-try has, Taylor argues, 'managed to make its own relationship to goods—the trendy—increasingly dominant' (ibid.: 421; for a similar argument see McGuigan 2009; for a critique see Cronin 2004 a and b).

The concept of 'cool' is a prominent feature of the self-promotional discourse of advertising practitioners as well as of critical accounts of advertising (Nancarrow et al. 2002). It is predominantly employed in the form of either a quality that actually exists out there and can be discovered (the 'abstract essentialist' view, as Heath and Potter 2005: 194 call it) or as 'consumerist mirage', manufactured by the marketing and advertising industry purely for commercial purposes (most prominently Baudrillard 1970, 1981). A leading proponent of the former view is Malcolm Gladwell (1997), who in his highly influential essay 'The Coolhunt' explained that the key to coolhunting was 'to look for cool people first and cool things later', since while 'cool things are always changing', cool people were 'constant'. His essay (and, even more so his subsequent bestseller *The Tipping Point*) described and at the same time further legitimised the idea that certain people not only possess highly valued (sub)cultural capital, but also that these people can be utilised for promoting brands. The idea of 'influencer marketing'—popularising products and brands by specifically targeting 'trendsetters' who would then be mimicked by the mainstream—positioned advertising practitioners as 'apex coolhunt-ers': as influentials who know how to influence the influentials (see Watts 2011). The claim that cultural trends originate in the special cultural capi-tal of trendsetters has been questioned (most forcefully by Watts 2011), but with the arrival of online 'viral marketing' it has become even more popularised as a common-sense explanation for how ideas and content spread throughout social networks (whether online or offline).

Yet ironically, as Potter (2010) argues, technology—and particularly the Internet—has eradicated the reason for 'coolhunting' by effectively eliminating the time span 'cool' subcultures need to establish themselves before their style and values are propagated throughout the mainstream culture. And this means, Potter (2010: 124) writes,

> … there is no longer a mainstream versus a counterculture; there is only the 'hipstream'. The mass-media ecosystem has disappeared and the prevailing aesthetic is not cool but quirky, dominated by unpredictable and idiosyncratic mashups of cultural elements that bear no meaningful relationship to one another.

In other words, cultural trends have become so fleeting that the idea that 'coolhunters' could possibly identify a developing trend and then promulgate and commercially exploit it before culture has moved on appears to be far-fetched.

An instructive example of how brands acknowledge and respond to this development is 'Pepsi Pulse', the soft drink manufacturer's interactive, social media-driven 'cheat sheet for pop culture' (Hernandez 2012). Pepsi Pulse is the brand's latest promotional vehicle for representing and communicating the meaning of the 'Pepsi Generation'. Pepsi Pulse is a digital real-time platform featuring trending pop culture and entertainment news, tweets by celebrities and brand followers as well as some original content such as special deals and celebrity challenges. With this platform Pepsi positions itself as a curator of popular culture. The rationale behind this strategic move is, as Pepsi's global head of digital Shiv Singh explains, that 'brand wars are being fought in news feeds and streams' (Hernandez 2012). The more deeply integrated Pepsi is with broader pop culture trends, Singh argues, the better the company does (Ha 2012). The distinctive aspect of Pepsi Pulse is that the platform merely channels cultural artefacts and sentiments around the brand. As a consequence, the brand subjects itself to algorithmic gatekeepers for selecting meaningful, 'cool' items to be featured on its 'cultural dashboard'. This approach eliminates two risks at the same time: the brand will never be too late in associating itself with relevant cultural trends, and it will never get it wrong (as long as the algorithms pick up the correct signals).

Thus, the meaning of Pepsi's 'Generation Next' is now mostly determined by an algorithmically filtered social media 'hipstream' instead of being shaped by the taste preferences and the tacit sense for the 'cool' of the cultural intermediaries in advertising agencies. Similarly, social media sentiment analysis offers marketers a cost-efficient and real-time alternative to advertising practitioners' cultural knowledge for assessing their brand's (and that of their competitors') relation to popular culture. The goal of sentiment analysis—the aggregation and automated analysis of consumer created content on social media sites, blogs and online forums for their affective quality is, as Andrejevic (2013) writes, pre-emptive and productive. It aims to minimise the circulation of negative affect and to maximise emotional investment and engagement around the brand. This is achieved by replacing representation with correlation. Algorithms sidestep meaning while simultaneously creating 'actionable insights'. Thereby they replace advertising practitioners' cultural knowledge with an algorithmically produced 'real-time focus group report'.

Algorithms also challenge advertisers in the area of identifying 'influentials': Companies such as Klout, PeerIndex or Facebook's Social Graph, which algorithmically quantify people's influencer status according to the degree of their embeddedness within social media networks, provide marketers with (supposedly) more reliable ways for identifying taste makers and trendsetters than human coolhunters. While until recently corporations hired advertisers and cultural experts to produce insights into how brands were understood and performed within cultural life, it is now also algorithms that serve as taste experts and coolhunters. The critical difference, though, is that the human coolhunters were seeking some specific authentic meaning they could channel into the strategic planning and positioning of brands. Algorithms, in contrast, don't need to know what 'cool' means. They only need to have the ability to make appropriate judgements about how to assess and broker attention by way of determining meaningfulness of content in relation to (individual) consumers. In this capacity algorithms have become part of the broader meaning-making process in advertising. Pepsi Pulse is thus the first of many instances in this book where marketers and advertisers shift from identifying specific meanings to creating media machinery for managing meaning in real time. The mechanics of coolhunting, rather than being a tool for locating appropriate brand meanings, become the brand.

Algorithmic Meaning Making

One of the most celebrated scenes of the *Mad Men* series is a presentation by creative director Don Draper to representatives of Kodak. His agency is tasked with selling a new Kodak slide projector in a competitive pitch. Draper decides to load the device with pictures of his family, featuring intimate, emotional moments of his personal life. He accompanies the pitch with a reflection on the projector's role in reliving nostalgic memories, framing it as an elaborated 'time machine' (Dean 2010).

When Kodak introduced the slide projector in 1962 it was celebrated as a dazzling innovation. As Rawsthorne (2013) notes:

> The Carousel checked many of the boxes of a successful 1960s consumer product. It was more convenient than its predecessors and was designed in a snazzier style that hinted at technological wizardry. Critically, it combined the chance to show off for whoever was clicking the button with an opportunity for self-expression. Millions of people used their Carousels to tell their own versions of their life stories, or their families', just as aristocrats had done for centuries by commissioning artists to commemorate their personal landmarks. No wonder so many of us (at least those of us who are over 30) have vivid memories of watching family slide shows on Kodak Carousels, and of the individual slides that came to define our perceptions of the past.

Fast-forward 50 years to the 'Museum of Me', a 2011 advertising campaign for the computer processor manufacturer Intel. The campaign is built around an interactive, personalised video that draws on an individual user's social media profiles and connections for creating their own 'visual archive of their social life' in the style of a museum exhibition. In the video users are taken on a tour through different rooms of the museum which 'exhibit' personal photos, videos associated with the users' profiles, location information, a collection of status updates, the profile pictures of friends and other content posted to their wall. As the project's website explains:

> By visualizing elements such as your Facebook friends, photos and Likes, The Museum of Me reveals who you are as a reflection of your social graph. This visual experience links to the core value of Intel, which connects people through their digital lives. The experience led users to share their museum photos, which created significant WoM [Word of Mouth] on Facebook. (Projector 2011)

The similarities between these two cases and technologies are striking, as are the differences. Particularly interesting is the way technology transforms the practice of meaning making and the selection of meaningful information or artefacts. In the case of the slide projector it is the user who selects information from an existing archive of captured moments and orders them into a meaningful 'narrative', purposefully crafted to represent a certain overall idea and narrative of the user's life events and identity. In the case of the Museum of Me it is an algorithm that 'reveals' the users identity by selecting, ordering and displaying artefacts drawn from a widely dispersed archive of source material. What is represented to the user is not so much meaning, but a collection of items deemed to be meaningful, according to the software's code. This is an interesting and relevant difference, which draws attention to the role the materiality of media play in the process of meaning making. Informative in this context is German media theorist Friedrich Kittler and his analysis of the material and technological dimensions of meaning. Central to his account is the argument that meaning is fundamentally a matter of the storage, selection and processing of relevant data (Kittler 1990; Packer 2013). Bringing together central arguments of Foucault and McLuhan, he argues that the process of meaning making depends on discourse (the prescriptive frameworks that define what kinds of knowledge are considered valid and relevant) and media technology (institutions as well as technologies of access). Adopting this perspective in the context of social media, Langlois (2014) writes, 'both the practices of meaning making and the substance of meaning are material and technological first and foremost, and the technological and material context determines what constitute meaningfulness and meaninglessness' (ibid.: 9). Consequently, the analysis of meaning turns from being a question of interpreting (representational) content to a question of analysing the material, social and technological processes that condition the practice of interpretation itself (Langlois 2014). The relevance of such an approach becomes particularly apparent in the context of the algorithmically produced assemblage and distribution of content evident in the case of the Museum of Me. This campaign is not just an isolated example, but paradigmatic for the trend of personalised, social media-based commercial communication. As Langlois (2014: 18) argues:

> Whereas older media forms were primarily designed to format meaning—both in the constitution of signs and the designing of specific practices of making sense—online participatory media are concerned with the automated

production and circulation of meaning. This means a radical decentralisation, displacement and recasting of the human elements in the process of meaning making.

At the heart of this decentralisation is the move towards the personalisation of (promotional) content. This takes place, first, in terms of delivering user-generated content on social media platforms and, secondly, in terms of algorithmically determined content assemblage as well as the delivery of personalised advertisements through programmatic advertising platforms. One of the central claims of Facebook, for instance, is that its usability and acceptance depends on the selection and delivery of those pieces of content out of the vast pool of artefacts that individual consumers will find relevant. This requires the social media platform to develop algorithms that—although not being able to understand meaning—nevertheless determine meaningfulness. Online, meaning making is thus ultimately not only a question of semiotics, but also depends on the codes which determine what content is made visible and the protocols that structure the circulation of content through social networks.

Advertising campaigns like the Museum of Me should therefore be understood not so much as texts but as interfaces—as devices that mediate between software processes and cultural representations. Langlois (2014), by drawing on Deleuze and Guattari (1987), suggests we regard the processes of meaning production and circulation in the digital environment as being regulated by 'meaning machines'. She defines meaning machines as

> a range of technocultural processes that, by working with, through and around signs, organize the relationships, mediations, and translations between data input, information, linguistic symbols, cultural practices of communication, and users. (Langlois 2014: 68)

Similarly, Bucher (2012) suggests that the infrastructure underlying social media platforms like Facebook should be understood as 'technicity', a term and theoretical concept describing 'the ways in which technologies embody "mentalities" or modes of framing the relations between living and nonliving processes' in order to achieve certain ends (Bucher 2012: 12). Attention and meaning is then best understood as being grounded in a 'sociotechnical milieu' (Bucher 2012), emerging out of the interaction between users and technology.

In this context, a campaign like the Museum of Me serves as an illustrative example. It shows how the production and circulation of meaning on social media platforms incorporates multiple disparate actors, materials and processes, turning it into a form of mediation that is ultimately best analysed from a technocultural perspective. As an advertising campaign, the Museum of Me performs a kind of algorithmically driven 'double-assemblage'. It not only assembles content for the personalised 'exhibitions' presented to consumers; as users share the campaign on social networking sites, it also assembles a network of users, which subsequently becomes visible to the brand. Thus, the algorithms involved perform a function that goes beyond putting the right ad in front of the right person—they assemble culture and sociality. Instead of treating advertising as a practice of symbolic meaning making, the creators of the Museum of Me (the Japanese advertising agency Projector) turned advertising into what would best be described as the 'techno-cultural management of meaningfulness', based on the utilisation of the algorithmically determined nature of content flows on social media networks. The role of the creators of the campaign was thus not so much an in-depth understanding of consumers and culture, but of code. Summarising this shift succinctly and provocatively, WPP's Martin Sorrell suggested that, alongside advertising creatives, algorithms should also be able to win awards at the Cannes Lions International Festival of Creativity, the advertising industry's most prestigious awards ceremony (Whitman 2014).

CONCLUSION

The new commercial logic of the post-exposure audience marketplace and the interrelated ideological reconfiguration of marketing as value co-creation force the advertising industry to reconsider its practices and professional ideology. The tropes of the 'death of advertising' and the 'empowered consumer' are the adaptive discursive responses to these processes. In the digital media environment advertising practitioners do not only need to adapt to the requirement of marketers to produce 'engagement', but also to the logic of algorithmic media platforms. As a consequence, advertisers are increasingly interested in understanding the protocols that guide how consumers engage with and use technology. The move here is from understanding the specific meanings humans attribute to products and brands toward understanding how humans live their lives within a responsive digital infrastructure. More important than uncovering insights by 'exploring' the human unconscious (Vance Packard's main concern) will be advertising practitioners' competence in navigating the 'technological unconscious'—a term used by Thrift (2004) to describe the 'black box' nature of code and the central role of algorithmic processes as they increasingly address, correlate and anticipate social relations. Consequently, if advertisers are understood to be acting as cultural intermediaries, this intermediating role does not rely so much any more on advertisers' tacit, privileged insights into the specifics of consumer culture. Instead, advertisers intermediate by developing and deploying technocultural devices, such as algorithms, for the management of the open-ended meaning-making processes of popular culture. Following the logic of the personalised 'engagement economy' (McGonigal 2008) and its reliance on data, the task of advertising has become broader and simultaneously more technical and cultural. It not only deals with the production of symbolic meaning, but it also involves three additional important aspects: (1) to recruit audiences into the digital infrastructures that manage attention and assign value; (2) to increase the intensity and frequency of audience participation in these platforms, and (3) the development of interfaces, devices and technicities of attention and stimulation that act as—or connect to—already existing infrastructures for the management of attention.

Thus, as we will discuss in Chapter 2, the elicitation and structuration of consumer participation has become a central objective underlying the industry's reconceptualisation of advertising. We call this reconceptualisation the 'participation paradigm'. The participation paradigm signifies a clear step beyond understanding advertising exclusively as a practice of textual representation. Instead, the industry increasingly focuses on governing the context of meaning making by means of technocultural processes.

Note

1. This endorsement is featured on the back cover of the 2001 edition of Ewen's book.

References

Andrejevic M. (2013). *Infoglut: How Too Much Information Is Changing the Way We Think and Know*. New York: Routledge.

Arvidsson, A. (2004). On the 'Pre-History of the Panoptic Sort': Mobility in Market Research. *Surveillance & Society*, 1(4), pp. 456–474.

Baudrillard, J. (1970). *The Consumer Society*. Paris: Gallimard.

Baudrillard, J. (1981). *Simulacra and Simulation*. Ann Arbor: The University of Michigan Press.

Beckett, A. and Nayak, A. (2008). The reflexive consumer. *Marketing Theory*, 8(3), pp. 299–317.

Bourdieu, P. (1984). *Distinction: A social critique of the judgement of taste*. London: Routledge.

Bruns, A. (2008). *Blogs, Wikipedia, Second Life, and Beyond. From Production to Produsage*. New York: Peter Lang.

Bucher, T. (2012). A Technicity of Attention: How Software 'Makes Sense'. *Culture Machine*, Vol. 13. Accessed December 12, 2015. Available at: http://www.culturemachine.net/index.php/cm/article/viewArticle/470

Burrowes, T. (2010). 'The Sad Tale of 'The Last Advertising Agency on Earth', *Mumbrella*. Accessed December 12, 2015. Available at: http://mumbrella.com.au/the-sad-story-of-the-last-advertising-agency-on-earth-21477

Campaign (2014).'Maurice Levy plots "diplomatic" solution for the future of Publicis.' *Campaign*. Accessed December 12, 2015. Available at: http://www.campaignlive.co.uk/news/1301398/.

Castillo, M. (2015). 'How to Advertise to the Millenial Who Hates Advertising', *Adweek*. Accessed December 12, 2015. Available at: http://www.adweek.com/news/technology/how-advertise-millennial-who-hates-advertising-162868

Cova, B., Dalli, D. and Zwick, D. (2011). Critical perspectives on consumers' role as 'producers': Broadening the debate on value co-creation in marketing processes. *Marketing Theory*, 11(3), pp. 231–241.

Crogan, P. and Kinsley, S. (2012). Paying Attention: Towards a Critique of the Attention Economy. *Culture Machine*, Vol. 13. Accessed December 12, 2015. Available at: http://www.culturemachine.net/index.php/cm/article/view/463

Cronin, A. M. (2004b). Currencies of Commercial Exchange: Advertising Agencies and the Promotional Imperative. *Journal of Consumer Culture*, 4(3), pp. 339–360.

Dean, W. (2010). 'Mad Men: season one, episode 13', *The Guardian*. Accessed December 12, 2015. Available at: http://www.theguardian.com/tv-and-radio/tvandradioblog/2010/jun/17/mad-men-season-one-episode-13-finale

Davenport, T. H. and Beck, J. C. (2001). *The Attention Economy: Understanding the new currency of business*. Cambridge, MA: Cambridge University Press.

Dean, J. (2010). *Blog theory: Feedback and capture in the circuits of drive*. Cambridge: Polity.

Deleuze, G. and Guattari, F. (1987). *A Thousand Plateaus: Capitalism and Schizophrenia*. Minneapolis: University of Minnesota Press.

Doyle, E. (2015). 'Why 84% Of Millenials Don't Trust Traditional Advertisers', *B&T*. Accessed December 12, 2015. Available at: http://www.bandt.com.au/advertising/84-millennials-dont-trust-traditional-advertisers

Ettema, J. S. and Whitney, D. C. (1994). The money arrow: An introduction to audiencemaking. In Ettema, J. S. and Whitney, D. D. (eds.), *Audiencemaking: How the Media Create the Audience*. Thousand Oaks: Sage, pp. 1–18.

Ewen, S. (1976). *Captains of Consciousness: Advertising and the Social Roots of Consumer Culture*. New York: McGraw-Hill.

Featherstone, M. (1991). *Consumer culture and postmodernism*. London: Sage.

Frank, T. (1997). *The Conquest of Cool*. Chicago: Chicago University Press.

Garfield, B. (2010). 'Anthropology of Ad Agency Summed up in 2 minutes flat: Ad for FITC Design and technology Festival Sums up Chaos Scenario in Far Less Than 90,000 Words', *Advertising Age*. Accessed December 12, 2015. Availableat:http://adage.com/article/ad-review/garfield-anthropology-ad-agency-summed-2-minutes/143120/

Garfield, B. (2009). 'Ad Age Advertising Century: The Top 100 Campaigns', *Advertising Age*. Accessed December 12, 2015. Available at: http://adage.com/article/special-report-the-advertising-century/ad-age-advertising-century-top-100-campaigns/140918/

Gladwell, M. (1997). 'The Coolhunt', *The New Yorker*. Accessed December 12, 2015. Available at: http://gladwell.com/the-coolhunt/

Goldhaber, M. (1997). The Attention Economy and the Net. *First Monday*, 2(4). Accessed December 12, 2015. Available at: http://firstmonday.org/article/view/519/440

Goldman, R. (1992). *Reading Ads Socially*. London: Routledge.

Goldman, R. and Papson, S. (1996). *Sign Wars: The Cluttered Landscape of Advertising*. New York: Guildford Press.

Goodson, S. (2012). The Next Generation Brand. Forbes. Accessed December 12, 2015. Available at: http://www.forbes.com/sites/marketshare/2012/09/26/the-next-generation-brand/

Google. (2015b). 'Google Inc. Announces Fourth Quarter and Fiscal Year 2014 Report'. Google. Available at: https://investor.google.com/earnings/2014/Q4_google_earnings.html

Ha, A. (2012). 'Pepsi Puts A Pop Culture "Cheat Sheet" At The Heart Of Its New Campaign', *TechCrunch*. Accessed December 12, 2015. Available at: http://techcrunch.com/2012/04/30/pepsi-live-for-now/

Heath, J., & Potter, A. (2005). The rebel sell: Why the culture can't be jammed. Capstone: Chichester.

Hallinan, B. and Striphas, T. (2014). Recommended for you: the Netflix Prize and the production of algorithmic culture. *New Media & Society*. Published online before print. June 23, 2014, doi: 10.1177/1461444814538646

Haug, W. (1986). *Critique of Commodity Aesthetics*. London: Polity.

Havas Worldwide (2014). *Hashtag Nation. Marketing to the Selfie Generation.* Prosumer Report. Singapore: Havas Worldwide.

Heine C. (2015). 'Why Facebook's New Branding-Focused Tool Changes How Its Ad Can Be Targeted', *Adweek.* Accessed December 12, 2015. Available at: http://www.adweek.com/news/technology/why-facebooks-new-branding-focused-tool-changes-how-its-ads-can-be-targeted-167220

Hernandez, B. A. (2012). 'Pepsi Unwraps "Pulse" Digital Dashboard for Pop Culture', *Mashable.* Accessed December 12, 2015. Available at: http://mashable.com/2012/04/30/pepsi-pulse-live-for-now/

Hoffman, B. (2010). 'Gutless Ad Weasels', *The Ad Contrarian.* Accessed December 12, 2015. Available at: http://adcontrarian.blogspot.com.au/searc h?q=saatchi+and+saatchi

Hoffman, B. (2011) 'Rewriting History', *The Ad Contrarian.* Accessed December 12, 2015. Available at: http://adcontrarian.blogspot.com.au/2011/04/rewriting-history.html

Holt, D. (2002). Why Do Brands Cause Trouble? A Dialectical Theory of Consumer Culture and Branding. *Journal of Consumer Research,* 29(1), pp. 70–90.

Holt, D. (2004). *How Brands Become Icons: The Principles of Cultural Branding.* Boston: Harvard Business School Press.

Hood, J. M. (2005). *Selling the Dream: Why Advertising is Good Business.* Praeger Publishers: Westport.

IAB (2013a). 'IAB's Randall Rothenberg on "Advertising Is ___?", *YouTube,* 23 September. Accessed December 12, 2015. Available at: https://www.youtube.com/watch?v=6dIPSeex4OY&list=PL6aT9elthI51Eq1rFq1zC2 mIf5-qU61t2&index=3

IAB (2013b). 'What IS Advertising, Anyway?', *YouTube,* 28 October. Accessed December 12, 2015. Available at: https://www.youtube.com/watch?v=rrti4DFQJ5I

Jenkins, H. (2006). *Convergence Culture*: New York: New York University Press.

Jewish Business News (2014). 'Publicis Maurice Levy Wants To Disrupt Marketing.' *Jewish Business News.* Accessed December 12, 2015. Available at: http://jewishbusinessnews.com/2014/12/09/publicis-maurice-levy-wants-to-disrupt-marketing/.

Johnson, B. (2014). 'Revenue, Staffing, Stocks and Digital Show Growth for Agencies in 2014 Report', *Advertising Age.* Accessed December 12, 2015. Availableat:http://adage.com/article/agency-news/2014-agency-report-revenue-staffing-stocks-digital/292849/

Kapko, M. (2013). 'Adweek 2013: WPP's Sorrell Defines Modern Advertising as a Science, Not Art' *Click Z.* Accessed December 12, 2015. Available at: http://www.clickz.com/clickz/column/2296641/adweek-2013-wpp-s-sorrell-defines-modern-advertising-as-a-science-not-art

Katzenbach, C. (2011). Technologies as institutions: Rethinking the role of technology in media governance constellations. In M. Puppis and M. Just (eds.), *Trends in communication policy research*. Bristol: Intellect, pp. 117–138.

Klara, R. (2011). 'Perspective: Generation Appreciation', *Adweek*. Accessed December 12, 2015. Available at: http://www.adweek.com/news/advertising-branding/perspective-generation-appreciation-135561

Kittler, F. (1990). *Discourse Networks 1800/1900*. Stanford: Stanford University Press.

Kontrowitz, A. (2015). '10 Things you need to know now about programmatic buying: the 411 on buying digital ads without speaking to a single human, *Advertising Age*. Accessed December 12, 2015. Available at: http://adage.com/article/print-edition/10-things-programmatic-buying/298811/

Langlois, G. (2014). *Meaning in the Age of Social Media*. New York: Palgrave Macmillan.

Lee, H. J. and Andrejevic, M. (2014). Second-Screen Theory: From the Democratic Surround to the Digital Enclosure. In Holt, J. and Sanson, K. (eds.), *Connected Viewing: Selling, Streaming & Sharing Media in the Digital Age*. New York: Routledge, pp. 40–61.

Leiss W., Kline, S., Jhally, S. and Botterill, J. (2005). *Social Communication in Advertising: Consumption in the Mediated Marketplace*. London: Routledge.

Leymore, V. Langholz (1975). *Hidden Myth: Structure and Symbolism in Advertising*. London: Heinemann.

Marshall, J. and Vranica, S. (2015). 'In Cannes, Advertisers Scramble to Grasp Multiplying Digital Options' *Wall Street Journal*. Accessed December 12, 2015. Available at:http://blogs.wsj.com/cmo/2015/06/26/in-cannes-advertisers-scramble-to-grasp-multiplying-digital-options/

Marshall, J. (2013). 'Martin Sorrell: WPP Isn't an Advertising Company', *Digiday*. Accessed December 12, 2015. Available at: http://digiday.com/agencies/martin-sorrell-wpp-isnt-an-advertising-company/

McFall, L. (2004). *Advertising: A Cultural Economy*. London: Sage.

McGonigal, J. (2008). *Engagement Economy: The Future of Massively Scaled Collaboration and Participation*. Institute for the Future. Accessed December 12, 2015. Available at: http://www.ift.org/node/2306.

McGuigan, J. (2009). *Cool Capitalism*. London: Pluto.

McKelvey, F. (2014). Algorithmic Media Need Democratic Methods: Why Publics Matter. *Canadian Journal of Communication*, Vol. 39, pp. 597–613.

Moor, L. (2012). Beyond cultural intermediaries? A socio-technical perspective on the market for social interventions. *European Journal of Cultural Studies*, 15(5), pp. 563–580.

Morris, J. W. (2015). Curation by code: Infomediaries and the data-mining of taste. *European Journal of Cultural Studies*, 18 (4–5), pp. 446–463.

Nancarrow, C., Nancarrow, P. and Page, J. (2002). An Analysis of the Concept of 'Cool' and It's Marketing Implications. *Journal of Consumer Behaviour,* 1(4), pp. 311–322.

Napoli, P. M. (2011). Audience Evolution: New Technologies and the transformation of media audiences. New York: Columbia University Press.

Napoli, P. M. (2014). Automated Media: An Institutional Theory Perspective on Algorithmic Media Production and Consumption. *Communication Theory,* 24(3), pp. 340–360.

Noll, A. M. (2006). *The Evolution of Media.* Lanham, MD: Rowman and Littlefield.

Packard, V. (1957). *The Hidden Persuaders.* London: Pelican.

Packer, J. (2013). "Epistemology NOT Ideology OR Why We Need New Germans". *Communication and Critical/Cultural Studies,* 10 (2–3), pp. 295–300.

Peppers, D. and Rogers, M. (2004). Managing Customer Relationships. Hoboken: John Wiley & Sons.

Peppers, D. and Rogers, M. (2005). Return on Customer: Creating Maximum Value from Your Scarcest Resource. Singapore: Marshall Cavendish Business.

Perez, S. (2015). 'P&G's #LikeAGirl Ad Scores The Most Social Buzz During Super Bowl 2015', *TechCrunch.* Accessed December 12, 2015. Available at: http://techcrunch.com/2015/02/01/pgs-likeagirl-ad-scored-the-most-social-buzz-during-super-bowl-2015/

Potter, A. (2010). *The Authenticity Hoax. How we get lost finding ourselves.* Carlton North: Scribe Publications.

Prahalad, C. K. and Ramaswamy, V. (2004). *The Future of Competition: Co-creating Unique Value with Customers.* Boston: Harvard Business School.

Projector (2011). 'Case Presentation – 'The Museum of Me', *Projector.* Accessed December 12, 2015. Available at: http://www.projector.jp/awards/museumofme/en.html

Rawsthorne, A. (2013). *It's a Spaceship! No, It's a Time Machine.* Accessed December 12, 2015. Available at: http://www.nytimes.com/2013/01/21/arts/design/its-a-spaceship-no-its-a-time-machine.html?_r=0

Razorfish (2015). *Digital Dopamine. 2015 Global Digital Marketing Report.* New York: Razorfish.

Rietbroek, R. (2014). '2020 Advertising: Dynamic and Responsive', *The Wharton Future of Advertising Program.* Accessed December 12, 2015. Available at: http://wfoa.wharton.upenn.edu/perspective/robbert-rietbroek/

Rothenberg, R. (2013). 'The Definition of Advertising has never been more unclear' *Adweek.* Accessed December 12, 2015. Available at: http://www.adweek.com/news/advertising-branding/definition-advertising-has-never-been-more-unclear-152434

Rothenberg, R. (1988). 'Ad Agencies' Obsession With Winning Awards', *New York Times.* Accessed December 12, 2015. Available at: http://www.nytimes.

com/1988/06/06/business/the-media-business-ad-agencies-obsession-with-winning-awards.html.

Schwarzkopf, S. (2009). What was Advertising? The Invention, Rise, Demise, and Disappearance of Advertising Concepts in Nineteenth- and Twentieth-Century Europe and America. Accessed December 12, 2015. Available at: http://www.thebhe.org/publications/BEHonline/2009/schwarzkopf.pdf.

Serazio, M. (2015). Selling (Digital) Millenials: The Social Construction and Technological Bias of a Consumer Generation. *Television & New Media*, 16(7), pp. 599–615.

Shields, M. and Marshall, J. (2015). 'How The Super Bowl Resonated Across Digital and Social Media', *Wall Street Journal*. Accessed December 12, 2015. Available at: http://blogs.wsj.com/cmo/2015/02/02/how-the-super-bowl-resonated-across-digital-and-social-media/

Simonson, I. and Rosen, E. (2014). *Absolute Value: What Really Influences Customers in the Age of (Nearly) Perfect Information*. New York: Harper Collins.

Sinclair, J. (2012). *Advertising, the Media and Globalisation: A World in Motion*. London: Routledge.

Sinclair, J. (1987). *Images Incorporated: Advertising as Industry and Ideology*. London: Croom Helm.

Slater, D. (2011). Marketing as a Monstrosity: The Impossible Place between Culture and Economy. In: Zwick, Detlev and Cayla, Julien, (eds.), *Inside Marketing: Practices, Ideologies, Devices*. Oxford: Oxford University Press, pp. 23–41.

Smith Maguire, J. and Matthews, J. (2012). Are we all cultural intermediaries now? An introduction to cultural intermediaries in context. *European Journal of Cultural Studies*, 15(5), pp. 551–562.

Sorrell., M. (2014a). Don Draper wouldn't recognise 75% of what we do', Post on *LinkedIn*. Accessed December 12, 2015. Available at: https://www.linkedin.com/today/post/article/20140612121144-237838958-don-draper-wouldn-t-recognise-75-of-what-we-do?published=t

Sorrell, M. (2014b). 'Martin Sorrell on how the web shaped WPP: "Google is a friendlier frenemy now"', *Marketing Magazine*. Accessed December 12, 2015. Available at: http://www.marketingmagazine.co.uk/article/1284765/martin-sorrell-web-shaped-wpp-google-friendlier-frenemy-now-web25

Striphas, T. (2015). Algorithmic culture. *European Journal of Cultural Studies*, 18 (4–5), pp. 395–412.

Suich, A. (2014). *Little Brother. Special Report: Advertising and Technology*. The Economist, 13 September 2014, pp. 3–12.

Taylor, T. F. (2009). Advertising and the conquest of culture. *Social Semiotics*, 19(4), pp. 405–425.

Thrift, N. 2004: Intensities of feeling: Towards a spatial politics of affect. *Geogr. Ann., 86 B* (1), pp. 57–78.

Uricchio, W. (2011). The algorithmic turn: photosynth, augmented reality and the changing implications of the image. *Visual Studies,* 26(1), pp. 25–35.

Vargo S. and Lusch R. (2004). Evolving to a New Dominant Logic for Marketing. *Journal of Marketing,* 68(1), pp. 1–17.

Vestergaard, T. and Schroeder, K. (1985). *The Language of Advertising.* Oxford: Blackwell.

Watts, D. (2011). *Everything is Obvious* - *Once you know the answer.* New York: Crown Publishing Group.

Wernick, A. (1991). *Promotional Culture. Advertising, Ideology and Symbolic Expression.* London: Sage.

Whitman, R. (2014). 'Martin Sorrell Thinks An Algorithm Should Win A Lion', *Media Post.* Accessed December 12, 2015. Available at: http://www.media-post.com/publications/article/229216/martin-sorrell-thinks-an-algorithm-should-win-a-li.html

Williamson, J. (1978). *Decoding Advertisements: Ideology and Meaning in Advertising.* London: Marion Boyars.

ZenithOptimedia (2015). 'Google Strengthens Its Position As World's Largest Media Owner', *ZenithOptimedia.* Accessed December 12, 2015. Available at: http://www.zenithoptimedia.com/google-strengthens-position-worlds-largest-media-owner-2/

CHAPTER 2

Instructions: Producing Participation

Given the advertising industry's preoccupation with its own transformation, the purpose of this chapter is to investigate current conceptualisations of 'advertising' as well as the associated occupational ideology of advertising practitioners. This chapter is interested in the way advertising practitioners define, validate and give meaning to their work in the face of the changing media and marketing environment. Following Deuze (2006), the term 'occupational ideology' here refers to an established belief system that not only guides the production of meanings and ideas within a particular group of professionals, but which also represents and shapes this group's values and norms regarding the nature of acceptable work and its relation to social and political issues. The analyses of the advertising industry's self-representation and self-reflection presented in this chapter draws mainly from publicly available resource material. These include reports and self-promotional material published online or in print media, interviews with trade journals and other publications, industry talks and presentations as well as ethnographic field observations at professional gatherings and industry conferences. Employing a similar methodological approach in his influential study of the culture and industrial reflexivity of Hollywood film/video production workers, Caldwell (2008: 3) referred to these sources as 'deep' texts, rituals and spaces.

In his extensive ethnography of film and television production in Los Angeles, Caldwell (2008) develops a conceptual framework for examining the work of cultural production. His concepts of industrial self-theorising, private and public disclosures, trade rituals and deep texts are useful

© The Author(s) 2016
S. Brodmerkel, N. Carah, *Brand Machines, Sensory Media and Calculative Culture*, DOI 10.1057/978-1-137-49656-0_2

theoretical anchor-points that we use throughout our analysis of advertising in this book. Caldwell (2008) dispels the idea that we should aim to find 'an "'authentic" reality "behind the scenes"' of media and cultural production. Instead we should examine the 'critical industrial' practices of producers. Cultural producers construct and express 'theories' that explain how and why they do what they do as part of their work. Caldwell calls the practice of creating a shared knowledge base of explanations and values that inform production 'industrial self-theorising'. Cultural producers' narratives about their work are presented in a variety of private, bounded or public disclosures and they vary depending on the context and audience. The way creatives talk to each other in the private space of an advertising agency differs from the way they present issues at industry conferences, in trade magazines or on public television programmes. They tailor their contributions depending on whether they imagine they are explaining their work to colleagues, industry peers or a wider public audience. Media and cultural industries are unique in their capacity to use their own professional skills and techniques to construct carefully staged representations of their profession. As Caldwell (2008: 35) observes, 'the industry now constantly speaks to itself about itself, sometimes in public'. These publicly and semi-publicly disclosed narratives serve multiple purposes: to create a shared knowledge base within the profession, to position oneself relative to competitors in the industry or to argue for the broader public legitimacy of the industry and its outputs. Our analysis of the self-reflexivity of the advertising industry thus does not claim to reveal the 'authentic' essential truth about what advertising is and how it is supposed to be practised. Rather, it illuminates the discursive and contested nature of the concept of 'advertising' and the industry's occupational ideology.

ACTIVATING ADVERTISING

In 2010, Tom Bernardin, Chairman and CEO of the iconic advertising agency network Leo Burnett, and Global Chief Creative Officer Mark Tutssel published a book called *HumanKind*. The book is the self-promotional distillation of the new philosophy the agency leadership team developed in response to the changing business and media environment that had developed throughout the first decade of the 21st century. As such it is illustrative and paradigmatic of the advertising industry's recent reconceptualisation of the fundamentals of its craft. In a five-minute video address to stakeholders explaining the agency's reconfiguration as a 'humankind communications company', Tutssel summarised the new strategic positioning (Morrissey 2011). 'With the extraordinary impact of technology and the growth of populations we realize we have to change the way we communicate', Tutssel explained. HumanKind was, Tutssel continued, inspired when the agency 'first experienced the powerful wave of user-generated content, as people were empowered by the Internet'. As a result of this empowerment the industry had to realise that 'ad agencies and clients don't create iconic brands, people do'. Furthermore, so Tutssel argued, 'brands are no longer competing against each other, but with the whole of popular culture'. Having set the scene, Tutssel then summarised the core of the agency's new definition and guiding principles of advertising practice:

> We know that creativity is most powerful when it creates what we call humankind acts, not just advertising. These acts of human-centred brand ideas or experiences do more than just sell product: [...] They activate and amplify the human purpose and create content that is of human interest—stimulating, rewarding, engaging, relevant and—above all—useful. [...] This approach unites all the marketing disciplines and media channels around an idea that creates participation, and its success is measured by the level of its impact on behaviour. [...]To engage people, brands will need to balance complete clarity and consistency of meaning with breathtaking spontaneity of behaviour. (Morrissey 2011)

And in an interview with the online industry journal PSKF Leo Burnett's Chief Strategy Officer, Stephen Hahn Griffiths, elaborated on these key principles:

> Maybe it's not so ambitious to shoot for a brand that can change the world, particularly if you structure participation effectively. [...] To win people's involvement, you need a compelling purpose-driven idea that gets people to pay attention. [...] We talk a lot about the evolution of planning [...] and how it points to behavioral insights, which in turn gives you permission to tap into other aspects of life that they're consuming, like media, content, and technology, rather than simply what they are buying. [...] The most successful campaigns become a part of the social fabric, an extension and enabler of who people are. [...] It's not that we make people feel and think differently, we drive action and behavior change. (Aziz 2011)

Self-promotional rhetoric aside, the HumanKind philosophy is an illustrative example of how the advertising industry reconceptualises advertising around a number of key themes, which together represent a clear departure from a model of advertising based predominantly on symbolic persuasion. We articulate these key themes as: everything is media; effective advertising is ongoing real-time engagement; effective advertising expresses and amplifies a brand's commitment to social values; effective advertising is actionable; brands are open and reflexive platforms; and effective advertising provides utility.

The key themes of the participation paradigm have become the new orthodoxy of how advertising practitioners conceptualise the task of advertising in a participatory media environment. For example, in an article for the British industry magazine *The Drum*, Havas Media CEO Paul Frampton summarised the most discussed issues of 2014's Cannes Lions festival (the 'Academy Awards' of the advertising industry). There was, he writes, 'a great deal of conversation around the need for relevant and engaging content' (Frampton 2014). He also noticed 'a pleasing amount of momentum behind "humanising" advertising and brands doing good'. Advertisers acknowledged the need to regard mobile phone marketing as 'post-digital', requiring 'utility and value to lead', and the need for advertising to develop 'better data solutions and systems to better serve people' (Frampton 2014). Frampton's observations also reflect the growing pressures of disintermediation on the advertising industry. He writes:

> I overheard a lot of conversation around emerging crowd sourced approaches to TV production which will undoubtedly disrupt the creative community in the same way PPC disrupted media agencies. [...] Creativity and data, ideas and maths have had an uncomfortable relationship for years but I feel that this year in Cannes the power of combining these has been more widely recognised. The values of the entertainment industry on the one hand and the start up industry on the other are forcing marketers and agencies to look at the world through a different lens.

Similarly, in an article published in *Marketing Magazine*, DDB CEO Chris Brown summarised how brands and agencies needed to respond to this 'period of great change' caused by the fragmented, participatory media environment (Brown 2014). According to Brown, the context in which agencies now operate has changed from 'a linear well-defined path to purchase where advertising and marketing had a clear role, to a multifaceted and multi-layered customer journey where the many and varied interactions and experiences all positively and negatively affect both brand reputation, advocacy, and ultimately, sales'. Key to 'winning the age of customer experience', as Brown argues, is the 'use of data, both big and small, as well as experience design and high-end UX capabilities'. He then identifies four fundamental rules that are essential for creating these 'compelling experiences'. First, advertising needed to 'provide utility' by creating data-driven, tailored and 'more personalised valuable experiences that are more engaging and effective'. Secondly, advertising had 'to leverage the power of emotion to help create an enhanced experience with a brand'. With 'the explosive growth of social media and content marketing', Brown argues, 'the opportunities to tell stories as part of direct and indirect brand experiences have become a strategic priority'. Thirdly, brands had to 'deliver and sustain a reputation that demonstrate its positioning for the "greater good" beyond sales'. And, last but not least, brands needed to respond to consumers' demand to be provided with personalised, relevant and unique content in line with consumers' likes and dislikes, purchase behaviours and demographic profiles'.

A similar line of argument is put forth by Ogilvy & Mather's General Manager Phil Whitehouse, who argues that 'customer experience is the new brand' (Whitehouse 2014). It is imperative for brands, he suggests, to 'share the same values as the customers they seek'. Since the Internet had heralded 'a new era of brand transparency', companies had to demonstrate these values and regard them as 'the lights that guide every execution across all touchpoints'.

The widespread adoption of key themes of the participation paradigm is also evidenced by the 'philosophies' featured on the websites of leading advertising agencies. Below is a selection of 'mission statements' from five leading advertising agency networks that illustrate this participatory rhetoric and demonstrate how it operates as an established paradigm in the industry.

Whybin\TBWA creates and manages brand behavior in the modern world through Disruptive ideas brought to life across the Media Arts landscape. (Whybin\TBWA Sydney 2015)

Today technology makes the truth more transparent than ever. There are maybe two places in the world that consumers seek out advertising: on Times Square and online. And telling the truth well online is key. Online, Truth Well Told is truth well shared. So McCann is now dedicated to creating campaigns, platforms and content that consumers will actively seek out and engage with. (McCann Worldgroup 2015)

Tell a great story and people will listen. Let them live it and they'll believe. That's the ambition of SapientNitro's Storyscaping. Storyscaping is how we help our clients create meaningful experiences that tell their story in ever-present ways—by marrying imagination with systems thinking. The power and intimacy of story is enabled through a vast interconnection of technologies and platforms that weave into the lives of connected consumers and make it ever-actionable. (Sapient Nitro 2015)

We make ideas for every medium (and quite often invent new ones) to get our message to the right people, in the right place, at the right time. We understand today's advertising game and we love creating work that people genuinely like to engage with. (George Patterson Y&R 2015)

As one of Australia's largest and most diverse integrated communication agencies DDB helps clients transform their businesses by using an understanding of humanity, technology and creativity to change behaviour. (DDB Sydney 2015)

The following section articulates the main characteristics and discursive framings of the participation paradigm by drawing on a variety of industry sources. In the chapters to follow these key themes are then further analysed, contextualised and subjected to a comprehensive critical analysis.

The Participation Paradigm: Key Themes

Everything Is Media

The fragmented media environment requires marketers and advertising agencies to consider every point of contact between a brand and a consumer as a promotional media channel. In the view of advertising agencies everything is a potential advertising channel, and consequently the traditional separation between promotional disciplines has dissolved. Given the premise that every touchpoint communicates, advertising professionals increasingly consider the materiality of media technology, their affordances in terms of data capture and the affective responses they are likely to elicit when experienced by consumers. This new way of conceptualising branding and media planning follows a widely popularised marketing literature arguing that businesses' competitiveness in the 21st century requires the delivery of 'experiential' value to consumers at all levels of a company's activities (Pine and Gilmore 1999; Schmitt 1999). As Henry Jenkins (2006) observes, the idea of 'brand experience' has become central to the affective economics of cultural life, a process largely driven by media proliferation and audience fragmentation. As Moor (2003: 46) notes:

> Although proponents of the 'experience economy' tend to rationalize their emphasis on providing 'experiences' in terms of a particular understanding of consumers (e.g. that consumers now 'need' more experiences because they take services for granted), from a critical point of view it is more useful to see it as emerging from new understandings (and new structures) of media.

Given this premise, the main task of media planning in advertising agencies has changed—from managing the efficient exposure of audiences to mass-media messages to conceptualising and planning the affective components of consumers' media engagement. Instead of focusing on the delivery of the largest possible audience at the lowest possible cost, communication planners approach media from the perspective of media ecology, considering the specific affordances of all consumer touchpoints (not just traditional or paid media) and trying to align media channels so that they mutually stimulate each other and 'guide' consumers through the so-called purchase funnel towards purchase and beyond (Collin 2014).

Closely aligned with the concept of the 'experience economy', brand consultants and media planners increasingly engage in 'multisensory marketing', moving away from the hegemony of the visual and redefining media as 'sensory touch points' (Lindstrom 2005; Marks 2008). In what Howes (2004) calls 'the sensual logic of late capitalism', marketers and advertising professionals consistently try to invent 'new modes of implanting the body and senses of the consumer in the world of goods' (Howes 2004: 290). This management of experiences attempts to design contexts of consumption that are based on a complex set of sensory, cognitive, affective, behavioural and relational responses (Schmitt 1999). The media touchpoint framework is about the mapping, classification and ordering of emotional needs of consumers throughout the trajectory of a consumption experience, to provide appropriate marketing messages and media experiences at each stage of consumer decision-making and brand interaction. Consequently, media planners have expressed a renewed interest in the 'poetics of media' (McStay 2013: 132), the way media are understood and used as sensational expressions in themselves as well as the role media and materiality play in managing and modulating different stages of unfolding media experiences. As Malefyt and Morais (2012) argue, marketers and advertising agencies have created new territories of consumer–advertiser engagement, which are characterised by the proliferation of sensory-ordered media and 'dislodge formally dominant forms of mass media and cultural frames of analysis from the privileged positions of visual and auditory hierarchies' (ibid.: 73). Advertising has lost, Malefyt and Morais suggest (2012), its once-held dominance as a public discourse and system of signs. Instead, the emerging forms of interactive, personalised experiences at the individual level promise advertisers 'a new realm of consumption in the private sensory experience of the consumer's mind and body' (ibid.: 73). The central position that this 'phenomenology of media' now occupies in the advertising industry's conceptualisation of creativity has, for instance, been paradigmatically summarised by Lee Clow, Director of Media Arts with TBWA and legendary creative behind the iconic Apple advertising campaigns of the 1980s and 1990s:

> I don't call what we do advertising any more. I call what we do Media Arts. I believe everything a brand does is media and the art of telling stories using everything from the Internet to painting a message on a wall is the broad definition of our future. (Clow 2009)

Effective Advertising Is Ongoing Real-Time Engagement

Brands are now commonly considered to be players and competitors in the broader field of entertainment and popular culture. Thus, advertisers argue that the dynamics of popular culture require marketers and advertising agencies to respond to current events and shifting trends immediately. The reflexive, real-time micro-management of brands is becoming increasingly important, forcing brands—in the words of Tutssel—to 'breathtaking spontaneity of behaviour'. This 'real-time principle' has led to advertising professionals questioning the relevance and effectiveness of the industry's privileging of the so-called 'big ideas'—the single creative concept that unites all creative executions and ensures message consistency for the time the campaign runs and across the different media channels used.

A leading proponent of this trend is Kevin Roberts, the outspoken (and now former) CEO of Saatchi & Saatchi. In several of his speeches and blog posts he claims that traditional, strategic marketing thinking is dead and that marketers and advertising agencies must adapt to the so-called VUCA world, a world characterised by extreme volatility, uncertainty, complexity and ambiguity. To be successful in this new media environment, Roberts argues, brands have to produce small ideas on a continuous basis. He explains:

> The context for winning in business is no longer 'new.' We live in the always-on, impulse-led, instant *Age of Now* [emphasis in original]. Life is digital, mobile and it goes down NOW. [...] Thanks to data, robots and automation, consumers are easier to shoulder-tap than ever. But tapping is not swaying, converting or holding consumers to your cause in their ballistic cycle of: See it, Search it, Shop it, Share it. To win love, to hold loyalty, a brand must move at the speed of culture. It must be live, inspiring people to participate in a conversation of real-time relevance, pulsing and connecting and growing each moment. (Roberts 2014)

Calle Sjoenell, Chief Creative Officer of Ogilvy & Mather (New York) agrees with Roberts' assessment. In his contribution to 'Advertising 2020'—a project initiated by Wharton University collecting the views of advertising professionals and industry thought leaders on what advertising could or should look like in 2020—he suggests that clients and agencies have to work 'more like a news agency, constantly adapting and making new media cross all media' (Sjoenell 2012). He envisions the production of advertising to be centred around a

> ... new department called The Making Department that is a mix between media, creatives, planners, technologists and producers who spend most of their time tweaking campaigns in real time instead of revising campaigns long before launch. The era of 9–12 months campaign planning will be rendered pretty much useless since it's hard to predict the economy, market and the media landscape that long in advance. The media acceleration is just too fast and it looks like it is speeding up even more. (Sjoenell 2012)

Gareth Kay, Chief Strategy Officer at Goodby, Silverstein and Partners, comes to a similar conclusion. In his contribution to Wharton's Advertising 2020 project he argues that the future of advertising is likely to lie in advertising agencies 'breaking the tyranny of the big idea and embracing small', since producing many small, intimate ideas instead of one 'big idea' reduces risk and at the same time makes brands 'stickier' and appear more 'personal' (Kay 2013). Bradley Moore, Director of Digital at McCann (Australia), agrees. He argues that owing to the rise of digital media, the big idea is becoming a thing of the past. He suggests that brands instead ought to embrace the concept of the 'long idea' to be able to engage with the 'always-on', hyper-connected consumer of today. These 'long ideas' are, as Moore (2013) explains, not structured and utilised in the form of traditional, periodical advertising campaigns, but executed by way of the ongoing creation of short stories and smaller pieces of content that do not necessarily resemble ads, but are part of a continuous 'always-on-strategy'. Another important aspect of the long idea, according to Moore (2013), is to consistently monitor the sentiment expressed around brands, since social listening enabled brands 'to be more responsive to consumers' needs'. What is here promoted as an increase in customer service as the result of the large-scale mining of consumer feedback is of course also intended to minimise the impact of negative feedback and to more generally shape and structure the affect flowing around brands. As Andrejevic (2013: 57) notes, these strategies of detailed tracking are not just designed for monitoring audience feedback, but 'to modulate its volume and circulation by intervening pre-emptively, adjusting in real time so as to alter the information landscape'. In the digital enclosure, audiences are treated as a probe and subjected to continuous randomised experiments with the aim of calibrating affective flows in a way that further increases engagement and consumption. Sentiment analysis promises—and is at the same time premised on—constant adjustment. This real-time modulation has the ability to 'bring the anticipated consequences of the modelled future into the present in ways that account for the former, and thus alter the latter' (Andrejevic 2013: 57). The techniques of sentiment analysis can thus also be understood as a prime example of the turn towards processes of algorithmic meaning making which we discussed in Chapter 1—as a partly automated system of semio-technology that replaces the knowledge of cultural intermediaries and the logics of representation with the statistical power of correlation.

Advertising Expresses and Amplifies a Brand's Commitment to Social Values

In the view of many advertising professionals, social media has rendered brands transparent to consumers. As a consequence, static managerial and administrative brand management approaches are considered ineffective. The participation paradigm, as expressed in the HumanKind philosophy, requires brands to create 'acts of human-centred brand ideas or experiences', as Tutssel argues. In this imagined world of brand transparency, the task of advertising agencies shifts from creating symbolic brand images to the amplification and socialisation of brand activations and real-world interactions. Brands, as well as advertising agencies, need to create 'acts, not ads'. In this view, advertising agencies become what could best be described as 'mediators of responsibilisation'. Advertising professionals consider themselves to be important actors in the process of the responsibilisation of the social field (Barnett et al. 2008) as they are tasked with translating the brand's proclaimed social commitment into engaging activations. Advertising is thus constructed as a form of education, sensitising consumers to forms of consumption that will foster their own as well as the collective good.

This discursive framing reflects the broader trend of what Shamir (2008) calls a 'moralization of markets'. This describes the push of neoliberal governance to delegate social-moral questions away from civic institutions to business actors, which simultaneously grounds social-moral concerns in the instrumental rationality of capitalist market relations and economises morality. He writes:

> As a technique of governance, responsibilization is therefore fundamentally premised on the construction of moral agency as the necessary ontological condition for ensuring an entrepreneurial disposition in the case of individuals and social-moral authority in the case of institutions. Neo-liberal responsibilization is unique in that it assumes a moral agency which is congruent with the attributed tendencies of economic-rational actors: autonomous, self-determined and self-sustaining subjects. (Shamir 2008: 7)

The moralisation of markets recodes socio-moral practices and notions of moral duty as business opportunities. Not surprisingly, advertising practitioners urge brands to seize these opportunities. Consequently, it becomes the task of branding and advertising to increasingly pre-empt symbolic spheres that used to be occupied by religion, civic institutions and institutionalised politics. The participation paradigm openly encourages the development of a supposedly socially responsible 'brand culture' (Banet-Weiser 2012) in which brands position themselves as seemingly more easily accessible and responsive sites for consumers to express social and political concerns and desires than political parties or other players in the field of institutionalised politics (Simon 2011). Instead of getting engaged in institutionalised forms of political participation, consumers are incentivised to voice their opinions through marketplace activities and brands. 'Brand culture' thus serves as the main optic 'through which to understand not simply the ways in which politics itself becomes branded but also how consumers who act politically within political brand cultures are encouraged to see themselves as activists' (Banet-Weiser 2012: 136). In brand culture, brands thus become governing bodies in the Foucauldian sense, shaping not only brand–consumer relationships but also relations within society (Heilbrunn 2005). We will return to this issue in Chapter 3.

Effective Advertising Is Actionable

Advertising has, as Tutssel argues, to be 'measured by the level of its impact on behaviour'. This view is echoed in almost all of the above-mentioned agency mission statements. Advertisers ascribe effectiveness to work 'that people genuinely like to engage with' (George Patterson Y&R), that 'weave [s] into the lives of connected consumers and make [s] it ever-actionable' (Sapient Nitro), that consumers 'will actively seek out and engage with' (McCann) and that will 'change behaviour' (FCB). This increased focus on activating audiences is a result of the economic logic of the post-exposure audience marketplace, which requires media publishers and advertisers to not only deliver an attentive, but also an active audience. As discussed in Chapter 1, owing to the proliferation and growing importance of 'engagement metrics', effective advertising has to be 'actionable' in terms of prompting interactivity that ensures the 'auto-production of audience commodities' (Lee and Andrejevic 2014: 44). Consumers have to be provided with media content and social platforms that make them engage freely in interactive communications and thereby allow advertisers to close the 'circle of monitored consumption' (Lee and Andrejevic 2014)—from exposure to promotional content to the analysis of audience responses and user-generated content to the tracking of subsequent consumption behaviour.

Brands Are Open and Reflexive Platforms

Given the demands placed on brands to engage in real-time communications with consumers, to gauge and modulate affect across a broad variety of consumer touchpoints, and to position themselves as politicised platforms and facilitators of market responsibilisation, brands are no longer conceptualised as stable, marketer-defined entities. As both Tutssel and Hahn Griffiths suggest, the 'power' to determine a brand's image now rests with consumers, forcing marketers and advertising agencies to incorporate consumer collaboration into brand management strategies. As a consequence, as Hahn Griffiths argues, effective advertising and brand communication is about finding ways to 'structure participation effectively'. Participation appears to be invoked here as the reflexive deployment of strategies for enlisting the creative and collaborative potential of consumers around the brand as a responsive and culturally embedded facilitator of consumer co-creation. In a presentation to the Institute for Practitioners of Advertising, the UK's leading trade organisation for the advertising industry, Patricia McDonald, Chief Strategy Officer with Isobar, stresses the same point. Advertisers should think about their consumers as actors taking on a variety of roles—'collaborators, saleforces, promoters and co-creators' (McDonald 2012). Consequently, the strategic campaign planning process within agencies has had to change accordingly. Advertisers have to understand, she argues, that business problems are 'a behavioural change in disguise' and that the most pressing strategic issue is how to structure participation. Strategic thinking has to revolve around the following key question: 'what we are going to make or do that will enable the behaviour we want to see?' (McDonald 2012). Similarly, for BBH Labs, the R&D unit of the agency network BBH, conceptualising brands as open, reflexive platforms requires a different understanding of the role, form and function of advertising. They write:

> In that context, 'advertising' can be reimagined—less linear messaging and more 'bread crumbs' to get involved with a brand: utility, service or entertainment-based building blocks unlocked in return for NPD & testing, trial or loyalty. Jargon like 'co-creation' disappears as we simply take for granted the fact that the people who buy our products are producers too.

For BBH Labs, the future of advertising and branding lies in the creation of so-called 'win-win-win platforms':

> 'Win-win-win' platforms are a simple shorthand we use to describe when a brand, its users and a benevolent, culturally important party or cause are connected by a campaign and everyone wins. The whole is truly greater than the sum of its parts. (Exon 2012)

The advertising industry's participation paradigm is thus not only a response to the economics of the post-exposure audience marketplace, but also an extension of the already mentioned reconfiguration of marketing as 'value co-creation' (Prahalad and Ramaswamy 2004), 'collaborative marketing' (Peppers and Rogers 2004, 2005) or the 'service-dominant logic of marketing' (Vargo and Lusch (2004).

Advertisers' discourse regarding the supposedly empowered consumer, engaging freely and for his or her own benefit with branded 'win-win-win platforms' and activations, is quite obviously paradoxical (the consumer is free to act, but only within the parameters set by advertisers). Yet it establishes a seductive ideological imaginary in which marketers and advertisers do not engage in marketing any more (at least not in the way it is conventionally understood: as a form of consumer control), and where the creation of value has been democratised (Zwick and Bradshaw 2014). Thus, the narrative of the 'empowered consumer' represents the necessary ideological framing of this new form of marketing and advertising predicated on consumer engagement. The utopian imaginary of consumer empowerment and of frictionless, mutually beneficial market relationships between brands and consumers has been intensely debated and criticised. The main focus of these critical accounts has been on the question to what extent the supposedly symmetric partnership between consumers and brands is in fact an asymmetric regime of exploitation, turning consumers' activities and skills into a source of freely provided labour (Scholz 2013; Terranova 2000; Zwick et al. 2008; Andrejevic 2013; Fuchs 2011). We will return to the question of value co-creation and audience commodification in Chapter 5, where we will outline how the productivity demanded of consumers in a mode of branding that simultaneously rests on participation and computation can be situated in relation to critical accounts of audience labour.

Effective Advertising Provides Utility

A widely shared belief among advertising professionals is that in the new media environment advertising itself has to provide utility. As Tutssel argues, 'above all', advertising has to be 'useful'. Advertising is thus constructed as a qualitatively new kind of value exchange between companies and consumers. Until recently, this value exchange has been conceived as a relationship in which consumers' attention is rewarded, first, with free editorial content provided by media publishers and, secondly, with the informational or entertainment value of the representational content of the ads themselves. In the digital environment however, these 'rewards' for the audiences' attention are considered insufficient. Instead, advertising had to reorganise itself around the 'unifying principle of utility', as Fred Pfaff and Art Cannon from the agency Fred Pfaff argue in *Advertising Age*:

Advertising giants built the brand business on sentiment, which falls short in an age where I want to do something. Marketing can't just communicate your ethos anymore; it has to deliver access to your brand through mechanisms that let people experience the value in everyday life. That means the brand job only starts at aspiration and has to incorporate a range of technologies for realization. (Pfaff 2013)

A key driver of this reorganisation, they argue, is the smartphone, which has changed consumer expectations in terms of the utility they expect from brands. Brands therefore have to leverage this 'unprecedented infrastructure of delivery and activation'. While media 'has always been perceived as being part of an activation chain', brands had to realise that it 'now has to be the chain'. Similarly, Richard Tobaccowala, Chief Strategy Officer of VivaKi, argues in his contribution to Wharton's Advertising 2020 project that one of the two key practices for building brands in 'the connected age' was to leverage social network advocacy by engaging people through 'utilities and services that solve problems or provide value' (Tobaccowala 2012). Also for Wharton's Advertising 2020, Nigel Morris from Aegis Media writes:

The future of advertising and communications will move from channeling brand messages to designing and creating valuable consumer-brand interactions. But they will only be valuable to brands if the brand delivers relevant utility or enjoyment at the right time, place and social or physical context to the right people. (Morris 2012)

The reason why utility is promoted so enthusiastically as the new 'unifying principle' for the industry is that it represents the shortest path to enacting the central requirement of the participation paradigm. If consumers are reconfigured as active, empowered participants, the mentality of collaboration and democratised value creation needs to be translated into a set of tangible technologies and techniques (Beckett and Nayak 2008), demonstrating this supposedly new spirit of co-creation and value exchange. Additionally, as we will explain in more detail later in this chapter, the focus on 'useful' devices opens up new opportunities for the government of consumer behaviour. And, last but not least, it allows the advertising industry to latch onto the positive aura surrounding the Silicon Valley ideology purporting the emancipatory potential of new information technologies (Barbrook and Cameron 1996; Davis 2015).

In the imagination of advertisers, utility can come in various different forms, ranging from the manufacturing of sociality to the provision of real-time news or the introduction of new tracking technologies, to name a few. Celebrated recent examples of 'utility-providing' advertising are Domino's 'Pizza Tracker', Johnson & Johnson's 'Hello, my name means' campaign or Charmin's 'Sit or Squat' app. Domino's Pizza Tracker is a GPS-driven monitoring app that allows customers to follow the journey of a pizza delivery driver in real time. According to CEO Don Meij the app was inspired by 'the uberfication movement' and also lets consumers see the name, face and biography of the driver—a move that allegedly provides a 'new level of engagement between our customers and our delivery drivers that's never been seen before in the takeaway food industry' (Digital Life 2015). Johnson & Johnson 'Hello, my name means' campaign aims to help future parents choose a name for their baby with an algorithmic driven web search tool. Once users have typed in a potential name, the tool pulls dynamic and real-time information on the topics people with this particular name are talking about on various social media platforms, what kind of music they listen to, what careers they have followed, how popular they are on social networks and even their digital humour. As the agency explains, this information is then presented 'in a completely intuitive interface' and also translated into a short video users can share, using 'Big Data to the benefit of the consumer' (Little Black Book 2014). And Charmin's celebrated 'Sit or Squat' app is a consumer-generated and -curated GPS directory for finding clean bathrooms in various cities.

Applications, interfaces and devices like these have become the main means by which advertisers attempt to elicit and structure consumer participation. One of the most illustrative cases of recent years is Nike's 'Fuelband', a marketing project based upon a self-tracking device that allows its wearers to track their physical activity, steps taken daily and number of calories burned. The information from the wristband is integrated into the Nike+ online community and phone application, allowing wearers to set their own fitness goals, monitor their progress and compare themselves to others within the community. It also enables Nike to develop personalised marketing and advertising programmes. For example, the 'Year in Nikefuel' campaign allowed users to 'take a look at key metrics of your daily and weekly movement last year and see how your Nike+ FuelBand activity stacks up to the Nike+ FuelBand community' (Nike 2015). In addition to that, over 100,000 users received a personalised one-minute film illustrated by a French designer with content based on the particular user's activity data including location, weather and individual Nike+ data (Nike 2014).

Fuelband and similar sensor-equipped devices are now at the centre of Nike's product and marketing strategy. They form a whole interdependent ecosystem of data-collecting devices and the subsequent brokerage of sociality on established social media sites such as Facebook as well as Nike's own social apps and platforms. Nike has also partnered with start-up companies that tap into FuelBand data, offering opportunities for finely targeted marketing. For example, Sprout allows users to integrate their FuelBand data into employer-sponsored fitness programmes, and HighFive uses real-time activity data to deliver relevant coupons and other offers (Fowler and Banjo 2013). Simultaneously, Nike's marketing spending was reported to be moving away from traditional media, with a more than 40 % decline in spending on print and TV advertising in recent years (Cendrowski 2012).

Nike's Fuelband paradigmatically illustrates why advertisers would argue that utility has to replace the management of symbols as the 'unifying principle' around which advertising had to reorganise itself. The main promise of the technological manifestations of 'utility'—applications, interfaces and connected devices—is that the combination of user experience design (also known as 'choice architecture'), elements of gamification, online sociality and big data analytics allows for behavioural engineering. Advertisers regard these applications and devices as a convenient and efficient short cut—instead of trying to change the way people think by means of symbolic persuasion, they aim at directly changing consumers' behaviour with the help of choice architectures that provide positive feedback and structure participation. Consumers are invited to think of themselves as rational, free and empowered participants (after all, trying to extract as much additional value out of the company–consumer relationship is a sign of consumer savviness) while acting in a clearly defined and incentivised rule-space. In Chapter 3 we will argue that this 'new behaviouralism' is a response not only to the interactive media environment, but also to the rising popularity of a behavioural mode of governance that promises the fulfilment of neoliberal imaginaries by constructing consumers for a new 'neoliberalism after markets' With this phrase Boeckler and Berndt (2012: 429) tentatively describe the attempts to restabilise the belief in the free market after the financial crisis that unfolded in 2008 by shifting the emphasis from deregulating markets to regulating human behaviour. 'Once again', they write, 'homo economicus is being resurrected, but this time not only as a precarious effect of sociotechnically distributed practices, but also as a psychologically and neurobiologically engineered human body' (Boeckler and Berndt 2012: 424).

The Participation Paradigm: A Summary

The overall picture that emerges from these examples and the industry's discourse is that practitioners are framing advertising as a practice that is fundamentally about the design, amplification and socialisation of experiences. This new conceptualisation of advertising is less concerned with symbolic meaning making based on representations and more interested in governing the contexts in which meaning is being made. Key objectives of this mode of advertising and branding are the productive instigation and utilisation of consumers' affective labour and the circulation of flows of affect around the brand. Taken together, the key themes of the participation paradigm paint a picture of advertising that is deeply invested in the manipulation of user interfaces and the physical environment. Advertising turns into an exercise in creating frictionless choice architectures that stimulate and channel brand and consumption experiences. Therefore, advertising practitioners are now more and more engaged in the project of producing brands to operate as *brand machines*—a network of human relationships mediated by a digital media environment that coordinates and orchestrates action, generates data and shapes flows of attention over time and space. As advertising agency Leo Burnett suggests, brands should be regarded as 'the connective tissue between new technology and real people' (Leo Burnett and Contagious 2013). The aim for advertisers is therefore not so much to engage in semiotic persuasion, but to recruit the 'empowered' consumer by enabling performances and relationships within which consumers express values, feelings and affects. Advertisers increasingly design spaces, interfaces, technological devices and infrastructure that manage the way we register our lives, identities and relationships in the databases of social media.

CONVERGING CULTURES: ADVERTISING CREATIVITY, SILICON VALLEY-STYLE

A particularly instructive example of how this new thinking has been put into practice is VW's 'SmileDrive' campaign. Promoted as 'the first social app that maximizes fun on every drive', the campaign was built around the idea of allowing drivers to build a social network that enabled them to 'share fun moments and connect on the road and beyond' (Art Copy & Code 2015b). The app not only recorded the core data of each trip a user made (ranging from total miles logged and the time spent on the road to the weather conditions during the drive)—it also allowed users to add status updates, photos and other content to a shareable 'SmileCast travelogue'. As an affective component, the so-called 'PunchDub' digitised the old game where passengers punch each other in the arm when they drive past another VW. Integrating gamification elements, SmileDrive also rewarded drivers with achievement badges after late-night rides or particularly long journeys. It provided users with an overall 'SmileScore', summarising all the badges, punches and other accomplishments in an overall metric score customers could use to compare their rides and compete for higher scores. And, last but not least, the 'Find my Car' feature helped keep track of the car when parked, storing its exact location.

VW's marketing department and Deutsch LA, the lead agency behind this campaign, described the initiative as a 'platform for social enjoyment' and a 'social app that offers entertainment and utility'(Art Copy & Code 2015b). The project was, as Winston Binch, Chief Digital Officer at Deutsch LA, explains, 'about facilitating remarkable experiences and not just about "ad-talking" and "putting a message out there"'. Thus, the functionality of SmileDrive as well as the justification for its development features all the characteristics of the participation paradigm: the creation of sociality, the gamification of everyday tasks and the delivery of affective, personalised experiences to be registered and shared in the databases of social media. From the perspective of VW, the project helped the brand to elicit and structure consumer participation, to channel the flow of affect around the brand and to generate ongoing streams of data and consumer intelligence.

Particularly noteworthy about SmileDrive is that it is part of Google's ongoing *Art, Copy & Code* project, an initiative aiming to 're-imagine the future of advertising' (Art Copy and Code 2015a). According to Google, advertising is 'in the middle of a second creative revolution, driven by technology'. At the core of this revolution is the addition of 'code' to the creative mix, which enables 'the re-imagination of everything'. Google outlines its view of the future of advertising by defining four key areas of investigation. First, the project will 'explore the world of connected objects', imagining how they can be made 'more entertaining' by 'bringing the personalisation and intelligence of the web to everyday things'. Secondly, the project will bring 'fresh thinking to established media', reimagining traditional media for the digital age. Thirdly, it envisages marketing becoming 'useful' by creating technological applications that leverage data and 'make people's lives easier', instead of just producing conventional ads. And, lastly, the project is about further developing and showcasing personalisation and targeting technologies, so that instead of creating messages aimed at audiences, consumer segments and personas', advertisers can 'simply talk to people the way they want to be talked to'. This project is not only an interesting indicator of how a technology company envisions the future of advertising, it also illustrates the convergence of two cultures: the blending of Madison Avenue's advertising thinking with Silicon Valley's processes, methodologies and myths.

Solving 'Real-World Problems'

With the advertising industry's focus on utility, applications and connected devices, it appears to adopt Silicon Valley's technology-driven effort to solve so-called 'real-world problems'. What its proponents would describe as the innovative application of technology for improving the human condition has been coined 'silicon salvation' (Hanrahan 2015) or 'solutionism' by critics—an 'unabashedly pejorative' term Morozov (2013: 4) uses to describe Silicon Valley's ideology to recast 'complex social situations either as neatly defined problems with definite, computable solutions or as transparent and self-evident processes that can easily be optimised'. What counts as solutions in the eyes of 'the newly empowered geeks and solutionists' (Morozov 2013: 6) are often technology-driven fixes to pseudo-problems and vices that are—when analysed in all their (social) complexity—rather virtues in disguise. In this sense SmileDrive can be regarded as a playful 'solutionist fix' for making boring commutes and solo-drives more entertaining. For the user, this 'utility', however, comes with the 'side effect' of increased surveillance and data-mining. SmileDrive is similar to Domino's Pizza Tracker application, which practically establishes an almost complete monitoring system of the company's delivery drivers under the moniker of providing 'customer value'. An even more instructive solutionist fix, predicated on a sensing environment, is the 'Pay-per-Laugh' campaign for the Spanish comedy club Teatreneu. In mid-2013, the Spanish government raised the tax on theatre tickets significantly, from 8 % to 21 %. As a result, theatres experienced a 30% decrease in audience attendance. Tasked with reversing this trend, the agency The Cyranos (part of the McCann World Group) developed an innovative and award-winning solution for Teatreneu. The agency installed iPads with facial recognition software in every seat in the theatre and got the comedy club to change the pricing system from a fixed price for tickets to a 'pay-per-laugh' scheme. The facial recognition software monitored audience members during the performance and charged 0.30 Euro for every detected smirk or laugh. According to the agency, after the introduction of this system the charged prices for tickets increased by 6 Euro compared to the previously charged fixed price, and a 35 % increase in audience attendance. Not surprisingly, the campaign attracted worldwide press coverage, and the pay-per-laugh scheme is reportedly being replicated by other venues (Brand Buffet 2014). To many the campaign appeared to be an ingenious solution to a business problem (after all, the campaign won a Cannes Lion). For example, the *Washington Post* featured an article by Dominic Basulto, a 'futurist' and blogger, who regarded Pay-per Laugh as simply 'a technologically enhanced version of "name-your-own-price" payment models, which 'takes away most of the risks for the consumer' (Basulto 2014). He also imagines taking this model further by replacing 'cumbersome' facial recognition technology with wearable devices that access a broad range of biometric data. He illustrates by way of a future scenario that one could imagine a risk-free dining experience, where consumers 'pay for a restaurant meal purely on the types of flavour sensations in your mouth or neurotransmitters triggered inside your brain'. Thus, in Basulto's account the campaign serves as a welcome example for illustrating the value of normalising the constant surveillance of populations and for framing social relations in neoliberal terms of individual value exchanges that need to be made as 'risk'-free as possible. Some commentators, however, regarded the campaign either as a satirical stunt or as a serious case of 'solutionism'. As for instance the *Guardian* pointed out, Pay-per-Laugh was

> ...flatly reductive for comedy, with its implication that the most valuable comedy is the comedy that generates most laughs. Were pay-per-laugh to take off, would any club ever again book experimental comics—the ones who risk deferring laughter, or withholding it; the ones who generate not quantity of laughs, but high quality? In any event, the last thing comedy needs is a mechanism to make everyone even more neurotic about how many seconds have passed since the last laugh. (Logan 2014)

Passive Participation: Anticipating the 'Commercial Surround'

Campaigns like Teatreneu's Pay-per-Laugh are, however, only a glimpse into the future of the 'passive-ication of interactivity' characteristic for the evolving 'sensor society' (Andrejevic and Burdon 2015). The distinguishing feature of the sensor society is the passive, distributed and always-on data collection enabled by sensors that form an interactive overlay on the physical environment and thereby integrate it into the digital enclosure. Media now increasingly function as oblique platforms for 'immediate, action-facilitating interconnection with and feedback from the environment' (Hansen 2012: 53). Often referred to as the 'Internet of Things', the automatic background monitoring of this developing sensing environment rests upon the interconnection between an increasing number of comprehensive sensing devices and the development of analytical infrastructures for generating actionable insights and detecting unintuitive correlations in the data-streams (Andrejevic and Burdon 2015). In the sensor society, this sensor-driven data generation and collection is thus inseparable from predictive analytics. The aim of the analytical infrastructure is to continuously fine tune the system's ability to reconstruct the past and predict the future.

According to a study by The Economist Intelligence Unit, the Internet of Things is the trend that is expected to have the biggest impact on marketing over the next few years (Martin 2015). More than half of the surveyed chief marketing officers and senior marketing executives expect the ubiquitous, always-on data generation by embedded devices to 'revolutionize marketing'. Almost as important and game changing, according to the study, will be real-time personalised mobile communication. Not surprisingly, the possibilities afforded by sensors and the Internet of Things plays a central role in the imagination of advertising professionals. For example, Russell Dubner, CEO of communications agency Edelman NY, writes for Wharton's Advertising 2020:

> The successors of wearable technology like Google Glass will blend the digital and physical worlds. Ambient connectedness to information and one another will force us to redirect advertising dollars from billboards and TV spots to the millions of people who are 'wired'. Opting in or out of brand communications will be more fluid based on a person's exact location and activity, shifting the current focus from hyper-local to in the moment. (Dubner 2013)

Tim Goodwin, Senior Vice President Strategy and Innovation at Havas, imagines the Internet as 'a connective ambient layer, in the background and all-knowing', allowing advertisers to buy 'micro-moments to serve hyper-relevant ads' (Goodwin 2015). Along these lines Bruce Neve, CEO of the media planning and buying agency network Starcom MediaVest, develops the following lively description of a future morning ritual:

As I walked into the bathroom, the body scanning sensors could tell I had a rough night. Sure enough, looking into the mirror, it displayed an ad for Tylenol (extra strength) which was dynamically inserted as sponsor of my morning sports video highlights. In addition, a coupon offer from Nabob coffee was presented along with my daily agenda which I dropped into my mobile watch. (Neve 2013)

Many of the key features of the advertising industry's participation paradigm—the focus on utility, media phenomenology, interface design and connected devices—thus need to be located not only in the context of the post-exposure audience marketplace and the idea of value co-creation, but also in the anticipated 'commercial surround' (Lee and Andrejevic 2014) of the sensor society. In this commercial surround, almost every activity—from watching television to brushing your teeth—is folded 'into the monitored embrace of a digital enclosure' in which 'one's activities are recorded, stored and mined for marketing purposes' (Lee and Andrejevic 2014).

What appears to dominate the discourse of advertisers and the imagination of cultural critics alike is a future scenario resembling the famous scene in the Hollywood movie *Minority Report*, in which the main character (played by Tom Cruise) is served personalised virtual ads based on a sensing environment that identifies passers-by using retina scans as he walks down a mall. This is, however, not the only possible usage scenario of sensors and sensing infrastructures. Advertisers are keen to utilise sensors not only for serving 'hyper-relevant ads' in the 'micro-moments' of consumer susceptibility, but for creating affective brand experiences. Take for instance the 'AFL Alert Shirt' campaign by the Australian pay TV channel Foxtel. To get loyal subscribers of Foxtel's sport channels closer to the action of Australian Rules Football games (AFL), the agency CHE Proximity developed a sensor equipped AFL Shirt that is able to receive real-time game data and convert it into haptic sensations simulating the live sporting contest (Campaign Brief 2014). As CHE Proximity's executive creative director Leon Wilson explains:

Up until now fans have only been able to connect with their team on an emotional level. Now they can physically feel every impact, rush of adrenalin, or anxious heart beat. (Campaign Brief 2014)

A similar idea was conceived and implemented by Ogilvy & Mather Argentina. The agency developed a belt for the baby cosmetics brand Huggies that would allow men to feel their unborn baby's kicks by the real-time transmission of movement data of the baby in the mother's belly (Kiefaber 2013).

While some might dismiss these device-centred campaigns as innovative yet inconsequential 'gimmicks', we would rather argue that they serve as early indicators of a future trajectory of advertising practice as well as the industry's changing business model. Devices such as the AFL Alert Shirt or Huggie's Baby Belt illustrate a form of advertising based not only on the premise of providing 'utility', but also on the 'affect amplification' of bodily responses. Advertising is here conceived of not as the provision of information or the elicitation of emotions based on symbolic, textual representations. Rather, advertising takes the form of 'useful' material devices that directly stimulate, modulate, amplify and transmit users' affective responses to experiences and real-world interactions. The brand does not address consumers on a cognitive level, but instead invites them to play directly with corporeal forces. That way the brand becomes connected to consumers' most intimate moments, positioning itself not symbolically, but by modes of affective affordances and intensities and the gratification consumers gain by engaging with these devices. Importantly, these affective responses can be transformed into digital signals and stored in databases for future reference. Thus, consumers become transparent not only in terms of their interests (as in the case of behavioural tracking and targeting on the Internet), but also with regard to their embodied responses to lived experiences. It takes little effort to imagine future devices and usage scenarios for this kind of 'sensing' advertising, particularly since many mobile phones (for instance the latest iPhones) already have the capacity to sense users' mood (University of Alabama at Birmingham 2015). Furthermore, given the popularity of so-called fitness trackers and wearable technology of all sorts, brands might in the near future decide not to send out motivating (and promotional) messages, but 'motivational stimuli'. Again, the critical aspect here is that biometric information is not the impulse triggering the delivery of a traditional ad, but an impulse triggering another impulse.

In terms of the industry's business model, advertisers again appear to be taking their cues from Silicon Valley, venturing into the field of developing creative technology and design-driven product innovation. As Vincent Teo, former digital planning director at Proximity/BBDO, argues, advertising agencies are suffering from an 'exodus of good digital talent' who find it difficult to accept a business model 'where the work is focused on outputs rather than outcomes that provide true value by solving a real-world problem through a product/service utility and experience' (Teo 2013). To reverse this trend and to avoid disintermediation by Silicon Valley start-ups, advertising agencies need to find a new model for commercialising creativity and creating intellectual property. In Teo's view, agencies have to go beyond producing ads and toward 'helping brands enable stories through a culture of agile technology innovation focused on creative problem solving and making useful things' (Teo 2013). Quite a few major agencies have adopted this view and have begun to launch innovation labs and product innovation arms, among others Deutsch LA, Droga 5 and the aforementioned BBH Labs.

Matt Baxter, CEO of UM Australia, summarises the advertising industry's repositioning succinctly:

> Increasingly, we ask our clients to come to us with any sort of business problem which requires creative thinking. We are positioning ourselves far more in the creative solution space than in the advertising or media space. (Mills 2014)

Y&R Group managing director Andrew Dowling agrees:

> Innovation can be technology but should encompass our whole business and it shouldn't be exclusive to technology, it can involve product development or changes to business models. (Mills 2014)

A particularly instructive example of this way of approaching advertising is Havas' 'Fundawear' project for the condom company Durex (Havas Worldwide 2013). The agency solved one of the 'problems' couples experience when they are in a long-distance relationship by developing internet-connected underwear that allowed couples to 'touch each other' by transmitting vibrations to the underwear via a smartphone app. The campaign not only won a Cannes Lion and attracted worldwide media coverage, but also represents an illustrative case study of a mode of branding that is not so much based on expressing the meaning of a brand symbolically, but where the value of the brand is performed affectively. Advertisers are thus now best understood as semio-technologists developing brand machines. By this we mean branded and culturally relevant applications, interfaces, devices that act as—or connect to—already existing infrastructures for the management of attention in networks of human relationships. The sensing environment of the Internet of Things forces advertisers to approach advertising and media not only from a 'Barthesian' perspective of semiotics, myth and ideology, but increasingly from the perspective of media phenomenology, post-phenomenological technological mediation and a 'Kittlerian' perspective on media power based on the collection, storage and processing of information. As Packer (2013: 295) notes, 'digital media power is first and foremost epistemological, not ideological'. Drawing on the media theory of the German theorist Friedrich Kittler, he contends that media power is 'founded upon the ability to capture, measure, and experiment with reality'. Coming from a similar perspective, Andrejevic and Burdon (2015) urge critical researchers to redirect their attention to the infrastructural nature of the sensor society and the way the materiality of media infrastructure impacts and shapes power relationships. We would argue that the participation paradigm of the advertising industry represents a ground zero for critical investigation along these lines, and the following chapters will develop this argument in more detail.

Conclusion

The advertising industry's participation paradigm reframes the definition of advertising in several ways. Instead of relying on one-way, interruptive message delivery through mass media channels, the participation paradigm revolves around inviting user participation, enabling message personalisation, turning products into media channels and embedding the product and brand deeply into the social flow and mediation of everyday life. Campaigns such as VW's SmileDrive, but even more so Nike's Fuelband or Durex's Fundawear exemplify a new and so far under-researched direction of data-based advertising and branding. These brands envision Internet-connected products and devices not so much as receivers of traditional advertising messages, but as socially embedded 'affect switches' that calibrate attention and affect. In Chapters 4 and 5 we will explain in detail how these products and devices have already become part of a larger ecosystem of media experimentation aiming to expand the sensory capacities of media. In this world advertising and branding work not so much by means of semiotic persuasion, but as a 'field of attention, attraction and affect', something which is 'experienced in a lived and embodied place, time, field of movement and action' (McStay 2013: 4). Nike's Fuelband and Durex's Fundawear are illustrative examples of a new mode of advertising and branding that rests on digital media's epistemological power in the sense of Kittler's media processes: the sensor-driven collecting, storing and processing of data. The participation paradigm thus turns advertising and branding into a process that relies on the participation and social relations that brands stimulate and manage, which are embedded within a calculative and predictive media apparatus. In this mode of branding, participation is not only expressive in the sense of consumers producing synmbolic content; it also takes on affective and experimental dimensions. Participation involves making the body available to the sensory and stimulatory capacities of media infrastructure and brand machines.

As a consequence, advertising and branding are becoming simultaneously more data-driven and more culturally embedded. This point tends to be overlooked and under-theorised in contemporary critical accounts of online consumer participation. While the seminal critical accounts of advertising working in the tradition of textual analysis tended to focus exclusively on the symbolic, contemporary critical accounts of digital technologies predominantly analyse and theorise the practices and consequences of data mining in terms of consumer surveillance and exploitation. Contemporary advertising, however, works at the intersection between data, the cultural-symbolic and media materiality. In other words, critical analyses of contemporary advertising need to pay closer attention to the question how advertising, consumer participation and technology are interrelated in orchestrating qualitative experiences that create value for brands.

Such a critical account will be developed in detail in the rest of this book. Chapter 3 begins this analysis by focusing on advertisers' renewed interest in the manipulation of the material environment. We argue that advertisers not only regard 'choice architectures' as interfaces for manipulating consumer behaviour, but also frame and justify these tactics by conceptualising the contemporary consumer as simultaneously advertising savvy, psychologically flawed and affectively impressionable.

References

Andrejevic M. (2013). *Infoglut: How Too Much Information Is Changing the Way We Think and Know*. New York: Routledge.

Andrejevic, M. and Burdon, M. (2015). Defining the Sensor Society. *Television & New Media*, 16(1), pp. 19–36.

Art Copy & Code (2015a). Art Copy & Code, *Google*. Accessed December 12, 2015. Available at: http://www.artcopycode.com/

Art Copy & Code (2015b). 'Volkswagen SmileDrive', *Google*. Accessed December 12, 2015. Available at: https://www.thinkwithgoogle.com/campaigns/volkswagen-smiledrive.html

Aziz, P. (2011). 'How One Agency Created A Brand Strategy Toolbox Inspired By The Need For Change', *PFSK*. Accessed December 12, 2015. Available at: http://www.psfk.com/2011/10/humankind-a-brand-strategy-toolbox-inspired-by-the-need-for-change.html#ixzz1bjLa5hkW

Banet-Weiser S. (2012) *Authentic TM: The Politics of Ambivalence in a Brand Culture*. New York: New York University Press.

Barbrook, R. and Cameron, A. (1996) [1995]. "The Californian Ideology". *Science as Culture*, 6.1 (1996), pp. 44–72.

Barnett, C., Clarke, N., Cloke, P. and Malpass, A. (2008). The elusive subjects of neo-liberalism. *Cultural Studies*, 22(5), pp. 624–653.

Basulto, D. (2014). 'An innovative new payment model that's no laughing matter', *The Washington Post*. Accessed December 12, 2015. Available at: http://www.washingtonpost.com/news/innovations/wp/2014/10/14/an-innovative-new-payment-model-thats-no-laughing-matter/

Beckett, A. and Nayak, A. (2008). The reflexive consumer. *Marketing Theory*, 8(3), pp. 299–317.

Boeckler, M. and Berndt, C. (2012). Geographies of circulation and exchange III: The great crisis and marketization 'after markets'. *Progress in Human Geography*, 37(3), pp. 424–432.

Brand Buffet (2014). 'Pay-per-Laugh The Cyranos McCann Worldgroup Europe Barcelona Cannes Lions 2014 Winner', *YouTube*, 17 June. Accessed December 12, 2015. Available at: https://www.youtube.com/watch?v=V0FowbxEe3w

Brown, C. (2014). 'Winning in the age of customer experience: the Rule of Four', *Marketing Magazine*. Accessed December 12, 2015. Available at: https://www.marketingmag.com.au/hubs-c/winning-in-the-age-of-the-customer-experience-the-rule-of-four/

Caldwell, J. (2008). *Production Culture. Industrial Reflexivity and Critical Practice in Film and Television*. London: Duke University Press.

Campaign Brief (2014). 'Foxtel launches game changing technology that physically connects AFL fans + Fox Footy lovers to their teams in a new app via CHE Proximity', *Campaign Brief*. Accessed December 12, 2015. Available at: http://www.campaignbrief.com/2014/03/foxtel-launches-game-changing.html

Cendrowski, S. (2012). 'Nike's new marketing mojo', *Fortune*. Accessed December 12, 2015. Available at: http://fortune.com/2012/02/13/nikes-new-marketing-mojo/

Clow, L. (2009). 'Creatives 2009: Lee Clow', *Advertising Age*. Accessed December 12, 2015. Available at: http://adage.com/article/special-report/creatives-2009-lee-clow/137378/

Collin, W. (2014). 'Why agencies should focus on reciprocity rather than engagement', *Mumbrella*. Accessed December 12, 2015. Available at: http://mumbrella.com.au/reciprocity-rather-than-engagement-256181

Davis, M. (2015). E-books in the global information economy. *European Journal of Cultural Studies* 18, (4–5), pp. 514–529.

DDB Sydney (2015). 'About Us', *DDB Sydney*. Accessed December 12, 2015. Available at: http://ddb.com.au/sydney/about-us/

Deuze, M. (2006). 'What is journalism?: professional identity and ideology of journalists reconsidered'. *Journalism*, 6(4), pp. 442–464.

Digital Life (2015). 'Domino's driver-tracking lets you follow a pizza from the oven to the door', *Sydney Morning Herald*. Accessed December 12, 2015. Available at: http://www.smh.com.au/digital-life/digital-life-news/dominos-drivertracking-lets-you-follow-a-pizza-from-the-oven-to-your-door-20150507-ggw857.html

Dubner, R. (2013). 'Advertising 2020: Where Hyper-Relevance Rules', *Wharton Future of Advertising Program*. Accessed December 12, 2015. Available at: http://wfoa.wharton.upenn.edu/perspective/russelldubner/

Exon, M. (2012). 'Part 3: Advertising is dead, long live advertising', *BBH Labs*. Accessed December 12, 2015. Available at: http://bbh-labs.com/part-3-advertising-is-dead-long-live-advertising/

Fowler, G. A. and Banjo, S. (2013). 'Nike FuelBand Partners Tailor Ads to Your Movement', *Wall Street Journal*. Accessed December 12, 2015. Available at: http://blogs.wsj.com/digits/2013/06/20/nike-fuelband-partners-tailor-ads-to-your-movement/

Fuchs, C. (2011). Web 2.0, Prosumption and Surveillance. *Surveillance and Society*, 8(3), pp. 288–309.

Frampton, P. (2014). 'Reflecting on Cannes Lions', *The Drum*. Accessed December 12, 2015. Available at: http://www.thedrum.com/opinion/2014/06/28/reflecting-cannes-lions-havas-medias-paul-frampton-what-we-really-learned-years

George Paterson Y&R (2015). 'We are GPY&R', *George Paterson Y&R*. Accessed December 12, 2015. Available at: http://www.gpyr.com.au/

Goodwin, T. (2015). 'Intimate Data Will Be Key to the Internet of Things', *Advertising Age*. Accessed December 12, 2015. Available at: http://adage.com/article/digitalnext/intimate-data-key-internet-things/297005/

Hanrahan, B. (2015). 'The Anthropoid Condition', Los Angeles Review of Books. Accessed December 12, 2015. Available at: https://lareviewofbooks.org/interview/the-anthropoid-condition-an-interview-with-john-durham-peters/

Hansen, M. B. N. (2012). Ubiquitous sensibility. In Packer, J. and Crofts Wiley, S. B. (eds.), *Communication Matters: Materialist Approaches to Media, Mobility and Networks*. Milton Park: Routledge, pp. 53–65.

Heilbrunn, B. (2005), 'Brave new brands: Cultural branding between Utopia and A-topia', in Schroeder, J.E. and Salzer-Moerling, M. (eds.), *Brand Culture*. London: Routledge, pp. 103–117

Howes, D. (2004). Hyperesthesia, or, The Sensual Logic of Late Capitalism. In Howes, D. (ed.), *Empire or the Senses*. Oxford: Berg, pp. 281–303.

Jenkins, H. (2006). *Convergence Culture*: New York: New York University Press.

Kay, G. (2013). 'The Future of Advertising Could Be Small', *Wharton Future of Advertising Program*. Accessed December 12, 2015. Available at: http://wfoa.wharton.upenn.edu/perspective/garethkay/

Kiefaber, D. (2013). 'Huggies Makes Pregnancy Belt for Men So They Can Feel Their Baby Kicking', *Adweek*. Accessed December 12, 2015. Available at: http://www.adweek.com/adfreak/huggies-makes-pregnancy-belt-men-so-they-can-feel-their-baby-kicking-150277

Lee, H. J. and Andrejevic, M. (2014). Second-Screen Theory: From the Democratic Surround to the Digital Enclosure. In Holt, J. and Sanson, K. (eds.), *Connected Viewing: Selling, Streaming & Sharing Media in the Digital Age*. New York: Routledge, pp. 40–61.

Leo Burnett and Contagious. (2013). 'The Future of Advertising: How brands can embrace miraculous new technologies to change our daily lives', *Slideshare*, 11 October. Accessed December 12, 2015. Available at: http://www.slideshare.net/LeoBurnettWorldwide/the-future-of-advertising-27113780

Lindstrom, M. (2005). *Brand Sense: Sensory Secrets Behind The Stuff We Buy*. London: Kogan Page.

Little Black Book (2014).'DM9DDB Helps Mothers Pick Baby Names with New Tool for Johnson's', *Little Black Book*. Accessed December 12, 2015. Available at:http://www.lbbonline.com/news/dm9ddb-helps-mothers-pick-baby-names-with-new-tool-for-johnsons/

Logan, B. (2014). 'Pay-per-laugh: the comedy club that charges punters having fun', *The Guardian*. Accessed December 12, 2015. Available at: http://www.theguardian.com/stage/2014/oct/14/standup-comedy-pay-per-laugh-charge-barcelonaLury, C. (2004). *Brands: The logos of the global economy*. Routledge: London.

Malefyt, T. de Waal and Morais, R. J. (2012). *Advertising and Anthropology. Ethnographic Practice and Cultural Perspectives*. London: Berg.

Marks, L. U. (2008). Thinking Multisensory Culture. *Paragraph* 31(2), pp. 123–137.

Martin, C. (2015). '51% of Marketers See Internet of Things as Biggest Impact Trend', *Media Post*. Accessed December 12, 2015. Available at: http://www.mediapost.com/publications/article/256903/51-of-marketers-see-internet-of-things-as-biggest.html?utm_source=newsletter&utm_medium=email&utm_content=readmore&utm_campaign=85575

McCann Worldgroup (2015). 'The McCann Story', *McCann Worldgroup*. Accessed December 12, 2015. Available at: http://mccann.com.au/about/the-mccann-story/

McDonald, P. (2012). 'Briefing for Participation', *Planning in High Heels*. Accessed December 12, 2015. Available at: http://planninginhighheels.com/2012/07/02/briefing-for-participation-4/

McStay, A. (2013). *Creativity and Advertising. Affect, Events and Process.* London: Routledge.

Moor, L. (2003). "Branded Spaces: The Scope of New Marketing." *Journal of Consumer Culture*, 3(1), pp. 39–60.

Moore, B. (2013). 'The big ideas is dead, long live the long idea', *McCann*. Accessed December 12, 2015. Available at: http://mccann.com.au/the-big-idea-is-dead-long-live-the-long-idea-by-bradley-moore/

Morris, N. (2012). 'Convergence is Shaping the Future of Communications', *Wharton Future of Advertising Program*. Accessed December 12, 2015. Available at http://wfoa.wharton.upenn.edu/perspective/nigelmorris/

Morrissey, B. (2011). 'Leo Burnett's one small step for humankind', *Adweek*. Accessed December 12, 2015. Available at: http://www.adweek.com/adfreak/leo-burnetts-one-small-step-humankind-11727

Morozov, E. (2013). To Save Everything, Click Here: The Folly of Technological Solutionism. New York: Public Affairs.

Neve, B. (2013). '24 Hours in 2020', *Wharton Future of Advertising Program*. Accessed December 12, 2015. Available at: http://wfoa.wharton.upenn.edu/perspective/bruce-neve/

Nike (2015). 'Year in Nike Fuel', *Nike*. Accessed December 12, 2015. Available at: https://yearinnikefuel.com

Nike (2014). 'Can you outdo you year wth Nike+?', *Nike*. Accessed December 12, 2015. Available at: http://news.nike.com/news/can-you-outdo-your-year-with-nike

Packer, J. (2013). "Epistemology NOT Ideology OR Why We Need New Germans". *Communication and Critical/Cultural Studies*, 10 (2–3), pp. 295–300.

Pfaff, F. (2013). 'Why Marketers Need to Reorganize Around the Most Powerful Behavior Principle of All: Utility', *Advertising Age*. Accessed December 12, 2015. Available at: http://adage.com/article/guest-columnists/utility-powerful-behavior-principle/240860/

Peppers, D. and Rogers, M. (2004). Managing Customer Relationships. Hoboken: John Wiley & Sons.

Peppers, D. and Rogers, M. (2005). Return on Customer: Creating Maximum Value from Your Scarcest Resource. Singapore: Marshall Cavendish Business.

Pine, J. B. II and Gilmore, J. H. (1999). *The experience economy: Work is theatre and every business is a stage.* Boston: HBS Press.

Prahalad, C. K. and Ramaswamy, V. (2004). *The Future of Competition: Co-creating Unique Value with Customers.* Boston: Harvard Business School.

Roberts, K. (2014). 'Winning in the Age of Now', *Saatchi & Saatchi*. Accessed December 12, 2015. Available at: http://www.saatchikevin.com/speech/winning-age-now/

SapientNitro (2015). 'Storyscaping', *SapientNitro*. Accessed December 12, 2015. Available at: http://www.sapientnitro.com/en-us.html#services/storyscaping

Schmitt, B. H. (1999). Experiential marketing. Journal of Marketing Management, 15, pp. 53–67.

Scholz, T. (2013). Introduction: Why Does Digital Labour Matter Now? In Scholz, T. (ed.), *Digital Labour: The Internet as Playground and Factory*. New York: Routledge, pp. 1–11.

Shamir, R. (2008). The age of responsibilization: on market-embedded morality. *Economy and Society*, 37(1), pp. 1–19.

Simon, B. (2011), 'Not going to Starbucks: Boycotts and the out-sourcing of politics in the branded world'. *Journal of Consumer Culture*, 11(2), pp. 145–167.

Sjoenell, C. (2012). 'The Year 2020', *Wharton Future of Advertising Program*. Accessed December 12, 2015. Available at: http://wfoa.wharton.upenn.edu/perspective/callesjoenell/

Teo, V. (2013). 'The Digital Agency of the Future', *Click Z*. Accessed December 12, 2015. Available at: http://www.clickz.com/clickz/column/2282117/the-digital-agency-of-the-future

Terranova, T. (2000). Free labor: Producing culture for the digital economy. *Social text*, 18(2), pp. 33–58.

Tobaccowala, R. (2012). 'What could/should "advertising look like in 2020?', *Wharton Future of Advertising Program*. Accessed December 12, 2015. Available at: http://wfoa.wharton.upenn.edu/perspective/rishadtobaccowala/

University of Alabama at Birmingham (2015). 'Sensor-packed smartphones can read your mood, guard your data, and wreak havoc in the wrong hands', *ScienceDaily*. Accessed December 12, 2015. Available at: http://www.sciencedaily.com/releases/2015/02/150224154743.htm

Vargo S. and Lusch R. (2004). Evolving to a New Dominant Logic for Marketing. *Journal of Marketing*, 68(1), pp. 1–17.

Whitehouse, P. (2014). 'Experience is the new brand', *Storyhooks*. Accessed December 12, 2015. Available at: http://storyhooks.6revs.com/2014/10/24/experience-is-the-new-brand/

Zwick, D., Bonsu S. and Darmody A. (2008). Putting Consumers to Work: 'Co-creation' and new marketing govern-mentality. *Journal of Consumer Culture*, 8(2), pp. 163–197.

Zwick, D. and Bradshaw, A. (2014). Capital's New Commons: Consumer Marketing and the Work of the Audience in Communicative Capitalism. In McGuigan, L. and Manzerolle, V. (eds.), *The Audience Commodity in a Digital Age: Revisiting a Critical Theory of Commercial Media*. New York: Peter Lang, pp. 157–172.

CHAPTER 3

Impulses: Engineering Behaviour

One of the most celebrated campaigns of recent years has been VW's award-winning 'Fun Theory' (Volkswagen 2009), developed by DDB Stockholm. To promote the German car manufacturers' environmental credentials, the agency—as a video case study explains (Escudero 2010)—decided against developing a conventional advertising campaign. Instead, DDB orchestrated the campaign around a series of real-life experiments that tested the proposition that people's behaviour can be changed most effectively by providing fun, engaging and enjoyable experiences. For example, the agency converted the staircase in a Stockholm subway station into working piano keys to encourage commuters to take the stairs instead of the escalator. In another experiment waste bins were equipped with sound effects to make rubbish disposal more fun. VW also sponsored an open competition for consumers to send in their ideas of how to change people's behaviour for the better by providing the incentive of 'fun'. The winning entry out of the more than 700 submissions proposed a 'Speed Camera Lottery'—an initiative that automatically entered every speed limit-obeying person driving past the speed camera into a lottery funded by revenue generated from speeding tickets issued. Videos of the experiments became a viral marketing success, accumulating more than 20 million views on YouTube shortly after having been released (Hepburn 2011).

This campaign exemplifies many of the key features of the participation paradigm described in the previous chapter. It arguably provided, to use the aforementioned phrase of BBH Labs, a 'win-win-win platform'. It connected the brand, consumers and a 'benevolent cause'. It encouraged

© The Author(s) 2016

S. Brodmerkel, N. Carah, *Brand Machines, Sensory Media and Calculative Culture*, DOI 10.1057/978-1-137-49656-0_3

action, managed to turn consumers into producers and, by way of viral marketing, into content distributors. Michael Bugaj, Social Media Director of DDB Stockholm, enthusiastically summarised these key features on the agency's blog, highlighting the way the campaign not only strengthened the bond between consumers and the brand, but also how it 'empowered people to change' and how it made the world 'a little bit better', and thereby benefited everyone involved (Bugaj 2011).

What makes this campaign particularly instructive is not only the extent to which it conforms to the key features of the participation paradigm, but even more so its application of a specific behaviour change philosophy underlying what DDB calls 'communication that empowers people to change'. The central premise that people's behaviour can be more effectively modulated by manipulating the environment in which they make decisions and act (here in the form of adding 'fun' to the functionality of everyday objects) rather than by persuasive appeals and ideological interpellations is the characterising feature of what has been called the 'behavioural turn' taking hold in policy-making circles (Leggett 2014; Yeung 2012; Jones et al. 2010, 2013; Whitehead et al. 2011; Pykett et al. 2011). The recent emphasis on behaviour change as the central objective of policy interventions—instead of influencing attitudes and preferences by providing information—has been sparked predominantly by the interrelated research in the fields of behavioural economics, neuroscience and behavioural psychology. The main thrust of this research is a problematisation of human rationality and decision-making underlying neoclassical economics. While standard economic models view market actors as rational utility maximisers, behavioural economists regard human decision-making as 'predictably irrational' (Ariely 2008) because of hardwired cognitive flaws. What emerges from the accounts of behavioural economists is the image of a citizen-consumer whose rational decision-making capacity is constrained by mental heuristics and cognitive biases, and whose preferences are not exogenous and stable, but susceptible to social norms and—most importantly—to the framing effects of the surrounding choice environments (whereby 'environments' are not restricted to purely architectural concerns, but include physical settings in general, user-experience interfaces of analogue and digital devices, the psychological framing of choices on registration forms and so on).

Since these cognitive flaws are considered to be responsible for welfare-minimising decisions on the part of citizen-consumers, many behavioural economists advocate government interventions that aim to counteract these heuristics and biases by providing de-biasing 'choice environments'. The mechanics of the Fun Theory campaign follow logically from this line of thinking: Rather than trying to convince people with traditional persuasive appeals to improve their health by taking the stairs instead of the escalator, the agency decided to 'nudge' people's behaviour through direct interventions in the 'choice environment' (for example the novelty of the piano staircase). In that, the Fun Theory campaign paradigmatically illustrates the paradoxical nature of the new behaviour change agenda and its underlying view of the human mind—the campaign's competition invited the supposedly empowered, co-creating citizen-consumer to become part of the subtle manipulation of other citizen-consumers' behaviour (but supposedly in their best interest).

The aim of this chapter is to analyse how advertisers have come to utilise behavioural economics in order to construct an image of the contemporary consumer that conforms to the central premises and ideological requirements of a participatory media system. Together with governments and economists, marketers and advertisers are important actors in the discursive framing and enactment of the consumer. Marketing theories and advertising conceptualisations 'perform, shape, and format the consumer' (Cova and Cova 2012: 149), trying to render the fragmented and volatile nature of markets and market actors manageable. They pursue, as Zwick et al. (2008) argue, the development of ideological imaginaries, management techniques and modes of relating that bring about consumer populations suitable for the respective modes of capitalist production. Thus, these discourses and imaginaries are historically, socially and culturally contingent, and interrelated with the development of marketing theories and advertising conceptualisations.

We argue that by incorporating central concepts from behavioural economics and the neurosciences, advertisers mobilise the image of the contemporary consumer as a post-rational human subject. This conceptualisation attempts to uphold the idea of consumer empowerment while at the same time framing consumers as manageable by way of exploiting psychological flaws that are assumed to be a universal feature of the human mind. It paradoxically integrates notions of consumer empowerment, human irrationality and market responsibilisation in such a way that it serves as a moral justification for the utilisation of a wide range of technologies of social influence and control.

IMPULSES, NUDGES, AGENCEMENTS

McStay (2013) draws attention to the fact that advertising creativity cannot be reduced to just an exercise in representation, but also needs to be understood and analysed as a sensational event. Following Žižek (2014: 5), we can define an 'event' as an 'effect that seems to exceed its causes'. McStay points out that limiting the analysis of advertising to its semiotic dimension means missing the event-like nature of advertising with its context-dependency and the affective corporeal experiences it often aims to elicit. When advertisers argue that 'everything is media', they refer to exactly such a phenomenological approach to media and media ecology. The aim is to explore the affective affordances of the material environment and the interaction between the physical and the digital for modulating affective intensities. One only needs to think here of creative forms of outdoor advertising that incorporate and playfully utilise the surrounding environment: The impact of such advertising 'texts' cannot be fully explained by an abstract semiotic analysis; it rather requires taking into account their context-bound affective affordances in terms of stimulation and sensation. A significant part of contemporary advertising should thus be understood as impulses and triggers of sensational experiences that emerge out of an embodied engagement with the material environment, real-time interactions in virtual environments, or co-creative mediations between the analogue and the digital realm. As McStay (2013: 78) writes:

> Advertising events are then not simply representations, but are better seen as processes, occasions, interactions, and bodily in that advertising is able to affect us, and, increasingly, we are more overtly able to affect it.

Rather than merely being the practice of representation and semiotic persuasion, many forms of advertising should be regarded as the practice of creating forms of 'biotechnical engagement' (McStay 2013)—assemblages of human and non-human actors and the sequencing of mediated experiences in such a way that they modulate affect and encourage interaction.

This view reflects our notion of affect as we outlined it in the introduction: as autonomous, embodied qualities that can be stimulated as well as narrated symbolically and discursively. Affective advertising thus works at the intersection of the symbolic and the affective, representing the interaction of representation, embodiment and technology.

   Such a conceptualisation echoes to a certain extent the aim of the 'new economic sociology' to move debates away from the sociology of marketing to a sociology of 'market-things' (Cochoy 2007, 2010; McFall 2009; Boeckler and Berndt 2011). The term 'market-things' here refers to the mundane and often ignored infrastructure that enables economic action. This infrastructure includes devices and ordinary objects that 'equip people with the tools and skills necessary to operate as producers and consumers in free markets, often without seeming to do very much at all' (McFall 2009: 279). Cochoy (2008) offers the example of the shopping trolley to illustrate how this 'trivial device' contributes to shaping exchanges in supermarkets. The trolley becomes part of an 'agencement', a term Callon (2005) uses to describe the collective character of assemblages of textual elements, material entities, social practices and technical protocols through which subjectivity is enacted and action framed. Thus, the new economic sociology shares with behavioural economics the distrust in the rational agent presupposed by neoclassical economics. It also converges with McStay's view of advertising as a form of 'biotechnical engagement'. If actors are agencements, agency does not rest with a single element, but arises out of the interaction of these elements. This is what behavioural economists would describe as framing effects of the surrounding choice environment. Understanding economic action, then, requires 'moving away from the privileging of language and discourse and an attendant neglect of the socio-technical, material and corporeal elements of agencements' (McFall 2009: 274).
   Returning to the example of the shopping trolley, it becomes apparent that many of this trivial device's 'contributions to consumer cognition' (Cochoy 2008: 20) are what behavioural economists would call 'nudges'. For instance, the device itself reinforces consumers' commitment to the purchasing process; it acts as an instrument that 'encourages for a time the accumulation of things without calculation' (Cochoy 2008: 21); and—because of its size—it regulates the amount of items consumers purchase, substituting 'the budgetary constraint of the consumer with a volumetric one' (Cochoy 2008: 21). 'Nudges' like these have become key elements in the advertising industry's attempts to guide people's behaviour not by means of semiotic persuasion, but at the 'surface level' of user experience design and the development of deliberate choice architectures. They have also become a defining feature of the 'behavioural turn' in governance and policy-making, aiming to steer the decision-making of the post-rational consumer-citizen towards less self-defeating outcomes. As the coming section illustrates, advertisers are

happily adopting the main premises of the behavioural turn and its underlying assumptions regarding the nature of the human mind and its complex interface between the rational and irrational. For the advertising industry, aligning itself with the model of the 'predictably irrational' human subject proposed by behavioural economics and the neurosciences is a tempting proposition: It allows advertisers for the first time since the heyday of psychoanalytically inspired motivational research to draw on a recognised scientific field for establishing a holistic view on the consumer's mind and their susceptibility to (promotional) stimuli.

Mobilising the Post-rational Citizen-Consumer

A particularly instructive example of the advertising industry's new emphasis on integrating the findings of behavioural economics and the neurosciences into its theorising and self-promotional discourse is the Marketing Science Ideas Exchange (MSiX)—an annual conference 'dedicated to the interface between behavioural science and marketing'(MSiX 2015). MSiX attracts attendees from a wide range of disciplines and industries: advertising practitioners, consultants, policy-makers and researchers. Thus, the conference represents the broad spectrum of disciplines engaged in the behaviour change agenda adopted by governments and marketers. For example, MSiX 2015 featured speakers such as Harvard Business School professor Michael Norton with his keynote address on 'brand transparency', advertising practitioners such as Sam Tatam from OgilvyChange (an agency specialising in behaviour change campaigns using behavioural science), and Australia's Shadow Assistant Treasurer Andrew Leigh, talking on how to use behavioural economics to shape public policy and people's behaviour. Leigh used his talk to run the audience through the fundamental premises of behavioural economics: contra to prevailing neoliberal orthodoxies human rationality is bounded; the physical and procedural design of everyday environments has the power to negatively impact on people's rational decision-making faculties; and there is a patterning to people's irrational decision-making, which opens up opportunities for governing and 'nudging' these decisions. He explained the dual-system framework of the mind,[1] suggested by Nobel-prize winning psychologist Daniel Kahneman (Kahneman 2011; Tversky and Kahneman 1974), according to which the act of decision-making is processed by either one of two separate systems of the mind.

According to Kahneman's model, the so-called System 1 consists of thinking processes that are intuitive, automatic, experience-based and relatively unconscious. System 2 is more reflective, controlled, deliberative and analytical. Leigh then summarised and illustrated some of the most commonly featured heuristics and cognitive biases: the 'availability bias', which is said to make us prone to predicting the frequency of an event based on how easily an example can be brought to mind; the 'endowment effect', which makes us place higher value on objects we own than objects we do not own; and 'hyperbolic discounting', which makes us care more about immediate benefits and costs than those in the future. Most importantly, he drew attention to how policy-makers could exploit these cognitive flaws for 'nudging' people towards more rational decisions.

These nudges can broadly be classified into three categories (Yeung 2012). First, policy makers can use so-called anchors and default settings. For example, data shows that the number of organ donors depends to a large extent on whether the decision to become a donor is framed as an opt-in or an opt-out choice (Ariely 2008). Secondly, people's decisions can be nudged by way of deliberately designed choice environments. For instance, cafeteria owners could improve their customers' health by deliberately placing healthy food at easily accessible places and thereby nudge customers towards better food choices (Thaler and Sunstein 2008). Thirdly, people could be provided with deliberation and 'responsibilisation' tools—ranging from mandated cooling-off periods to voluntary pre-commitment mechanisms (for example, pre-set budgets that gamblers can use to counter impulsive gambling). As with many of the other presentations, the talk mostly offered a retelling of the behaviour change gospel and recitation of the most popular case studies. The conference also featured panel discussions on 'clever data' and a talk on 'evolutionary rationality' by Jason Collins from the financial consultancy PwC, trying to convince the audience that evolutionary psychology can provide marketers not only with proximate but with ultimate explanations for consumer behaviour (Collins 2015). Also not missing was a presentation on neuroscience and an (unsuccessful) live demonstration of neuroimaging. The aim of the demonstration was to show how a subject's brain encoded key story elements of a TV commercial by the Australian telecommunications provider Optus into long-term memory. The principle was explained by data generated in similar experiments prior to the conference. The speakers showed graphs that visualised the intensity of activity in certain brain regions second by second throughout the experience of watching an ad.

The peaks in the graphs indicated, as the presenters argued, the ad's key story elements. This knowledge could help advertisers to select visuals for poster campaigns or guide the editing process if different versions of the ad were required. It could also provide insights into associations that are central to a brand's image.

The conference themes and the conversations in the breaks arguably demonstrate the extent to which neuroscientific concepts are morphing into cultural truths about the supposedly post-rational human nature: cognitive biases are 'hardwired', cognition is a 'dual process' taking place either in 'System 1' or 'System 2', the 'lighting up' of certain areas of the brain reveal people's 'real' response to stimuli and so forth. The fundamental premise that unifies these different approaches, and which makes them so attractive to policy-makers and advertisers alike, is that they all promise a way out of the impasses of representation. Neuromarketing and associated 'neurocultures' (such as neuroeconomics, neurolaw and neuroeducation) are constructed and popularised as techniques that enable researchers, marketers and advertisers to circumvent the messy and unreliable realm of representation and cut straight to the underlying interior 'truth' supposedly revealed by directly observable behaviour or measurable brain activity. Instead of having to deal with complex and potentially contradictory accounts of consumers' perceived reality, neuromarketing promises direct access to an unmediated, pre-social set of meanings and desires (Andrejevic 2012: 211). While neuromarketing promises to provide quantifiable insights into the 'real' nature of citizen-consumers' brains and how they respond to certain stimuli, behavioural economics is praised as a tool for predicting and steering the behaviour of citizen-consumers without having to engage in education or symbolic persuasion. Thus, these neurocultures are promoted as efficient and effective ways to bypass the conscious reflection of consumers, regardless of their media-savviness. Exemplifying Žižek's (1999) observation regarding the generalised scepticism of savvy non-dupes, many of the conference talks exhibited a naïve belief in positivism and a 'retreat to the body as the haven of truth' (Peters 2001: 712). For advertisers and marketers, behavioural economics and associated neurosciences have become the latest technologies of 'ironic revelation'. These are tools and methods that purport to reveal certain, otherwise hidden aspects of individual consciousness and that ironically reveal the contrast between what a person thinks to be the case and the underlying 'truth' the technology or behaviour analysis supposedly confirms to be the case (Schneider and Woolgar 2012). In other words, these neurocultures are neo-Freudian in the sense that they again place the interrelationship between the conscious and the unconscious at the centre of attention, establishing a guild of experts and authorities claiming to have privileged access to the 'truth' of human nature and the drivers of people's behaviour. At the same time the consumer is constructed as a post-rational, 'unknowing, unreliable entity who (which) can only (reliably) be spoken on behalf of by others with access to the appropriate technology' (Schneider and Woolgar 2012: 185).

ADVERTISERS AS CHOICE ARCHITECTS

Behavioural economics is widely promoted as a game-changer for the advertising industry. Rory Sutherland, Vice-Chairman of Ogilvy Group UK and keynote speaker at MSiX 2014, summarised the value of the new behavioural and neurosciences in a pre-conference video address, predicting that in the coming years this 'psychological revolution' will lead to a significant improvement of marketing practices. In fact, as Sutherland argues, if the advertising industry had not responded with a 'kind of paranoid flight from any mention of unconscious processes' in response to the accusations voiced by Vance Packard's *Hidden Persuaders*, it had sparked this revolution already two or three decades ago (Mumbrella 2014).

In his role as the President of the industry association Institute of Practitioners in Advertising (IPA) in the UK, Sutherland made an inquiry into behavioural economics the central plank of his term (Institute of Practitioners in Advertising 2010). The IPA is regarded as one of the world's pre-eminent trade bodies for marketing communications agencies. The IPA has over 270 of the UK's agencies in membership, which together handle an estimated 85 % of all UK advertising spend (V-On 2013). Since 2009 the IPA has established a Behavioural Economics Think Tank, a strategic partnership with a specialist Behavioural Science Group at Warwick Business School, has integrated behavioural economics as a 'fundamental pillar' (Institute of Practitioners in Advertising 2011) in its professional development training courses, run behavioural economics workshops and published three official IPA publications which are available to IPA members and the public. A special section on the IPA website contains further information in the form of bibliographies, videos, news and links to relevant blogs and websites. Furthermore, some agencies such as The Behavioral Architects (2015); Brainjuicer (2015) or The Irrational Agency (2015) now specialise in providing consumer research and marketing advice based on behavioural economics. Leading advertising agencies have also established behavioural economics units, for example Ogilvy Change (2015) or Draftfcb's Institute of Decision Making (2015).

The IPA presents behavioural economics as a new intellectual framework which is going to 'transform the practice of advertising' (Institute of Practitioners in Advertising 2009b) and as a game-changer for the industry which 'provides a fundamental rethink of the nature of marketing, whether for commercial advantage or social good'. In the view of Sutherland (2010: 7) it provides 'some badly needed common ground upon which agencies can make a common cause'. He argues that two reasons in particular should encourage advertising agencies to become thought leaders in the field of applied behavioural economics. First, as he points out, the nature of agencies' clients has changed significantly. In the 1950s, two-thirds of advertising budgets came from packaged goods companies, and, as Sutherland explains, since advertising these products required negligible behavioural change components, 'the persuasion model and the brand model worked perfectly well in that kind of area' (Institute of Practitioners in Advertising 2009b).

Nowadays, however, more than two-thirds of advertising budgets come from service providers such as telecommunication services or insurance companies. In addition, advertising agencies deal with an increasing number of government and social marketing campaigns such as initiatives to encourage people to give up smoking or obesity prevention campaigns. These kind of campaigns, Sutherland argues, require advertisers 'to make a much bigger behavioural ask, and the role that actual persuasion plays in those things as opposed to technology or perhaps interface design and experience design may be much, much smaller' (Institute of Practitioners in Advertising 2009b). Secondly, Sutherland suggests, the new focus on behavioural economics allows advertisers to utilise the opportunities of new media technologies that 'work not through persuasion nor impressions but through engagement and involvement, media which are experiential, media which are timely or contextual'. He urges the industry to embrace the affordances that persuasive technologies provide for behaviour change initiatives. Understanding and utilising interface design are at least equally important, Sutherland argues, to understanding the techniques of proposition-driven persuasion (Institute of Practitioners in Advertising 2009b).

This view is shared by other leading industry figures. Matthew Craemer, former editor at large of *Advertising Age*, summarised this point succinctly, arguing that 'user experience is the new 30-second spot' (Creamer 2012). In the view of Simon Lawson, Business Director and

Communications Strategist at PHD (Melbourne), behavioural economics has already gained widespread acceptance in the advertising community, with advertisers now looking 'en masse to the lessons of behavioural economics' (Lawson 2014).

Gareth Kay, in his previously mentioned contribution to Wharton's Advertising 2020 project, agrees. He argues that advertising ought to follow the central paradigm of user experience design, which aims to become frictionless to the point of invisibility. In his words, advertising agencies 'need to celebrate radical simplicity, the invisibility of powerful design and the stuff that "just works"'. But he also urges the industry to apply the concepts of user experience design based on behavioural economics more stringently:

> One of the most important pieces of academic work in the last few decades has been in the field of behavioral economics. It's hugely important to advertising [...] but despite increasingly popular books on the subject (*Nudge* by Sunstein and Thaler is as good a place as any to start) we tend to ignore its most basic premises. One of these is that big behavioral change can occur through small actions. (Kay 2013)

This call to focus on 'small actions' through experience design and choice architectures needs to be understood as not just a prompt to utilise an additional promotional tactic: it rather represents a paradigm shift in the way the industry theorises effective commercial communication.

Behavioural Engineering

The so-called 'academic-practitioner gap' has become a recurring theme in the history of marketing and advertising (Hunt 2002; Nyilasy and Reid 2009). However, there used to be a consensus on a few fundamental aspects with regard to the way advertising was considered to work. One of these was the broadly accepted view that advertising needs to influence consumers' attitudes, beliefs and feelings about the advertised product or service. Reinforcing or changing consumers' attitudes was deemed to be the necessary precursor to subsequent behaviour change. Based on this belief, marketing research developed numerous idealised 'hierarchy of effects' models that identify and delineate the different steps consumers run through when making purchase decisions. The most famous of these is the so-called AIDA model, which was proposed as early as 1903 by the door-to-door salesman E. St Elmo Lewis. It suggests that advertisements work by taking consumers through several sequential steps of cognitive and affective processing: attention, interest, desire and action (Schrape 2014). First, advertisers need to make sure that consumers notice the ad. Then the ad needs to promise certain advantages that raise consumers' interest and make sure that a desire arises (based on a rational cost–benefit analysis and/or an emotional response to the symbolic content of the ad) upon which consumers then hopefully take action.

Thus, central to academics' as well as advertising practitioners' understanding of how advertising works used to be the belief that the behaviour of consumers derives from an instilled attitude. In short, attitude change precedes behaviour change. The current focus on choice architectures and on leveraging people's hardwired cognitive biases, however, turns this model on its head. A fundamental tenet of the 'nudge philosophy' is the promise of changing people's behaviour without having to change their attitudes first. It is exactly the non-conscious nature of 'nudges' that ensures their effectiveness. Behaviour change occurs without any preceding change in attitude. Rather, attitude change is said to follow behaviour change.

As Laurence Green, Chairman of the advertising agency Fallon argues:

> Our impulse to understand behavioural economics, then, is a helpful corrective to lazy or narrow thinking; a reminder that attitudes to a brand will often follow rather than lead behaviour change and that an advertising campaign is one answer, not always the answer. (Green 2010)

An opinion piece published in the UK magazine *Director* succinctly summarises this paradigm change (Simms 2010: 30):

> But behavioural economics also has much to offer the wider business sphere, if marketers are prepared to slay sacred cows, not least the supremacy of brand communication and the notion that attitudes and perceptions automatically translate into behaviour. In reality, the choices people make are far less likely to be influenced by the rational or even emotional content of the communications message than by more immediate factors, such as how the questionnaire is designed or where on a Web page a particular button sits. Such small things, which are cheap and easy to do, have a disproportionate impact on choice, and therefore sales.

One of the most ardent proponents of this 'new behaviouralism' in advertising is Adam Ferrier, a trained psychologist, Chief Strategy Officer with Cummins & Partners and curator of the MSiX conferences. In his book

The Advertising Effect he outlines the new behaviour change agenda in advertising (Ferrier and Flemming 2014: 5):

> Over the last 15 years, advertising has been transformed by the internet, technology advancements, social media, data and smartphones. It's become interactive. However, in a fully interactive media landscape, advertisers can influence and change behaviour more effectively. How? They involve the consumer. [...] Advertising is starting to understand that action changes attitude faster than attitude changes action.

Thus, in Ferrier's (2014: 40) view, 'advertising's new frontier is to make people act first and think later'. He therefore develops a model of advertising that does not rely on changing attitudes, but rather changes behaviour through activating consumers. In his account he draws heavily on key findings of behaviouralism and behavioural economics as well as cognitive and social psychology, combining elements of classical conditioning (as proposed by the early behaviourists, namely B.F. Skinner, John B. Watson and Ivan Pavlov), the utilisation of social norms and elements of cognitive design. Getting consumers to adopt or change behaviour is most likely, Ferrier suggests, if communication campaigns provide the right incentives and reinforcements, utilise peer pressure and design choice environments in a way that consumers can perform the desired behaviour as easily as possible.

Most importantly, and key to his behavioural model of advertising, is the argument that behaviour change will lead to attitude change. Ferrier maintains, based on the principle of 'cognitive dissonance' (Festinger et al. 1956), that consumers feel the need to align their attitudes with their behaviour. If advertisers activate consumers to perform certain behaviours, these consumers are likely to adjust their attitudes accordingly. Therefore, he concludes (Ferrier and Flemming 2014: 41), 'when you involve people in your mission through action, they adapt their thoughts and feelings to make sense of the action'.

Ferrier illustrates his model with various examples. For instance, he describes an experiment he and his collaborators conducted at an industry conference (Ferrier et al. 2012). The objective was to investigate the impact of different forms of appeals on people's willingness to donate money to a charity for children. In the experiment the subjects were divided into four groups—one receiving facts and figures on the issue, the second an emotional message and the third being tasked with creating ideas for an advertising campaign for the charity. The fourth group acted as a control group and solved an unrelated puzzle before all subjects were asked for donations to the charity. The result—the highest donations came from the group that created the advertising campaign—is interpreted by Ferrier as evidence for the effectiveness of activating and involving people in marketing initiatives. He argues that a number of psychological principles led to this outcome. People felt, as Ferrier and Flemming suggest (2014: 38), 'a sense of ownership' of the charity, which made them feel more engaged with the message. Moreover, 'cognitive dissonance kicked in', which made subjects align their behaviour with their attitudes (which, subsequently, led to them donating more money). Third, 'people felt a sense of autonomy', which 'circumnavigates resistance'.

In Ferrier's model, strategic advertising planning is presented as an exercise in identifying and applying the correct activations at important and relevant points of consumers' decision-making process. Altogether, he identifies ten activations (he suggestively calls them 'action spurs') of particular relevance to advertisers, many of which are based on cognitive biases identified by behavioural economists. The task for advertising then is to design and utilise participatory and interactive environments, gamified experiences and useful applications in ways that leverage these cognitive biases to the benefit of the client. As Ferrier and Flemming (2014: 205) conclude, advertising is 'moving from interruption and forced projection to promotion that relies on peer-to-peer recommendations—or that it gives as much as it takes, such as creating apps or games'. Thus, their account not only summarises the participation paradigm in all its registers (from the need to 'engage' audiences to the necessity to 'provide utility'), it also distils it into a pragmatic how-to formula for managing the contemporary consumer. In essence, the behaviour change agenda presented by Ferrier and other self-declared choice architects promises the possibility to guide people's behaviour without having to engage too much in the unreliable world of symbolic persuasion. As in the case of neuromarketing, citizen-consumers remain manageable, regardless of their level of media-savviness and familiarity with conventional advertising appeals. What matters is the design of relevant and effective interfaces, activations and choice architectures.

Benevolent Manipulators

The central premise of behavioural economics—that people's decision-making can be influenced by the purposive design of the environment and the appeal to social norms—is nothing new to advertisers. 'Nudges' have been employed by advertisers and retailers for decades in order to affect consumers' purchase decisions (just think of all the chocolate bars conveniently placed at the check-out counter or the aforementioned case of the shopping trolley). But in the digital enclosure the turn towards 'nudges' has taken on a new quality. Furthermore, what is novel is that behavioural economics is invoked as a moral justification for the application of these behaviour change interventions, grounded in its model of the predictably irrational human nature. One of the main reasons for the popularity of behavioural economics among policy-makers is that leading proponents have popularised nudging policy interventions under the banner of a so-called 'libertarian paternalism'. In their 2008 bestseller and new 'policy bible'(Schüll and Zaloom 2011: 530), *Nudge: Improving Decisions about Health, Wealth and Happiness*, Chicago University professors Richard Thaler and Cass Sunstein describe libertarian paternalism as a non-partisan and pragmatic approach to policy-making.[2]

The central argument of libertarian paternalists is that policy makers should regard themselves as choice architects who—by taking into account the systematic imperfections in human judgement—can organise the contexts in which people make decisions in a way that human decision-making is de-biased and 'nudged' into the right, welfare maximising direction. 'Nudges' are supposed to exploit cognitive biases so that people make the choices they would make had they all the analytical abilities of the archetypical rational decision-maker postulated by neoclassical economics. In the view of Thaler and Sunstein these interventions are 'libertarian' not only because they guide people towards decisions that are (supposedly) in their best interests, but also because they don't change economic incentives or foreclose the option for people to take a different path of action. Moreover, since 'choice architectures' are 'inevitable', as Thaler and Sunstein (2008: 5) maintain, why wouldn't one design them in a way that leads to people making better decisions, as 'judged by themselves'? As Thaler and Sunstein (2008: 9) argue:

> By properly deploying both incentives and nudges, we can improve our ability to improve people's lives, and help solve many of society's problems. And we can do so while still insisting on everyone's freedom to choose.

So it is no surprise that Richard Thaler praised the Fun Theory campaign in an article published in the *New York Times*. Particularly impressed by the Speed Camera Lottery, the article provides several additional examples for how lotteries have provided 'positive reinforcement'. He concludes that 'if governments want to encourage good citizenship, they should try making the desired behaviour fun' (Thaler 2012).

The claim that libertarian paternalist interventions can simultaneously nudge people towards choices that are in their best interests and preserve their liberty to choose has attracted intense criticism (see for example Yeung 2012; Wilkinson 2013; Goodwin 2012; Rebonato 2014). These critics point towards the paradoxical nature of the argument that nudges supposedly don't forbid any options or change economic incentives, while their effectiveness rests entirely on the premise that people fail to exercise their power of reasoned self-deliberation. In the view of these critics, nudges should rather be regarded as subtle forms of manipulation and as inconsistent with the preservation of individual autonomy, because they aim to take advantage of people's tendency to act unreflectively (Yeung 2012; Wilkinson 2013).

This critical view rarely appears in the advertising industry's discourse, though. For example, the material on behavioural economics published by the IPA is characterised by a very selective reading and interpretation of the academic literature. In a central article the IPA's Behavioural Economics Consultant Nick Southgate paradoxically claims that 'people instinctively mistrust manipulative Choice Architectures', that 'Choice Architecture is, in fact, very hard to exploit' and that 'people can and do learn how to interpret, resist and play systems' (Institute of Practitioners in Advertising 2010: 15; 17). Furthermore, the IPA downplays the potential infringement of people's autonomy when being made subject to 'nudges'. For example, Southgate argues that the 'real power of Choice Architecture is not its ability to coerce, but its ability to persuade people that this is the best way to choose' (Institute of Practitioners in Advertising 2010: 25). This paradoxical position is probably best exemplified by the following quote:

> Once they get into Behavioural Economics, marketers will realise that consumers are smart, not illogical. But before long these marketers will be capable of predicting consumers' choices and actions. That will make for some very smart marketers. (Institute of Practitioners in Advertising 2009a)

Unsurprisingly, the advertising industry actively promotes its own activities in the light of the moral justification used by libertarian paternalists. For instance, the most prevalent observation when analysing the IPA publications is how the use of behavioural economics is presented as a win-win scenario for both clients and consumers. For example, a central section of one of the IPA's publications on behavioural economics outlines the industry body's 'vision of the future': 'Imagine a future where product and service innovations can be offered by IPA agencies to provide greater value-added service to clients, and their customers' (Institute of Practitioners in Advertising 2009a: 11). In a similar vein IPA President Rory Sutherland argues that behavioural economics will 'refresh our thinking and our talent pool and with it we can use ideas to turn human understanding into business and social advantage' (Institute of Practitioners in Advertising 2009b). And behavioural economics consultant Nick Southgate elaborates that 'our profession also amounts to a pledge to be benign Choice Architects designing choices for mutual benefit' (Institute of Practitioners in Advertising 2010: 15). He continues:

> ...the ultimate opportunity that Choice Architecture offers is to help people make better decisions. Decisions that leave them happier, more confident and with the outcome they most desire. [...] By mastering these skills we will be able to assist both brands and consumers and by doing so raise the value of our industry. (Institute of Practitioners in Advertising 2010: 29)

This benevolent attitude expressed by the IPA is in stark contrast to a common sense understanding of the objectives of marketing as well as to the findings of recent reports on the use of behavioural economics in commercial contexts. For example, in the UK House of Lord's report on Behaviour Change Richard Wright, Director of Sensation, Perception and Behaviour at Unilever, is quoted as stating that 'the reality [...] is that any business is in business to make money' and that opportunities to influence behaviour would be taken if they were a means to selling more products (House of Lords—Science and Technology Select Committee 2011). Similarly, a report by the Australian Communication and Media Authority, which analysed the Australian communications market through the lens of behavioural economics, comes to the conclusion that service providers used behavioural insights to their advantage, leaving consumers worse off (Xavier 2011).

The advertising industry, however, tries to present itself as 'benevolent manipulators' and Silicon Valley-style solvers of 'real-world problems'. The case studies that are circulated and celebrated are mostly the ones that combine the use of digital technologies and social media with a 'worthy cause'. Paradigmatic for this is the so-called 'Impulse Saver' app provided by the New Zealand division of the bank Westpac. The app is essentially a big red button that, when pressed, allows users to transfer a predetermined amount of money into a savings account. It also features the so called 'Cash Tank'—a depiction of a customer's bank balance as a fuel tank, with preselected 'full' and 'empty' settings. The campaign idea originated, as Colenso BBDO managing director Nick Garret explains, in a TED talk by Rory Sutherland, in which he 'lamented our lack of ability to save as impulsively as we spend' (Campaign Brief 2011). The agency responded by developing the Impulse Saver app in consultation with Sutherland.

The extent to which the advertising industry is trying to adopt and leverage the positive aura surrounding libertarian paternalism and Silicon Valley's solutionism is perfectly illustrated by again quoting Rory Sutherland:

> I still genuinely believe that if you can hand-pick six or seven people from the advertising and marketing industry, there aren't many problems in the world that those people could not either solve or at least define in a new, interesting way. (Sutherland 2014)

This is a telling example of what Ihde (2008) would call 'the idol of paradise'—an overenthusiasm for the potential benefits of technological (and psychological) interventions coupled with a neglect of the potential by-products and unintended consequences of technology's inherently non-neutral nature.

Consumers for a 'Neoliberalism After Markets'

The philosophy underlying libertarian paternalist policies arguably reconfigures citizen–state relations in significant ways, departing from some of the central tenets of neoliberal modes of governance. Modern forms of liberal governance are, as Foucault's concept of governmentality suggests, based on forms of power that operate not by coercion, but by shaping subjectivities. It is in this sense that power is understood to be 'productive'—it works 'through' subjects by way of discourses, regimes of truth and governing practices that guide identity formation itself (Lemke 2001). In advanced liberal modes of government, these discourses revolve around notions of 'choice', 'autonomy' and 'personal responsibility'. As 'creatures of freedom, liberty and autonomy', subjects of advanced liberalism do not only enjoy autonomy, but are obliged to 'enterprise themselves' and take on the role as active and empowered market actors, exercising choice to maximise their own welfare (Rose 2006: 158). In short, neoliberal forms of governance are premised on notions characteristic of a 'reflexive modernity' (Giddens 1990)—deliberation, rational choice and reflection.

At the same time, however, and somewhat in contradiction to the neo-liberal paradigm of individual autonomy, the interior lives of citizens have increasingly become objects of government interventions. As Rose (1999) observes, the 'psy sciences' (psychology, psychiatry, social work and teaching) have become more and more important in framing the intellectual context in relation to which we evaluate ourselves. For instance, the current behaviour change regimes of libertarian paternalism depart from neoliberalism's central tenets in significant ways. While neoliberalism aims to subject the state and society to the paradigms of economic science, libertarian paternalism attempts to govern by psychological and neuroscientific principles. Most importantly, it invites citizen-consumers to consider themselves as irrational, cognitively impaired, 'post-rational' human subjects (Pykett 2013).

The emergence and popularity of the post-rational citizen-consumer can be understood as an attempt to restabilise neoliberal policies after the global financial crisis that unfolded in 2008 (Pykett et al. 2011; Boeckler and Berndt 2012; Jones et al. 2013). For example, Boeckler and Berndt (2012) suggest that we are at a point where neoliberalism is entering a new stage the authors tentatively call 'neoliberalism after markets' (ibid.: 429). The central characteristic of this new stage is not a refutation of neoliberalism's radical market orientation, but a shift of regulation. Essentially, 'neoliberalism after markets' seeks to more purposefully govern individual behaviour. As Boeckler and Berndt (2012: 429) argue, 'emphasis is no longer on regulating or deregulating the market; rather the market is in the process of becoming perfect, again, by regulating human behaviour'. Similarly, for Jones et al. (2013: 170) the 'psychological governance' of libertarian paternalism represents a collection of neoliberal techniques that are utilised to act 'as correctives to those very social, ecological, economic and individual harms produced by neoliberalism in the first instance'. As these critics point out, behavioural economics as a discipline is not rivalling neoclassical economics; despite challenging the model of homo economicus, it ultimately preserves the assumption that freedom to pursue economic self-interest is the most efficient and effective way of organising a social economy. The identified problems with neoclassical rationality assumptions are merely regarded as a call to action to rationalise consumers' irrational exuberances. This, however, leads to the rather paradoxical conceptualisation of a citizen-consumer who is considered to be capable of exercising his freedom, autonomy and self-responsibility, but who at the same time needs expert guidance and support in the 'correct' exercise of that capacity (Pykett et al. 2011).

As Jones et al. (2013: 169) note:

> Here we see how it is the irrational, neoliberal subject, acting through their freedom, that must be tempered by yet more neoliberal techniques of governance, namely the mobilisation of behavioural expertise to steer those freedoms in directions that are less self-defeating and socially harmful.

Libertarian paternalism thus appears to take Foucault's concept of a liberal governmentality to the extreme (Schrape 2014). As Leggett (2014: 9) summarises:

> Nudge could even be seen as the 'highest stage' of advanced liberalism and the scientific discourses of late modernity. On this reading, nudge is the point at which the mechanics of human choice itself, in apparently even the most mundane settings, become scientised and subject to disciplinary interventions.

Thus, nudging governance represents a key instrument in the responsibilisation of markets, and advertisers try to position themselves as authoritative actors in this process. This mode of governance, as Shamir (2008: 13) notes, establishes a 'market of moral authorities' that 'brings together merchants of moral values and moral entrepreneurs of economic value'. The industry's focus on 'utility' in its participation paradigm is an instructive example of this: 'Useful' applications such as Westpac's 'Impulse Saver' often double as 'moralizing technologies' (Verbeek 2009). They represent an implicit injunction to govern oneself by adopting these tools of self-responsibilisation and to thereby ensure that one conforms to the ideal consumer subject required by neoliberal market doctrine.

At the very least, 'utility devices' help the advertising industry in their attempts to discursively construct media-savviness exclusively in terms of consumers' exercise of utility maximisation (who would forego that much added value?), and not in terms of an informed and critical understanding of the complexity of social/commercial environments and the inner workings of the almost completely commercialised digital enclosure. In addition to that, advertisers' and policy-makers' focus on 'nudges' and 'utility' arguably complements and reinforces a disposition of reflexive irony and ambivalence characteristic for the contemporary 'brand culture' (Banet-Weiser 2012). The more brands engage with the politics of social responsibility and the 'moralization of markets' (Shamir 2008), the more consumers' relationship with brands is defined by a 'living ambivalence' (Banet-Weiser 2012: 216). Brands are not simply a tool of a commercial culture that sells lived experiences, but they are an inextricable component of a commercial culture that *is* the lived experience. And, given brands' almost seamless integration into the lived culture of consumers, ambivalence turns into a disposition that can be productively utilised by brands (we will return to this argument in more detail in Chapter 6).

At the same time, the adoption of helpful tools such as the Impulse Saver is premised on moments of 'ironic insights' on part of the user. As argued earlier in this chapter, behavioural economics and the neurosciences can be understood as 'technologies of ironic revelation' (Schneider and Woolgar 2012) in that they reveal the contrast between what a person thinks to be the case and the underlying 'truth' the technology or behaviour analysis supposedly confirms to be the case. Thus, for people to become users of such 'moralizing technologies' such as the Impulse Saver, they first have to develop an ironic perspective with regard to their own rational faculties. Behavioural economics 'ironically reveals' the limitations of our rational decision-making capacities, and the adoption of 'nudging' tools therefore requires an ironic disposition toward oneself.

THE IRONY OF EXTREME REFLEXIVITY

This self-responsibilisation by means of nudging devices fits neatly with neoliberal principles of individualisation, privatisation and self-regulation. As critics of the behaviour change agenda note, the philosophy behind nudging is characterised by an inherent political agenda focusing on individual responsibility while neglecting larger and more complex societal effects that are potentially the actual root cause of certain problematic behaviours (Jones et al. 2010). The lack of gambling regulation might serve as an instructive example here: While the gambling industry is developing ever more advanced methods for creating addictive choice environments such as 'time-bending' casino ambience and 'flow'-inducing slot machine designs (Schüll 2012), governments are shy to intervene with hard paternalism (legislation). Instead, they claim to preserve people's liberty to gamble while at the same time 'protecting' problem gamblers by providing tools of self-responsibilisation (for example, the aforementioned voluntary pre-commitment schemes).[3] Similarly, the advertising industry is creating a discourse by which it tries to portray itself as an authority of market responsibilisation, while at the same time creating environments that aim to exploit consumers' 'predictably irrational' nature.

With regard to these issues, the paradigmatic nature of VW's Fun Theory becomes particularly apparent. As we argued at the beginning of this chapter, this campaign illustrates the paradoxical nature of the behavioural turn and its associated model of human (ir)rationality. It exemplifies not only the attempts of the advertising industry to counter the 'problem' of declining symbolic efficiency by nudging people's behaviour through purposefully designed infrastructure and choice architecture. It also reflects the broader zeitgeist in terms of how the governance of populations is imagined and legitimised. Advertisers appear here as 'orchestrators of market responsibilisation', individualising the potentially harmful effects of social complexity while at the same time privatising and commodifying the creative capacities and social concerns of citizen-consumers. Most importantly, the Fun Theory reveals the deeply ironic nature of this form of governmentality. If we take behavioural economics as a 'technology of ironic revelation' (Schneider and Woolgar 2012), the campaign then goes a step further by using this technology as the underlying mechanic for 'ironic activations'. By turning consumers into 'amateur nudgers', it creates an 'empowered consumer' and simultaneously an interactive, self-reflexive reminder of the limits of this empowerment. Citizen-consumers are invited to practise techniques of manipulation, completely aware that these and similar techniques might be practised on them as well. Leggett (2014: 13) draws attention to the 'striking' public nature of the behaviour change agenda. This transparency takes the reflexivity of modernity to its logical extreme and subjects the technologies of behaviour change not only to interrogation by its architects, but also by its intended subjects. He writes:

> To adapt Foucault, we might label such reflexivity as 'domesticated governmentality'. Behind Foucault's account of the conduct of conduct lay a critical intent: To unmask the complexity and pervasive extent of governing practices, with the hope of identifying sites of resistance. However, the theory and reception of nudge operate as if the policy establishment itself has embraced the ideas of governmentality, through an entirely explicit commitment to eroding any remaining boundaries between state, civil society and individual identities. (Leggett 2014: 13)

The public nature of the behaviour change agenda—as practised by governments as well as advertisers—thus serves not as an enabling tool of empowerment, encouraging critical reflexivity, but as an (ironic) instrument of governance itself (Leggett 2014).

CONCLUSION

As Zwick and his co-authors (2008) argue, marketers and advertisers are important actors in the discursive construction of the consumer. They pursue the development of ideological imaginaries, management techniques and modes of relating that bring about consumer populations suitable for the respective modes of capitalist production. The 'predictably irrational' human nature underlying the concept of libertarian paternalism articulates the citizen-consumer 'according to a modality of self-correction' (Boeckler and Berndt 2012: 430). We are invited to conceive of ourselves as post-rational human beings, at the same time in charge and in need of assistance. This model of the contemporary citizen-consumer appears to be well suited for neoliberal forms of governance, aiming for radical marketisation but wanting to keep options open for initiatives of behavioural engineering. At the same time, it proves extremely popular with advertisers. By adopting central tenets of the neurosciences and behavioural economics, and by aligning itself with the broader trend of 'nudging' governance, the advertising industry has found a conceptualisation of the modern consumer subject that responds simultaneously to the requirements of the industry's participation paradigm as well as with the broader ideological zeitgeist of a 'neoliberalism after markets'. This conceptualisation maintains the notion of the empowered consumer while at the same time providing advertising practitioners with (quasi)-scientific understandings of the bases of human decision-making, which they can utilise to lend legitimacy to their practice. This benefits the industry not only from the perspective of justifying creative work in terms of advertising efficiency, but often also from a moral perspective. Behavioural nudges are generally presented as helpful correctives of innate cognitive biases and therefore purportedly work in the citizen-consumers' best interest. The celebrated Fun Theory campaign is an illustrative example of this logic.

The 'new behaviouralism' taking hold in marketing and advertising appears to be a contradictory concept that imagines the contemporary citizen-consumer as a paradoxical hybrid: empowered by digital technologies on the one hand, fallible and 'predictably irrational' on the other. And, as we will outline in the following chapters, the more these essentially flawed yet 'empowered' consumers interact in the digital enclosure of the participatory media environment, the more predictable they become. The underlying premise of a model of advertising based on eliciting consumer participation is not so much the control of meaning, but to orchestrate and control consumers by way of carefully designed choice environments and activations, subtle nudges delivered by apps and devices, predictive data analytics and subsequent real-time delivery of relevant promotional pitches. Consequently, advertisers and marketers increasingly create hybrid media spaces that pre-configure consumer activities and experiences and encourage the online mediation of these experiences, all with the objective of gathering ever more data. The aim of the following chapters is therefore to analyse in detail how advertisers attempt to develop and manage technocultural forms of branding that bring together the physical and the virtual, data and culture.

NOTES

1. The dual-systems model has a long history in psychology, philosophy and 'folk models' of decision-making, but it is far from being universally accepted. In contrast to economists and behavioural psychologists, neuroscientists regard the brain as a unified, integrated decision-making apparatus. The widespread popularity of the dual-systems model is not only a result of familiarity, given its historic forerunners, but, as Schüll and Zaloom (2011) argue, it is a consequence of its ideological fit with neoliberal paradigms. In their view the dual-systems model 'sustains a longstanding tenet of liberal governance: the notion that every member of the polity can be expected to harbor the same essential capacity for rational evaluation' (ibid.: 530). This is in contrast to a single-system brain model which would not allow for the notion of 'a pristine site of rationality' which might be 'resuscitated with the right policy tool' (ibid.: 530). Thus, the preference for a particular model of the brain is a result of its potency for legitimising governmental interventions.

2. In recent years, the Obama-administration in the US and David Cameron's Conservative government in the UK have enthusiastically embraced this so-called 'Third Way' of governance promised by proponents of libertarian paternalism (Jones et al. 2010, 2013; Whitehead et al. 2011). The 'nudge philosophy' is also shaping government policy development in France, the Netherlands, Argentina, Brazil, New Zealand and Germany (Jones et al. 2013b). Supported by the so-called 'Nudge Unit' of the UK government, behavioural economics has recently also been adopted by the state government of New South Wales in Australia.

3. In Australia the supermarket giant Woolworths has recently even merged the voluntary pre-commitment option with a frequent gambling rewards card, which not only acts as a loyalty scheme to encourage more frequent gambling, but also allows marketing messages to be flashed up on the gambler's machine as they play. This enables gamblers to order drinks

from the gambling machine without having to interrupt the gambling session, for example. See Milligan (2015).

References

Andrejevic, M. (2012). Brain Whisperers: Cutting through the Clutter with Neuromarketing. *Somatechnics*, 2(2), pp. 198–215.

Ariely, D. (2008). *Predictably irrational: The hidden forces that shape our decisions.* New York: Harper Collins.

Banet-Weiser S. (2012) *Authentic TM: The Politics of Ambivalence in a Brand Culture.* New York: New York University Press.

The Behavioural Architects (2015). *The Behavioural Architects.* Accessed December 12, 2015. Available at: http://www.thebearchitects.com/home

Boeckler, M. and Berndt, C. (2011). Geographies of markets: Materials, morals and monsters in motion. *Progress in Human Geography*, 35(4), pp. 559–567.

Boeckler, M. and Berndt, C. (2012). Geographies of circulation and exchange III: The great crisis and marketization 'after markets'. *Progess in Human Geography*, 37(3), pp. 424–432.

Bugaj, M. (2011). 'Attracting Customers with a Social Mission', *DDB Blog.* Accessed December 12, 2015. Available at: http://www.ddb.com/blog/community/attracting-customers-with-a-so/

BrainJuicer (2015). *Brainjuicer.* Accessed December 12, 2015. Available at: http://www.brainjuicer.com

Callon, M. (2005). 'Why Virtualism Paves the Way to Political Impotence: A Reply to Daniel Miller's Critique of *The Law of the Markets.' Economic Sociology: European Electronic Newsletter*, 6(2), pp. 3–20. Accessed December 12, 2015. Available at: http://econsoc.mpifg.de/archive/esfeb05.pdf

Campaign Brief (2011). 'Westpac counters kiwis impulse spending via Impulse Saver app developed by Colenso BBDO in consultation with Ogilvy UK"s Rory Sutherland', *Campaign Brief.* Accessed December 12, 2015. Available at: http://www.campaignbrief.com/2011/03/westpac-counters-kiwis-impulse.html

Cochoy, F. (2007). A Sociology of Market Things: On Tending the Garden of Choices in Mass Retailing. In Callon, M., Millo, Y. and Muniesa, F. (eds.), *Market Devices.* Oxford: Blackwell, pp. 109–129.

Cochoy, F. (2008). Calculation, Qualculation, Calqulation: Shopping Cart Arithmetic, Equipped Cognitio and the Clustered Consumer. *Marketing Theory* 8(1), pp. 15–44.

Cochoy, F. (2010). Reconnecting marketing to 'market-things': How grocery equipment drove modern consumption. In Araujo, L., Finch, J. and Kjellberg, H. (eds.), *Reconnecting Marketing to Markets.* Oxford: Oxford University Press, pp. 29–49.

Collins, J. (2015). 'Please, not another bias! An evolutionary take on behavioural economics', *Evolving Economics*. Accessed December 12, 2015. Available at: https://jasonallancollins.files.wordpress.com/2015/07/msix-20150729.pdf

Cova, B. and Cova, V. (2012). On the road to presumption: marketing discourse and the development of consumer competencies. *Consumption Markets & Culture* 15(2), pp. 149–168.

Creamer, M. (2012). 'Marketing's Next Five Years: How to Get From Here to There', *Advertising Age*. Accessed December 12, 2015. Available at: http://adage.com/article/news/marketing-s-years/237616/

Durham-Peters, J. (2001). Witnessing. *Media, Culture & Society*, 23(6), pp. 707–723.

Escudero, J. (2010). 'Cannes Lion Grand Prix 2010 – VW The Fun Theory', *YouTube*, 29 June. Accessed December 12, 2015. Available at: https://www.youtube.com/watch?v=qUs2lBo2QjM

Ferrier, A., Ward, B., and Palermo, J. (2012). Behavior Change: Why Action Advertising Works Harder Than Passive Advertising. Working paper presented at *Society for Consumer Psychology: Proceedings of the 2012 Annual Conference, Las Vegas, Nevada, February 16 – 18*, Society of Consumer Psychology, USA.

Ferrier, A. and Flemming, J. (2014). *The Advertising Effect. How to Change Behaviour*. Oxford: Oxford University Press.

Festinger, L., Riecken, H. W., and Schachter, S. (1956). *When Prophecy Fails*. Minneapolis, MN: University of Minnesota Press.

Giddens, A. (1990). *The consequences of modernity*. Cambridge: Polity Press.

Green, L. (2010). 'Rory Sutherland's quiet behavioural revolution gives the status quo bias a nudge', *The Telegraph*. Accessed December 12, 2015. Available at: http://www.telegraph.co.uk/finance/newsbysector/mediatechnologyan-dtelecoms/media/8023044/Rory-Sutherlands-quiet-behavioural-revolution-gives-the-status-quo-bias-a-nudge-think-tank.html

Hunt, S. D. (2002). Marketing as a Profession: On Closing Stakeholder Gaps. *European Journal of Marketing*, 36 (March), pp. 305–312.

Ihde, D. (2008). *Ironic Technics*. Copenhagen: Automatic Press/VIP.

Institute of Decision Making (2015). *Institute of Decision Making*. Accessed December 12, 2015. Available at: http://www.instituteofdecisionmaking.com

Institute of Practitioners in Advertising (2010). We're all Choice Architects now. 2nd ed. London: IPA.

Institute of Practitioners in Advertising (2011). Let's get practical. London: IPA.

Irrational Agency (2015). *Irrational Agency*. Accessed December 12, 2015. Available at: http://www.theirrationalagency.com

Jones, R., Pykett, J. and Whitehead, M. (2010). Governing temptation: Changing behaviour in an age of libertarian paternalism. *Progress in Human Geography*, 35(4), pp. 483–501.

Jones, R., Pykett, J. and Whitehead, M. (2013). Psychological governance and behaviour change. *Policy & Politics,* 42(2), pp. 159–182.

Kahneman, D. (2011). *Thinking, fast and slow.* London: Allen Lane.

Kay, G. (2013). 'The Future of Advertising Could Be Small', *Wharton Future of Advertising Program.* Accessed December 12, 2015. Available at: http://wfoa. wharton.upenn.edu/perspective/garethkay/

Lawson, S. (2014). 'Can behavioural economics help improve agency relationships?' *Mumbrella.* Accessed December 12, 2015. Available at: http://mumbrella.com.au/can-behavioural-economics-help-improve-agency-relationships-198375

Leggett, W. (2014). The politics of behaviour change: nudge, neoliberalism and the state. *Policy & Politics,* 42(1), pp. 3–19.

Lemke, T. (2001). 'The birth of bio-politics': Michel Foucault's lecture at the College de France on neo-liberal governmentality. *Economy and Society,* 30(2), pp. 190–207.

McFall, L. (2009). Devices and Desires: How Useful Is the 'New' New Economic Sociology for Understanding Market Attachment? *Sociology Compass,* 3/2, pp. 267–282.

McStay, A. (2013). *Creativity and Advertising.* Affect, Events and Process. London: Routledge.

Milligan, L. (2015). 'Woolworths under fire from anti-poker machine groups for introducing gambling rewards card in pubs', *Australian Broadcasting Corporation.* Accessed December 12, 2015. Available at: http://www.abc.net. au/news/2015-09-17/woolworths-slammed-by-anti-pokies-groups-gambling-rewards-card/6784210

MSiX (2015). MSiX – Marketing Science Ideas Exchange, *MSiX.* Accessed December 12, 2015. Available at: http://www.msix.com.au

Mumbrella (2014). 'Rory Sutherland Announced for new Marketing Science Conference MSiX', *Mumbrella.* Accessed December 12, 2015. Available at: http://mumbrella.com.au/rory-sutherland-announced-new-marketing-science-conference-msix-231239

Nyilasi, G. and Reid, L. N. (2009). Agency Practitioner Theories of How Advertising Works. *Journal of Advertising,* 38 (Fall), pp. 81–96.

Pykett, J. et al. (2011). Interventions in the political geography of 'libertarian paternalism'. *Political Geography,* 30, pp. 301–310.

Pykett, J. (2013). Neurocapitalism and the new neuros: using neuroeconomics, behavioural economics and picoeconomics for public policy. *Journal of Economic Geography,* 13, pp. 845–869.

Rebonato, R. (2014). A Critical Assessment of Libertarian Paternalism. Journal of Consumer Policy, 37(3), pp. 357–396.

Rose, N. (1999). *Governing the soul: The shaping of the private self.* London: Free Association Books.

Rose, N. (2006). Governing "advanced" liberal democracies. In Sharma, A. and Gupta, A. (eds.), *The anthropology of the state: A reader.* Oxford: Blackwell, pp. 144–162.

Schneider, T. and Woolgar, S. (2012). Technologies of ironic revelation: enacting consumers in neuromarkets. *Consumption, Markets & Culture,* 15(2), pp. 169–189.

Schrape, N. (2014). Gamification and Governmentality. In M. Fuchs et al. (eds.), *Rethinking Gamification.* Lüneburg: meson press, pp. 21–45.

Schüll, ND. and Zaloom, C. (2011). The shortsighted brain: Neuroeconomics and the governance of choice in time. *Social Studies of Science,* 41(4), pp. 515–538.

Schüll, ND. (2012). *Addiction by Design: Machine Gambling in Las Vegas.* Princeton: Princeton University Press.

Shamir, R. (2008). The age of responsibilization: on market-embedded morality. *Economy and Society,* 37(1), pp. 1–19.

Simms, J. (2010). Nudge in the right direction. *Director* 64(4), p. 30.

Sutherland, R. (2010). Why Advertising Needs Behavioral Economics. AAAA Research Matters, Bulletin #7150. Accessed December 12, 2015. Available at: http://www.aaaa.org/agency/pubs/NewEssentials/Documents/Ad%20Marketing%20and%20Media/Behavioral%20Economics.pdf

Sutherland, R. (2014). 'Rory Sutherland's ADFX 2014 talk', *YouTube,* 9 September. Accessed December 12, 2015. Available at: https://www.youtube.com/watch?v=1R-wTKI4Was

Thaler, R. H., and Sunstein, C. R. (2008). *Nudge. Improving Decisions about Health, Wealth, and Happiness.* New Haven: Yale University Press.

Thaler, R. H. (2012). Making Good Citizenship Fun. New York Times, 13 February 2012. Accessed December 12, 2015. Available at: http://www.nytimes.com/2012/02/14/opinion/making-good-citizenship-fun.html?_r=0

Tversky, A. and Kahneman, D. (1974). Judgment under uncertainty: Heuristics and biases. *Science,* (New Series), 185, pp. 1124–1131.

V-On (2013). 'IPA Professional Development for Advertisers', *V-On.* Accessed December 12, 2015. Available at: http://www.v-on.com/work/case-studies/ipa-professional-development-advertisers

Verbeek, P. (2009). Ambient Intelligence and Persuasive Technology: The Blurring Boundaries Between Human and Technology. *Nanoethics,* (3), pp. 231–242.

Volkswagen (2009). The Fun Theory, *Volkswagen.* Accessed December 12, 2015. Available at: http://www.thefuntheory.com

Whitehead, M., Jones, R. and Pykett, J. (2011). Governing irrationality, or a more than rational government? Reflections on the rescientisation of decision making in British public policy. *Environment and Planning A,* Vol. 43, pp. 2819–2837.

Wilkinson, T. M. (2013). Nudging and Manipulation. *Political Studies,* 61(2), pp. 341–355.

Xavier, P. (2011). *Behavioural Economics and customer complaints in communication markets*. Report commissioned by the Australian Communications and Media Authority (ACMA) as part of the *Reconnecting the Consumer* public inquiry. Melbourne. Accessed December 12, 2015. Available at: http://www.acma.gov.au/webwr/_assets/main/lib310013/behavioural_econ-cust-complaints_report_exec_summary.pdf

Yeung, K. (2012). Nudge as Fudge. *The Modern Law Review*, 75(1), pp. 122–148.

Žižek, S. (1999). *The Ticklish Subject*. London:Verso.

Žižek, S. (2014). *Event: A Philosophical Journey Through a Concept*. New York: Melville House Publishing.

Zwick, D., Bonsu S. and Darmody A. (2008). Putting Consumers to Work: 'Co-creation' and new marketing govern-mentality. *Journal of Consumer Culture*, 8(2), pp. 163–197.

CHAPTER 4

I/O Devices: Conducting Interactions

M&C Saatchi launched the Clever Buoy experiment for the Australian telecommunications provider Optus in 2013. Clever Buoy uses the Optus network and Google to send messages to lifeguards at beaches warning them of the location of sharks. They envisage the device could be more broadly used to provide feedback from the ocean environment to beachgoers in communities around the country. Chief Marketing Officer Nathan Rosenberg explained that Optus sought to communicate the strength of the Optus network by building an application that would actually 'change the world' rather than just use traditional tactics like advertising or sponsorship (Google Creative Sandbox 2014). To realise this ambition the advertising agency suggested that they partner with Google.

As this example illustrates, the interplay between advertisers and media platforms extends beyond purchasing targeted advertisements to engineering media objects and processes. Roberta McDonald, Head of Creative Agency Engagement at Google, echoed this sentiment by describing the project as a 'valuable experience in learning' in how to use digital infrastructure to solve business challenges (Google Creative Sandbox 2014). Google, through initiatives such as *Art, Copy & Code* and *Think With Google*, invest in developing relationships with advertisers that explore ways to engineer their platform into marketing systems. Google particularly promote their capacity to use digital infrastructure to provide more context-aware and real-time calibration of social life. They frequently position this engineering effort as focused not on delivering customised information via a touchscreen but instead creating 'connected life platforms'

© The Author(s) 2016   97
S. Brodmerkel, N. Carah, *Brand Machines, Sensory Media
and Calculative Culture*, DOI 10.1057/978-1-137-49656-0_4

that modulate the interplay between living users and strategic interests of marketers (Eagle 2015).

The Optus Clever Buoy demonstrates how a previously inanimate object such as a marine buoy can be turned into an important transfer point or switch between media infrastructure and the social world. In this chapter we examine the efforts of advertisers and media platforms to smooth out the friction between living bodies and calculative media systems. The experimentation of advertisers with bespoke devices such as the Clever Buoy unfolds within a larger ecosystem of media experimentation. Just as advertisers are attempting to build a range of sensory touchpoints between consumers and brands, media platforms such as Facebook and Google undertake engineering projects that aim to expand the sensory capacities of media. The emergence of data-driven advertising and participatory media machinery is driven to some degree by the interplay between advertisers and media platforms. Media platforms evolve under the commercial imperative to provide value and utility to advertisers. For their part, advertisers become dependent on the capacity of these platforms to calibrate attention, action and affect.

This chapter analyses advertiser experiments with material devices such as buoys and beer bottles. While these devices are often small scale, bespoke and not always clearly linked to specific marketing objectives, they are nonetheless important examples of advertisers' responses to the changing media and business environment. They might represent the experimental vanguard in a market, yet whether they fail or succeed, they illustrate the trajectory of specific market formations (Cochoy 2012). The experiments and engineering projects we focus on here enable us to develop a conceptualisation of audience participation in a calculative media system. We pay particular attention to the interface between the living and open-ended capacities of the consumer and the technical protocols of media. The devices we purposively select and analyse are the 'sensory touchpoints' or 'affect switches' in a calculative mode of participation. These media devices and platforms do not function only, or even primarily, in a symbolic way, but rather act as transfer points for attention, attraction and affect in specific times and places. Each of these devices are brand machines in the sense that they coordinate the interplay between cultural and computational processes.

The illustrations that inform this account emerge partly from fieldwork over the past ten years. One of our earliest observations of advertiser experimentation with bespoke material devices was at the 2006 Big Day

Out music festival on Australia's Gold Coast. Among several activations on the site by Virgin Mobile was a series of insulated fibreglass domes on arched metal poles. The domes offered festivalgoers a soundproof bubble to hide in if they wanted to phone friends lost in the festival noise and chaos. Elsewhere on the site Virgin had erected a large screen where they invited festivalgoers to 'text the fest' by sending SMS messages to a designated number that would then post them on the screen for the audience to see. These were early experiments by brands in using material objects—some inanimate like the domes, others digitally networked like the screen—to orchestrate consumers' use of mobile devices in everyday cultural spaces (for a full account see Carah 2015). Virgin's domes are just one relatively obscure and long forgotten material object advertisers have created in the process of 'prototyping' the things we do with mobile devices such as cameras and phones. This chapter draws on fieldwork at cultural events where we observed the interplay between consumers and brands' devices and installations, together with a systematic analysis of material circulated on social media platforms, trade press and presentations at industry conferences. In particular, we draw on presentations by M&C Saatchi, DDB Worldwide and Facebook employees at Mumbrella 2014, Australia's largest media and marketing conference. This observation at industry conferences is complemented with an analysis of videos distributed by agencies, industry bodies and industry events.

SENSORY TOUCHPOINTS

Devices such as the Clever Buoy are an example of adventurous clients allowing advertisers to experiment with the sensory capacities and touchpoints of brands. In the process, these advertisers create applications that reshape what advertising is. This mode of advertising involves agencies producing material objects rather than symbolic content. It requires agencies to develop industrial and software design expertise and methodologies. In appearances at industry conferences and awards shows M&C Saatchi explained that the buoy came about in response to a brief from Optus to 'make the intangible tangible by bringing to life the strength of the Optus network'. The Clever Buoy was developed through a software and industrial research and design process. M&C Saatchi assembled a network of scientists who had developed techniques for identifying sharks and programmers who could build the software and hardware for the system. The advertising industry promotes projects such as Clever Buoy as 'future proofing' for agencies that can no longer sustain their business model by only producing content but must learn to use 'creativity' to solve business problems (Mills 2014). The emergence of these device, design and engineering based modes of advertising reshapes institutional relationships. New relations are forged between advertising and other sectors. Advertisers reach out to technical experts in software, hardware and industrial design. They develop partnerships with scientists working in universities or research organisations. Agencies also enter into new agreements with clients about intellectual property. Agencies tend to view the hardware, platforms and devices they develop as their intellectual property, licensing only their application to clients; whereas clients consider the material platforms and devices created to be specific to their brand, trying to prevent competitors gaining access to the media infrastructure they have invested in. Regardless of how agreements are reached about whether agencies or clients own the intellectual property attached to the material devices created, agencies develop capabilities in the design of material devices that transfer from client to client. As such, agencies iteratively become sites for a broad range of research and development in the use of media technologies to manage social, cultural and ecological processes.

In the case of the Clever Buoy, the material object created by the advertising agency is a sensor that collects, processes and transfers information. Clever Buoy is a system comprising several interconnected devices: a sonar unit, CPU, Optus satellites, Google networks and platforms, and mobile devices carried by lifeguards to receive alerts. It does not, however, convey a 'message' in the traditional advertising sense of providing information about the specific qualities of a product or its symbolic value in consumer culture. Rather, the object plays a role in orchestrating a network of generative relationships. The buoy helps to organise life on the beach and in doing so performs the capacities of the product, rather than representing them. The device stimulates and channels the transfer of affect in various ways. This includes the capacity of humans and non-humans to affect other living bodies. In this case, sharks become living participants in the mediation of a brand. The shark is harnessed as a stimulus that enables the brand to be *felt* and, by extension, create brand value. A shark becomes a stimulus in a media system that can respond to and manage transfers of affect. The network of media devices create reassurance by sensing the fear-transmitting shark. The capacity of media infrastructure to identify and mitigate risk constructs affective resonance around the brand. The shark is the necessary threat the brand's devices neutralise. Furthermore, the

Clever Buoy also demonstrates the utility and social responsibility dimensions of the industry's participation paradigm. The industry's solutions are presented as 'win-win-win': creating value for the brand, providing utility for the consumer and offering broader social benefits such as community safety and investment in innovation (Guerrier 2014).

While sceptics might quickly point out that an advertising 'experiment' such as Clever Buoy is not 'sales oriented' or even just an example of 'scam' campaigns made by agencies seeking industry awards (of which Clever Buoy won several, including a coveted Titanium Lion at the Cannes Advertising Festival), we argue that objects like this can be seen as indicative of the trajectory of advertising agencies and practices (Porter 2015). In his presentation at the industry conference MSiX in 2015, James Hunter, a highly awarded creative and founder of the agency Previously Unavailable, characterised advertising awards as 'a peer-review system for how advertising might work in the future'. This characterisation was met with widespread approval amongst conference attendees. In this spirit, we can critically map out the trajectory of media applications the buoy is part of. The current version of the buoy updates lifeguards at the beaches where the buoys have been installed. The rollout of the buoys is relatively small scale, and their broad-based utility is perhaps dwarfed by the international media coverage and industry awards they have garnered. Optus and M&C Saatchi, however, envision that the device could be rolled out more widely and serve as a platform upon which many consumer and environmental applications could be developed. This claim is defensible when considered in relation to the investment of Australian governments in shark detection systems. The New South Wales government, for instance, invested $16 million in a shark surveillance strategy in 2015, nearly half of which is set aside to trial new technologies (*Shark Year Magazine* 2015).

We can also envision how shark detection technologies such as Clever Buoy could be expanded from lifeguards to consumers. A consumer sitting on a beach might feel their smartwatch vibrate. The Optus app on the watch would alert them that a shark is approaching the beach. The range of sensory outputs the app harnesses might expand. A consumer in a beachside town could be alerted when the surf conditions were optimal. A surfer out in the water could be alerted when a change in weather was coming or when their length of time in the water plus their physical exertion indicate they ought to return to the beach to rehydrate and rest. Individuals could sync their apps so that parents or friends could always identify where each other was in the water. This range of applications can expand where the brand positions itself as an infrastructural underlay that augments the affective and sensory experiences of the beach. Via the buoy the brand orchestrates everyday activity, collecting and organising information from the surrounding environment and using that information to affect consumers with pulses and prompts delivered via a media network. The 'qualities' of the brand are not conveyed symbolically in the sense of the brand giving consumers information about their products and services that must be cognitively processed; they rather work affectively by establishing themselves as a network of utilities that shape how consumers experience everyday spaces and practices. Pulses and prompts delivered through a media network shape how consumers experience the utility of a brand and replace the persuading of consumers that specific rhetorical claims about a product or service are credible.

AFFECT SWITCHES

Advertisers are now involved in the creation of a range of bespoke material devices that orchestrate the interplay between consumers and media platforms. These bespoke devices are part of a proliferation of 'things' connected to media and internet infrastructure. An expanding number of everyday objects—cars, fridges, watches, shoes, household appliances and so on—are becoming enrolled in the Internet of Things. These things act as switches or transfer points that incorporate moments of everyday life into the apparatus of connectivity and computation facilitated by media platforms. As we have already indicated, collaborations such as Google's *Art, Copy & Code* illustrate the ways in which the experiments of advertisers with software and hardware design are interrelated with the broader research and development projects of large media platforms such as Google and Facebook. In significant ways, the imperatives of advertisers shape the development of media platforms. For instance, the transition of Facebook toward a mobile-first platform in recent years was driven by the imperative to develop a platform that seamlessly integrates advertising into the 'native' flow of content on the news feed of the mobile app. Bespoke material objects such as Optus' Clever Buoy are the curious and inviting 'ends' of advertisers' media infrastructure. They are often the touchpoint between the living body of consumers and their material cultural world and the interfaces, protocols and databases of media platforms. These devices offer compelling examples of the emergence of a mode of advertising that shifts its emphasis away from controlling the expression and attachment of particular ideas or qualities to a product and toward using media as devices for calibrating qualification or meaning making as an open-ended and continuous process.

The touchpoints between users and media platforms—be they the bespoke material devices advertisers create or mass-market hardware such as smartphones and virtual reality sets that platforms create—can be productively understood as *affect switches*. An affect switch transfers the capacity of a living being to affect into the calculative apparatus of media infrastructure. They are a kind of I/O device that converts sensory stimuli into computable digital information (pronounced 'eye-oh' and short for input/output). I/O designates any program, operation or device that transfers data into a computing system. A transfer of data is an output from one device and an input into another. For example, the keyboard translates the physical movement of the fingers into a series of digital commands in a software program. Similarly, the mouse translates the fine motor skills of the hand into digital data that moves a cursor on a screen.

Optus' Clever Buoy is an affect switch in the sense that it transfers the living movements of sharks into digital information that affects consumers. We have already encountered other affect switches in this book, such as Durex's Fundawear, which conveyed human touch from a smartphone app to underwear using haptic sensors, and Fox's AFL Alert Shirt, which conveyed the physicality of a football game to fans shirt with haptic sensors triggered by a smartphone app. In the next two chapters we will examine several objects that switch or transfer affect within a digital media system. The affect switch is a critically important component in the operation of brand machines that calibrate attention and action because it is the transfer point between the living body or social world and the calculative media system. Both advertisers and media platforms are engaged in the work of engineering these sensory touchpoints. Advertisers engineer touchpoints where they create objects such as buoys and bottles that stimulate consumers to register data or affect one another via a media platform. Media platforms engineer touchpoints where they develop interfaces and hardware that enable ever more aspects of lived experience to be opened up to the platform's capacity to watch and respond.

The word 'switch' has three useful meanings in this account. First, a switch is a material device that alters the flow and direction of an object or information such as an electrical current or a train on railway tracks. In computing, a switch is a 'program instruction' that makes a selection from a number of available paths (*Oxford English Dictionary* 2015). Switches engineer and govern the flow of objects and information in a system. Secondly, switching is an action whereby humans exert control via a system. Humans with the capacity to 'flick' a switch are able to coordinate movement in a system. They can affect the direction of an object, transmission of information, intensity of light or volume of a sound. To be 'at the switch' is to have the capacity to calibrate action in a system, to be able to prompt or stimulate action and attention in specified directions. Thirdly, switches imply choice on the part of participants. Participants can choose to switch in and out of a flow of information. Individual users might not be able to control what information is directed to them via a system, but they may be able to switch out of that flow altogether. Taken together, these definitions illustrate how a switch operates as a relational human–machine component in a system.

Affect switches are one part of a larger engineering effort to expand the sensory capacities of media (McStay 2013). The affect switch is the component of a brand machine attached to a living body, a kind of 'communicative prosthesis' that links the living capacities of the body to the decision-making capacity of media platforms (Andrejevic 2015). This capacity to harness the productive capacities of the body can be understood as affective labour. As argued elsewhere (see Carah 2014a, 2014b; Carah and Shaul 2015), affective labour can be understood in two registers: the deliberate narration of affects and the general capacity to sense and stimulate other bodies. It is no coincidence that the concept of affective labour emerges from accounts of modes of capital that are interdependent with networked, participatory and calculative information systems (Hardt 1999; Terranova 2000). These accounts illustrate how media networks depend on the social, creative and communicative capacities of humans. Media platforms are the product of the interface between technology and human users. Within these networks participants (or users, consumers, audience members, fans) are productive as both the creators of specific ideas and feelings and the generation of a general social network that is open to monitoring and modulation. Brands operate as 'computational loops' (Lury 2004) in these 'biotechnical' media systems (McStay 2013).

The affect switch is instrumental to a mode of advertising that doesn't rely on conveying a specific symbolic claim or quality as much as it aims to coordinate the living action of bodies. The affect switch is one part of advertisers' efforts to create media devices that track, respond to and modulate social relations in real time (Clough 2009; Dean 2010).

At a basic level, this mode of advertising needs users who register their social relationships on databases so that the friction between lived experience and media can be iteratively resolved. Consumers play the critical role of switching affect via media devices both to capture the attention of other users and to record those exchanges in databases. Media platforms depend on the affective capacities of users to channel social life through their apparatus. A switch is a component in engineered social systems that seeks to affect bodies toward a certain purpose, nudge them in a certain direction, or stimulate and intensify their attention. Switches conduct in both the sense of 'directing a performance' and 'allowing the flow' of affect in one or more directions. In the next sections we take beer bottles as one example of the creation of bespoke material objects by advertisers that act as devices for calibrating the interface between consumers and media infrastructure.

BEER BOTTLES AS AFFECT SWITCHES

Bespoke beer bottles are one example of the affect switches that advertisers are experimenting with. Beer bottles become more than just a container for the product, but an important I/O device in the media infrastructure of advertising. The bottle is the material object distributed by the brewer into the hand of the consumer and material context of consumption. The bottle is the touchpoint between the living body of the consumer and the brand. As such, alcohol brands already have an infrastructure for making themselves 'present' in the cultural context of consumption. The bottle travels from the brewer to the 'ends' of the distribution network. Once 'transferred' to the consumer at a bar or bottle shop however, the brewer traditionally 'loses sight' of its movement as it transitions into the affective zone of play that characterises alcohol consumption. As advertisers seek ways to extend their media infrastructure into these everyday consumption rituals the bottle emerges as a critical transfer point for the input and output of human affects and digital data. The Heineken Ignite, Strongbow StartCap and Grolsch Beacon are all examples of beer bottles that have been reformatted as I/O devices. These experiments leverage the presence of the beer bottle in consumption rituals as a point of connection with media platforms. Each imagines the bottle not only as a container for the product, or even as a symbolic device that carries a brand logo on its label, but rather as an I/O device that stores and transmits information between living bodies and media platforms.

In 2013, Heineken created a beer bottle designed to augment the experience of nightclubs. Pol Hoenderboom and Bart Mol, the creative directors at DDB and Tribal Amsterdam who developed the bottle, explained that they used a lean start-up approach to go from concept to prototype in ten weeks (DDB Worldwide 2013a, 2013b). They were asked by Heineken to develop a 'mobile solution that would connect their brand to consumers in clubs'. The 'smart bottle' they designed featured a custom 3D-printed base with LEDs, a microprocessor, accelerometer and wireless transmitter. Like many bespoke digital devices, the bottle is a composition of several devices that sense and transmit information. The agency also wrote a VJ software program that could control the LEDs in the bottles separately. The VJ software program was part of the media infrastructure of the nightclubs within which the bottles were embedded. The VJ software could stimulate the bottles to flash in certain rhythms or patterns in response to the proximity of other bottles or music being played by the DJ. The accelerometer and wireless transmitter worked as sensors that could stimulate the lights in the bottle to flash to the beat of the music and the movement of people in clubs.

Heineken claimed their intention was to create a mobile media device that captured people's attention in the club without them having to engage with the screen of the smartphone. They were distinguishing the bottle from attempts to engage with clubbers that interrupt the club experience. While delivering a piece of content via a video screen or smartphone momentarily dislocates the consumer from the club experience, the bottle integrates the brand into the rhythms of light, sound and bodily interactions clubs stimulate. The bottle augments the social interactions rather than interrupts them. While the brand doesn't interrupt the consumer via the smartphone, the bottle nonetheless stimulates the use of smartphones as part of the rhythms of club life. Clubbers react to the bottle by pulling their phones out, taking pictures and videos and circulating them through social networks. The smartphone might be seen retrospectively as the killer app in a diffuse effort to create a network of devices that orchestrate consumer action in an open-ended yet computable way.

Of critical importance here is that the Heineken Ignite bottle works in conjunction with the capacities of the smartphone, but doesn't attempt to deliver content via its screen. The advertiser creates a material device that stimulates a mode of participation interdependent with the sensory and calculative capacities of media. The bottle is a sensor that responds to sound and movement in the club. The flashing of the bottle prompts consumers to convert the sociality of the club into digital information they register on social media platforms. The bottle is an affect switch that senses sound and movement, transforming it into flashes of light that prompt consumers to interact with each other, capture images and circulate them as part of their enjoyment of nightlife.

The Heineken Ignite bottle can be understood as a switch in a larger 'engine' comprising living bodies, the media infrastructure of a club, smartphones and social media platforms (Cochoy 2012). Grolsch's Movie Unlocker bottle and Strongbow's StartCap more directly used the bottle as a device for triggering responses via a media platform (Strongbow 2012). Grolsch launched the movie unlocker bottle in the Russian market in 2013 (The Bench Cinema 2014). The cap of the bottle contained a Bluetooth beacon. When consumers opened the bottle the beacon was activated and could then be 'tapped' against any Bluetooth enabled media device to access a movie from a website developed by the brand. Yoni Solomon from Vibes noted that the 'beacons provide a fluid, easy mobile experience that promotes participation … when looking to drive commerce of any kind, the best practice is to create as frictionless an experience as possible' (Barris 2014). While the broad take-up of streaming services might rapidly diminish the value of accessing a movie free of charge online, the important development in this experiment is the bottle as a triggering device connected to a media platform. Taking the principle of the bottle as a trigger, we can see how the bottle could be used to stimulate other actions: production of content on a social media site, recording of data about purchases and bottle movements, access to exclusive live content or to events, the production of merchandise via a 3D printer, the recording of consumption patterns and so on. Once a bottle becomes a trigger in a media system it becomes a generic device for converting the human action of 'cracking open' a bottle of beer into a transfer of digital information. Once this ritual moment is connected to a digital platform potential innovations open up.

Strongbow's StartCap illustrates how bottles can become triggers that augment experiences in material cultural spaces such as bars and nightlife venues. The cap of the Strongbow bottles contained an RFID tag which, when the cap was popped, was activated and sensed by wireless scanners that were programmed to 'respond' to the tag. Popping the bottle of Strongbow could turn on music or trigger lights in the venue. Connected to apps on a smartphone, the cap could also trigger the production of check-ins or exclusive content on social media. Again, other innovations could follow, such as tracking consumption, triggering the provision of exclusive content, accruing rewards or benefits on an app, and so on. Once the beer bottle has an RFID tag in its cap it becomes part of a larger ecosystem of media devices. For beer brands, the bottle is the material object they send out into the world that spends time in the hands of consumers. Converting the bottle into a media device that can collect, store and transmit information enables the brand to orchestrate action in the times and places of consumption. In each case the capacity of the bottle to affect is interrelated with surrounding media devices and platforms: the smartphone, transmitters and receivers, content players and databases that trigger light and sound. Rather than produce content, the advertising agency reformats a material object as a media device. The bottles are affect switches that stimulate and register bodily capacities and human sociality. Affect switches like these beer bottles are another example of the 'passified' forms of participation we discussed in Chapter 2 (Andrejevic and Burdon 2015). In these formations, participation is valuable to advertisers not because we make conscious decisions to articulate our life narratives with a product, but simply because our movement through the social world involves 'flicking' or 'triggering' switches in a media system. The brand machine captures and converts these everyday bodily actions and expressions into digital information available for computation.

From Exposure to Engineering: Advertisers and Media Platforms

A key dynamic in the current emergence of interactive media technologies is the continuous negotiation that unfolds between media platforms and advertisers. As outlined in Chapter 1, this negotiation primarily centres on the construction and valuation of audience engagement. In a mass media system, conventions such as ratings systems were created to package and describe audiences. These conventions structured the relationship between media and advertising institutions. Media platforms such as Facebook and Google have created advertiser–platform relationships outside these conventions. Aside from the fact that they are not open to independent scrutiny of their analytics, these platforms have dramatically expanded the facets, qualities and moments of audience attention that can be assembled, calculated and valued (Lury and Moor 2010). The development of the interfaces, protocols and algorithms that govern interaction on media platforms are the outcome of agreements between media platforms, investors, advertisers and users about how attention is brokered and valorised.

The process of audience construction unfolding on these platforms is highly dynamic. Facebook does not provide advertising features as a finalised 'end product' to advertisers. Rather, the platform's advertising model emerges iteratively via ongoing interplay between platform and advertisers. Facebook and advertisers participate in continuous experiments to construct new configurations of audience attention, affect and action that can be made available for modulation via the platform. Speaking at the AANA Connect conference in Australia in 2014, Facebook's Head of Measurement and Insights in Australia Helen Crossley made a pitch to advertisers centred on the growing ability of the platform to conduct data experiments (Crossley 2014). Crossley's industry pitch echoed the statements of other Facebook representatives internationally where they promote their capacity to work with major brands to integrate data from Facebook, corporations' internal marketing databases and third parties in an effort to construct and leverage 'custom' and 'lookalike' audiences. Custom audiences enable advertisers to use their own in-house data to locate specific individuals on the platform. Lookalike audiences introduce an element of simulation, as Facebook creates audiences within its platform that match as closely as possible data the advertiser has about its current market.

The overlay between the data sets held by the platform, marketers and other third party data providers enables Facebook to simulate different configurations of audience attention and capacity. Much more than just enabling advertisers to target customised audiences at scale, Facebook offers an architecture for testing various audience compositions and mapping audience patterns in 'higher resolution'. Facebook offer marketers a means of 'enhancing' their markets by integrating data sets. In the USA, Facebook has opened up 'partner categories' where they enable firms to 'rent' data from other players in the Facebook ecosystem in order to develop more customised advertising. Crossley presented Facebook as a platform that applied its machine learning and algorithmic capacities to combine data from their platform, analytics companies and marketers. Facebook acts as a data broker and analyst, helping marketers to configure and locate custom audiences.

Facebook is not positioning itself as simply offering audience attention as a 'ready-made' product, but rather presents itself to marketers as a platform able to conduct experiments using data. Via these data experiments a new kind of 'audience' is emerging. In a mass media system an audience was sold as a mass of standardised attention: a group of individuals, paying attention at a particular moment in time, with various shared characteristics in a described concentration. For instance, a television audience could be described as having certain characteristics with regard to age, gender and income. From this construction of the audience commodity followed strategies of speaking to the audience as a collective. The audience was always, to some degree, a mass of undifferentiated attention. The iterative experiments conducted between advertisers and platforms such as Facebook attempt to shift the audience commodity from a describable unit of collective attention to a specifically customised moment where an individual is available to be stimulated or nudged.

Crossley predicted that Facebook's 'hyper-targeting' would end the concept of market segmentation by enabling advertisers to buy their exact audience at scale. An audience would no longer be a proxy simulation based on broad variables, but would constitute a number of specified individuals engaged at defined moments and locations via a chosen stimulus. The pitches of platforms such as Facebook and Google to industry audiences are characterised by an escalating series of claims about the capacity to stimulate the body of a consumer in a specific time and place in symbolic, cognitive, behavioural and affective ways. Critical to discern is that the platforms are shifting from selling 'more refined' or 'more customised' packages of audience attention as advertising space toward an architecture for modulating flows of data to capture particular moments of attention and stimulate specified actions. The effort to collect more data is accompanied by the equally important process of developing the tools, apps and interfaces that advertisers can use to enable more seamless interplay between their own marketing systems and Facebook's architecture for locating and intervening in everyday moments.

Facebook's growing capacity to experiment with a range of data to build custom and lookalike audiences stimulates the effort of brands to locate more moments to intervene in. If the public and scholarly perception of Facebook's advertising model has so far predominantly focused on its capacity to offer more refined targeting, the emergence of tools such as custom and lookalike audiences illustrates the effort to create a seamless integration of data between advertisers and the platform. The platform is working towards a data-driven experimental mode of advertising that dispenses with conceptual frameworks such as segmentation to intervene instead in specific moments triggered by the actions of specific individuals.

At this point, we can return to affect switches, for example the interactive beer bottles we discussed earlier in the chapter. The experiments of advertisers with bespoke material devices unfold in the larger engineering ecosystem of media platforms such as Facebook, Google, Twitter, Instagram, Snapchat, Tinder, fitness apps and so on. When an advertiser creates a bottle that flashes in response to the beat of a song in a club it is aiming to synchronise play between the living human body and a calculative media platform. The same effort is underway when a media platform's data scientists aim to simulate connections between consumers and brands at particular times and places. Each is working at the material and virtual interface between bodies and media systems. The flashing bottle might stimulate the playful capture and circulation of an image via a media platform such as Facebook, which in turn triggers calculations that determine connections between 'lookalike' individuals, moments and actions across the platform in real time that can be made available to advertisers.

The experiments advertisers conduct with material objects such as buoys and beer bottles happen at the sensory touchpoint between media platforms and the bodies of consumers. They make bodily capacities available to the data-driven calculations of the platform. This interplay between media platforms and advertisers is a form of 'media engineering' (McStay 2013: 130). Media platforms engineer the interplay between bodies and machines. As van Dijck (2013: 29) puts it, platform protocols, algorithms and interfaces limit and afford certain expressions and actions. Platforms are engaged in large-scale software and hardware engineering projects that aim to code sociality in ways that enable new configurations of audience attention, affect and action to be sold to advertisers. Advertisers are no longer confined to the production and circulation of symbols, but instead are adapting engineering approaches into their industrial routines. Advertisers create systems and objects that orchestrate social life. In this view, 'media are not simply blank vehicles for content, but represent an interaction of technical, intellectual, economic, institutional, biological, social, cultural and creative forces. They facilitate certain processes and deny others' (McStay 2013: 13). McStay (2013) clearly maps out how the capacities of media are expanding. Media are becoming more able to sense, stimulate and modulate a wide array of bodily affects. Media systems affect us with more than just content; they move beyond the screen to a variety of touchpoints with our bodies and everyday environments. Advertising is a key site where investment is made in ongoing experiments with the form, capacities and applications of media to human life.

The Vomit Problem

The escalating capacity of media platforms such as Facebook to offer advertisers opportunities to experiment with audiences is interrelated with the expanding sensory capacities of media platforms and devices. The bespoke I/O devices advertisers create are positioned at the interface between consumers and media platforms. These bespoke objects are just a few examples of the range of sensors that monitor and modulate the rhythms of everyday life (Andrejevic and Burdon 2015). Sensory objects are a critical component of media platforms because they enable platforms to expand their capacity to code and program social life. Sensors are the point at which media platforms become enmeshed with our bodies, homes, cars, public spaces and workplaces. The buoys and beer bottles we have considered are examples of these I/O devices that channel specific moments of attention and action within social life and natural environments into the calculative apparatus of a media platform. As much as these devices can be observed *in situ* as affecting the experience of the beach or the club, we can also understand them in relation to the data experiments Facebook enable advertisers to undertake.

Consider the case of Heineken Ignite. Heineken's advertising agency designs a media device that can be integrated into the social life of a nightclub. The object is a sensor that responds to the sound in the club environment and movement of clubgoers' bodies. The object creates an affective and sensory experience within the club between brand and consumers. But it also stimulates interconnections with calculative media platforms. Smartphones come out and images of the bottles are captured and circulated on Facebook and Instagram. The geo-locational data attached to those images could assign those individuals to a custom audience product made available immediately to Heineken, enabling them to intervene in the club experience in that moment, or to follow them up the next day, or the next time they are in a similar location. The flashing bottles stimulate the creation of images, which in turn prompts the creation of many forms of data. Images circulated might be tagged to reveal relationships between individuals and specific spaces. As the machine-learning algorithms of the media platform develop, the bottle itself might be a scannable code that immediately connects the image to a particular location and individuals. Other alcohol brands have experimented with turning their containers into scannable objects that can be recognised by smartphones. For example, Bundaberg Rum in Australia has launched a series of cans each with portraits of different iconic Australians. When two cans are held together and scanned by the app, image recognition software enables consumers to discover who the 'legend' is and see an exclusive digital video. They can also upload an image of themselves, which the app then manipulates to look like one of the iconic portraits (Sparks 2015). In each case the bottle is a significant object because it is part of the affective flow of drinking as a cultural practice. The bottle is a material object that facilitates rather than interrupts bodily exchanges. This is a highly significant quality of the bottle as an affect switch that engineers frictionless transfer between bodies and digital platforms. Bart Mol from DDB and Tribal Amsterdam explained that Heineken Ignite emerged from the observation that smartphones disrupt the social atmosphere of clubs. Therefore, they had to conceptualise a media device that would 'tap into the natural behaviour of people' in clubs. Rather than deliver content via a smartphone to the consumer, they created a device that would prompt clubbers to generate and circulate content and data.

The bottle can be understood as a switch in the larger platform ecosystem. The custom and lookalike audiences Crossley promoted to the advertising industry can be enhanced by material objects that stimulate the generation of digital information that links brands together with an expanding number of social moments and spaces. The more clubgoers interact with media platforms as part of the club experience, the more they register their location, proximity to brands, cultural moments and other consumers on the platform. This enables the platform to incorporate them in simulations of real-time lookalike or proximate audiences. They not only reveal themselves as available bodies in the club in that moment, but they also set up a vector from the club and the connection with a specific cultural experience and brand through to the larger data archive Facebook has about their interests, actions, movements and expressions over perhaps more than a decade of their lives. Sensory and stimulatory objects such as the Heineken Ignite bottle are part of a larger interplay unfolding between brands, bodies and media platforms. Critically, the bottle collects and transfers data and content as part of the rhythmic exchanges in the club. It is embedded within the club's body–machine circuitry and in turn connects the play of the dancefloor to the calculations of the database.

So far in this book we have seen a range of material objects work as affect switches between the living capacities of consumers and the calculative actions of media platforms: underwear, beer bottles, marine buoys, T-shirts and staircases to name a few. What these objects all share in common is the effort to expand the sensory capacities of brands, enabling them to incorporate a greater range of movements, actions, affects and sensations into the machinery of branding. In all cases these objects are dependent on a larger media platform or ecosystem. The RFID-tagged beer bottle relies on a media platform to trigger a sound or action. Sensor-rich underwear relies on the smartphone screen and app to transfer touch. The staircase in the railway station requires movement sensors to trigger sounds. The buoy relies on social media protocols and interfaces to provide information about shark movements. Just as advertisers experiment with devices that intervene in expanding facets of everyday life, platforms are also engaged in hardware engineering projects that aim to enable more seamless play with living bodies. Augmented reality projects such as Google Glass and Facebook's Oculus Rift illustrate the effort to imagine media as a machinery for simulating, intervening in and augmenting bodily experiences of reality.

The critique of the political economy of social media that has focused until now on the capacity of platforms to conduct surveillance and target advertisements is being rapidly outpaced by these platform developments. As Packer (2013: 297) puts it, digital 'media power is founded upon the ability to capture, measure, and experiment with reality'. Drawing on Kittler he argues that

> Media forge real power/knowledge relationships that reassemble the world. The breakthrough of digital media, as Kittler rightly pointed out, is that all media—all of reality—is now translatable. The world is being turned into digital data and thus transformable via digital manipulation. [...] the computational turn in advertising recognises that with enough data, the control of human behaviour can be worked upon piece by piece through constantly refining Kittler's key media processes—collecting, storing and processing data. No grand plans, aesthetic visions, or obfuscation is necessary.

Packer's point is that the ideological critique of advertising is not productive in an era where advertising does not depend on specific symbolic strategies or on creating broad, ideologically coherent 'ways of life' that consumers enter into. The first wave of critical scholarship about social media and advertising focused on either user-generated content or user-generated data (Andejevic 2010; Cohen 2008; Fuchs 2011). Users were exploited either because social media platforms could harness their productive capacities to create content that incorporated brands into their life narratives, or because their participation generated data that enabled more customised targeting. Following Packer and Kittler, however, we argue that we need to develop a critical account of media platforms that operate as experiments with engineering reality.

As much as these platforms are developing more sophisticated algorithms for brokering attention, and continuously A/B testing interfaces and protocol designs to increase engagement, they are also engaged in developing hardware that alters the entanglement between media and living bodies. The purpose of these engineering projects ultimately is to increase flows of revenue from advertisers by making bodies more available for modulation. The acquisition of the virtual reality start-up Oculus Rift by Facebook helps to illustrate the larger trajectory at play. Like the buoys and beer bottles we have considered so far, Oculus Rift is an affect switch, a technology aiming to smoothly integrate a media platform with the visual system of the body. The problem that Oculus Rift faced at the beginning was one that had bedevilled all virtual reality systems: they make the user feel like throwing up. Peter Rubin explained in his profile of Oculus in *Wired*, 'if you turn your head and the image on the screen that's inches from your eyes doesn't adjust instantaneously, your visual system conflicts with your vestibular system and you get sick' (Rubin 2014). Oculus Rift's engineers claim to have solved this problem since their headset is the first that successfully simulates 'parts of the human visual system directly'. Facebook's investment in Oculus Rift seems surprising if one views virtual reality as just a gaming device. The investment, though, indicates the trajectory Facebook envisage for their platform: a shift from sharing content to exchanging immersive experiences. Virtual reality is just one of a number of ways in which media platforms will interface directly with the human body's sensory capacities.

In his announcement of Facebook's acquisition of Oculus Rift, Mark Zuckerberg (2014) explained that when you put Oculus Rift on 'you enter a completely immersive computer-generated environment'. While its first applications would be in gaming, Zuckerberg gestured toward the rationale for a social media platform such as Facebook acquiring it:

> After games, we're going to make Oculus a platform for many other experiences. Imagine enjoying a courtside seat at a game, studying in a classroom of students and teachers all over the world or consulting with a doctor face-to-face—just by putting on goggles in your home. This is really a new communication platform. By feeling truly present, you can share unbounded experiences with people in your life. Imagine sharing not just moments with

your friends online, but entire experiences and adventures. These are just some of the potential uses. By working with developers and partners across the industry, together we can build many more. One day, we believe this kind of immersive, augmented reality will become a part of daily life for billions of people. (Zuckerberg 2014)

Zuckerberg told the magazine *Vanity Fair* that he acquired Oculus Rift because he believed that the next great computational platform was virtual reality devices with the capacity to 'communicate our full sensory experience and emotions to someone through thought' (Chafkin 2015). Facebook's experimentation with virtual reality is echoed by other major technology companies. Microsoft, Sony and Google have all invested in virtual and augmented reality projects and start-ups. Where virtual reality creates a fully immersive simulated environment, augmented reality—such as Google's Glass and Magic Leap projects—overlay digital simulations over human vision. Rather than view an opaque screen, see-through lenses augment human vision with digital information, visualisations and enhancements.

Zuckerberg explained to *Vanity Fair* that 'it's pretty clear that at some point in the future we're going to have glasses or contact lenses … that can give you some more sense of context of what's going on around you in the world' (Chafkin 2015). Zuckerberg envisions a seamless interface between his media platform and the living body of users. The hardware device of the platform might be glasses or even a thin contact lens, rather than a touchscreen. While this might be a decade away, the trajectory is toward the interfaces of media platforms augmenting our experience of everyday life. The interface will be a see-through screen laid over our human vision. As we look down a city street icons will appear above buildings the media platform predicts we might be attracted to because they sell our favourite beer or coffee, have good reviews, have a product it knows we are looking for, or that our friend is in there. Or perhaps, even stranger still, we could be informed about the gender composition of a club, or the relative health of the people inside a restaurant drawing on physiological information. If we visit a natural landscape we might be able to adjust the view to see what it looks like at different times of the day or year, or what it looked like when a friend visited it. Or we could look at an urban landscape and see how it changes over time. The screen of the smartphone is opaque; the interface of the next media platforms will be a translucent film that augments how our bodies encounter and affect the world around us.

Oculus Rift is commercially valuable and technically significant because in solving the 'vomit problem' it advances the effort to create seamless flow between the sensory capacities of the human body and the sensory devices of a media platform. As such it is a useful metaphor for the larger development of media platforms as immersive zones of play. Seen from this lens we can think of Facebook as a valuable media platform not only because it sells relevant formations of audience attention and enables advertisers to conduct data-driven experiments and simulations with potential markets, but also because it offers expanding opportunities to experiment with the human capacity to affect and act. The vomit problem is a metaphor for the creative problem-solving happening at the 'ends' of media infrastructure, where platforms connect with living bodies. Where advertisers and platforms work together to create new objects and associated modes of calibrating affect, action and attention, they are working to smooth out the interface between platforms and bodies. The notion of the vomit problem stands for any point of friction between the living body of consumers and the calculative capacities of a media platform.

The research and development activities of platforms such as Facebook, Instagram and Google focus in part on resolving points of dysmorphia between our bodies and media technologies. The investments they make are driven by the imperatives of advertisers seeking seamless integration into the flow and play of consumer life. The core business of media platforms is engineering human sensory and affective capacities, making them available to constant monitoring, modulation and modification. What advertisers' bespoke devices and platform-level hardware engineering projects have in common is the effort to engineer human experience in its many dimensions. Media platforms are calculative devices for sensing and processing data. The creation of devices that stimulate and orchestrate human capacities by both advertisers and media platforms configure media as a tool that collects, processes and experiments with information about embodied affect and social life (Packer 2013).

The activities of advertisers and platforms are each part of a larger effort to engineer the entanglements between bodies and media platforms. In some important ways these projects are strikingly similar to Schüll's account of 'annihilation' in the play between gamblers and poker machines. The poker machine and casino engineer an 'intimate entanglement between humans and technology' (Schüll 2012: 309). Just as the gambler seeks a kind of annihilation at the hands of the machine, the machine promises but never quite delivers in order to sustain the player's engagement with the machine in an unending loop of stimulus, response and adaptation. Schüll (2012: 153) describes the proliferating range of sensory devices incorporated in casinos and poker machines to calibrate the interplay between the body of the gambler and the calculative apparatus of the game. A range of devices from loyalty cards to facial recognition track players from machine to machine over time. The players' routines are registered as data that enables the machines to calibrate the rhythms of play in real time. Over time this capacity to calibrate becomes more finely tuned, and with that the ability to immerse gamblers in the 'zone of play' expands. Significantly, gambling engineering is both a software and hardware project: from the game play on the screen to the design of the casino. The same can be said of Facebook—from the flow of the news feed to the virtual reality headset to the indirect impact on the design of cultural spaces, such as nightlife venues (see Carah and Shaul 2015; Carah 2015). There is a useful analogy between the engineering effort of mediated gambling and the interplay between brands and media platforms. Mediated gambling involves a continual interplay between the creation of real-world spaces such as a casino, a range of I/O devices from the poker machine to the loyalty card to the gambler's body itself, and the data-driven algorithmic management of game play. Likewise, advertising also resembles this structure of stimulus and adaptation as a range of sensors are deployed to calibrate the social life, immersing consumers in a zone of play that makes their social capacities available to advertisers via interactive media platforms.

Our conceptualisation of the relationship between advertisers and platforms, and their respective media engineering projects, can no longer be confined to assessing the tools and conventions for packaging and targeting audience attention. Instead, the relationship between advertisers and media platforms is more productively understood as one driven by the mutual effort to engineer the interface between living bodies and lived experiences and flows of data-driven responsive media stimuli. These media engineering experiments unfold in multiple sites. Media platforms such as Facebook and Google invest in hardware engineering projects that aim to capture and simulate human capacities. Their investment in augmented and virtual reality technologies reveals their intention to make their platform an immersive interface between our bodies and the material and social world. These platforms are large nodes in a wider media engineering ecosystem. Start-ups emerge in continuous cycles with various attempts to expand the sensory capacities of media, and where the platforms see the value of their engineering know-how and achievements they seek to integrate them into their platform. Advertisers' attempts to create bespoke devices must be seen as part of this ecosystem too. Objects like the Heineken bottle or the Optus Clever Buoy are interdependent with media platforms. In the case of Clever Buoy it is technically dependent on media platforms to function; without Google the buoy would just be an inert object bobbing on the ocean's surface. Likewise, the Heineken Ignite bottle is dependent on media platforms that transmit data to the bottle to stimulate its lights in relation to media stimuli in the venue. We argue also that an object like Heineken Ignite can only be imagined in relation to media platforms. Media platforms undergird a culture where individuals seek to use devices to affect one another, and for those moments of affect to be archived in the databases of media platforms. The Heineken bottle emerges in a mode of advertising that is looking to stimulate the capacity to affect via media platforms.

This experimentation unfolding at advertising agency and platform level suggests that media platforms' role in reshaping advertising has surpassed simply offering more refined targeting of symbolic information for cognitive processing. The dynamic emerging between advertisers and platforms involves not just data-driven experiments but also experiments with the material hardware and sensory capacities of media. The media experiments of advertisers are part of a larger research and development ecosystem. The 'rivers of gold' that flow from advertisers into Facebook and Google fund the engineering efforts that expand the hardware and software capabilities of media. Where in the 20th century advertising's 'rivers of gold' funded quality newspaper journalism, they now fund media engineering projects. This is a critical shift. Revenue is no longer invested in the symbolic richness or quality of media but rather its capacity to interface with our bodies. For both strategically and critically minded followers of advertising, we need a political economy of communication that does not focus only on the capacity of media to control flows of symbols that humans process, but more importantly on the capacity of media platforms to calibrate bodily capacities more generally. The capacity of media platforms to calibrate affective intensity in real time is succeeding their capacity to act as socialising ideological tools that operate on broad populations to shape shared ways of life (Clough 2009). The vomit problem is a useful metaphor for this engineering effort, and its implications for how we understand what media are and how they enable what advertising is to undergo a dramatic shift.

Conclusion

So far in this book we have developed an account of various attempts by advertisers to 'code' or 'hack' around the friction between the specifically human characteristics of consumers and the calculative logic of marketers. In the turn to behavioural economics we see an effort to bypass what consumers 'think' in favour of what they 'do'. Rather than persuade rational human consumers, behavioural economics presupposes an irrational consumer who can best be influenced on the behavioural level. In the effort to engineer sociality using media platforms and bespoke material devices we observe advertisers' attempts to create a sensory 'zone' within which an expanding range of communicative moments and capacities are channelled into the calculative architecture of a media platform. Some of these devices remain clunky prototypes. In time, though, they may well be seen as the iterative first wave of attempts to code the living human body into a calculative real-time mode of advertising.

Advertising is embedded in a larger media engineering effort to reduce friction between the constantly morphing, creative capacities of consumers by more seamlessly tuning them into the capacities of media to watch and respond. Advertisers immerse consumers in a zone of play where their activity is wholly generative, rather than needing them to adhere to specific ideas or persuade them with specific messages. Advertisers approach consumers as productive units to be harnessed and calibrated, rather than to be persuaded or disciplined. With that in mind, advertisers and media platforms set about engineering a range of ways of reducing the friction between the open-ended playfulness of human experience and the calculative efficiency of media platforms that have always been imagined as market infrastructure. This engineering effort unfolds at the sensory touchpoints or moments of affective transfer between living bodies and media platforms.

Advertisers operate in a larger ecosystem of media engineering. Media platforms enable advertisers to use an expanding array of data both to target specified individuals and to simulate potential audiences. The relationship between advertisers and media platforms is developing in a context where media must be understood as a broad-scale engineering project to expand beyond media as a system for managing symbol-processing to a system for calibrating machine-body interplay. In the next chapter we position the emergence of advertising as a practice within an ecosystem of media engineering in relation to accounts of the participatory nature of branding. In doing so, we consider the purpose, productiveness and political value of participation in a media system geared to harness participation as an open-ended generative resource. We illustrate how a participatory mode of branding gradually shifts from using media to provide symbolic resources for participation to using media as an infrastructure for orchestrating participation in general. In Chapter 7 this leads us to consider how industry, policy and critical-activist conceptualisations of advertising as a solely representative or ideological process fail to properly describe advertising in the age of media engineering.

REFERENCES

Andrejevic, M. (2010). Surveillance and alienation in the online economy. *Surveillance & Society*, 8(3), pp. 278–287.

Andrejevic, M. (2015). 'Becoming Drones: Smartphone Probes and Distributed Sensing' (pp. 193–207) in Wilken, R. and Goggin, G. (eds.), *Locative Media*. Routledge: London.

Andrejevic, M. and Burdon, M. (2015). Defining the Sensor Society. *Television & New Media*, 16(1), pp. 19–36.

Barris, M. (2014). 'Grolsch leverages beacon-enabled bottle cap to build engagement in movie offer.' *Mobile Marketer*. Accessed December 12, 2015. Available at: http://www.mobilemarketer.com/cms/news/advertising/18358.html

The Bench Cinema (2014). 'Grolsch Beer: The Movie Unlocker Bottle'. *Vimeo* 2014. Accessed December 12, 2015. Available at: https://vimeo.com/102412875

Carah, N. (2014a). Brand value: how affective labour helps create brands. *Consumption Markets & Culture*, 17(4), pp. 346–366.

Carah, N. (2014b). Watching Nightlife: Affective Labor, Social Media, and Surveillance. *Television & New Media*, 15(3), pp. 250–265.

Carah, N. (2015). Algorithmic brands: A decade of brand experiments with mobile and social media. *New Media & Society*. Published online before print September 17, 2015, doi: 10.1177/1461444815605463

Carah, N., & Shaul, M. (2015). Brands and Instagram: Point, tap, swipe, glance. *Mobile Media & Communication*. Published online before print August 12, 2015, doi: 10.1177/2050157915598180

Chafkin, M. (2015). 'Why Facebook's $2 Billion Bet on Oculus Rift Might One Day Connect Everyone on Earth', *Vanity Fair*. Accessed December 12, 2015. Available here: http://www.vanityfair.com/news/2015/09/oculus-rift-mark-zuckerberg-cover-story-palmer-luckey

Clough, P. T. (2009). The New Empiricism Affect and Sociological Method. *European Journal of Social Theory*, 12(1), pp. 43–61.

Cochoy, F. (2012) 'The Pencil, the Trolley and the Smartphone: Understanding the Future of Self-Service Retailing Through its Sociotechnical History', in J. Hagberg, U. Holmberg, M. Sundström, M., and L. Walter (eds.), Nordic Retail Research, Emerging Diversity. Göteborg: BAS, pp. 215–233.

Cohen, N. S. (2008). The valorization of surveillance: Towards a political economy of Facebook. Democratic Communiqué, 22(1), pp. 5–22.

Crossley, H. (2014). 'The Future of Online Marketing', AANA Connect. YouTube, 20 May. Accessed December 12, 2015. Available at: https://www.youtube.com/watch?v=ceKvWJd8ALM

DDB Worldwide (2013a). 'Heineken: Ignite Story', YouTube, 28 May. Accessed December 12, 2015. Available at: https://www.youtube.com/watch?v=BvOSiX_yzws

Dean, W. (2010). 'Mad Men: season one, episode 13', The Guardian. Accessed December 12, 2015. Available at: http://www.theguardian.com/tv-and-radio/tvandradioblog/2010/jun/17/mad-men-season-one-episode-13-finale

van Dijck, J. (2013). The culture of connectivity: A critical history of social media. Oxford: Oxford University Press.

Eagle, A. (2015). 'The reimagination of daily life in 2015', Think With Google. Accessed December 12, 2015. Available at: https://think.storage.googleapis.com/docs/the-reimagination-of-daily-life-in-2015_articles.pdf

Fuchs, C. (2011). Web 2.0, Prosumption and Surveillance. Surveillance and Society, 8(3), pp. 288–309.

Google Creative Sandbox (2014). 'Lighting Talks 2014 Full Talk – Clever Buoys – a story of sharks, advertising & technology', YouTube, 18 June. Accessed December 12, 2015. Available at: https://www.youtube.com/watch?v=yB8Ztzdt97I

Guerrier, A. (2014). 'A New Value Framework for Creative Businesses – BBH Labs at SPOT Conference 2014', Slideshare, 25 May. Accessed December 12, 2015. Available at: http://www.slideshare.net/AgatheGuerrier/a-new-value-framework-for-creative-businesses-bbh-labs-at-spot-conference-2014

Hardt, M. (1999). Affective labor. Boundary 2, pp. 89–100.

Havas Worldwide. (2013). 'Fundawear', Havas Worldwide. Accessed December 12, 2015. Available at: http://www.havasworldwide.com.au/work-fundawear.html

Lury, C., & Moor, L. (2010). Brand valuation and topological culture, in Aronczyk, M. and Powers, D. (eds.), Blowing up the brand: critical perspectives on consumer culture. Peter Lang: New York, pp. 29–52.

McStay, A. (2013). Creativity and Advertising. Affect, Events and Process. London: Routledge.

Mumbrella (2014). 'Rory Sutherland Announced for new Marketing Science Conference MSiX', Mumbrella. Accessed December 12, 2015. Available at: http://mumbrella.com.au/rory-sutherland-announced-new-marketing-science-conference-msix-231239

Oxford English Dictionary (2015). 'Switch', Oxford: Oxford University Press.

Packer, J. (2013). "Epistemology NOT Ideology OR Why We Need New Germans". *Communication and Critical/Cultural Studies,* 10 (2–3), pp. 295–300.

Porter, M. (2015). M&C Saatchi's Optus Clever Buoy Wins Even More Global Recognition, *B&T.* Accessed December 12, 2015. Available at: http://www.bandt.com.au/marketing/mc-saatchis-optus-clever-buoy-wins-even-more-global-recognition

Rubin, P. (2014). 'The inside story of Oculus Rift and hwo virtual reality became reality', Wired. Accessed December 12, 2015. Available at: http://www.wired.com/2014/05/oculus-rift-4/

Shark Year Magazine (2015). 'NSW Shark Management Strategy: $16m for surveillance, deterrents, science and education.' *Shark Year Magazine.* Accessed December 12, 2015. Available at: http://sharkyear.com/2015/nsw-shark-management-strategy-16m-for-surveillance-deterrents-science-and-education.html

Sparks, H. (2015). 'Bundaberg Releases New Range of Innovative Cans', *Drinks Bulletin.* Accessed December 12, 2015. Available at: http://drinksbulletin.com.au/2015/09/bundaberg-releases-new-range-of-innovative-cans/

Strongbow. (2012). 'StartCap: The World's first digital bottle top remote controls a bar', *YouTube,* 12 November. Accessed December 12, 2015. Available at: https://www.youtube.com/watch?v=2mr_WfVYLZo

Terranova, T. (2000). Free labor: Producing culture for the digital economy. *Social text,* 18(2), pp. 33–58.

Zuckerberg, M. (2014). Untitled Facebook post, *Facebook.* Accessed December 12, 2015. Available at: https://www.facebook.com/zuck/posts/10101319050523971

CHAPTER 5

Infrastructure: Orchestrating Action

At Australia's largest media and marketing conference Mumbrella 360 in May 2014, a series of thought leaders from advertising, media and marketing came together to 'theorise' how their industries were changing. Evident in many of the presentations was the effort of advertising agencies and marketing consultancies to sell a participatory data-driven mode of advertising to brands. Facebook promoted the capacity of their data teams to generate insights by aligning client and Facebook data sets. Marketing consultancies spoke of their ability to use online devices to 'follow' consumers across various touchpoints from real-world retail to media consumption habits. Advertisers showcased their capacity to create material devices in design-based 'sprints'. 'New' media businesses such as Buzzfeed and 'old' media businesses such as free-to-air television both celebrated and bemoaned the changing relationship with advertisers who no longer wanted to buy only packages of attention from pre-determined audiences, but rather viewed media as platforms for orchestrating participatory, continuous and data-driven interactions with markets.

Amir Kassaei, the Chief Creative Officer of global advertiser DDB, presented himself as the omnipresent philosopher oracle of the event; his plane having only touched down from his previous engagement in the Asia-Pacific, he offered attendees maxims such as 'digital is not media, it's infrastructure' and 'creativity + humanity + technology = influence'. As each of these theories appeared on the screens behind him the audience raised their smartphones and tablets to capture images and circulate them through their social media networks. Early in his presentation Kassaei

© The Author(s) 2016   125
S. Brodmerkel, N. Carah, *Brand Machines, Sensory Media
and Calculative Culture*, DOI 10.1057/978-1-137-49656-0_5

played a video by comedian Louis CK that had recently 'gone viral'. CK recalls the case of a children's ballet performance that all the parents in the audience were busy filming on their mobile devices while the performance was on. CK provides a scathing commentary on this now all-too-familiar scenario: 'Everybody is watching a shitty movie of something that's happening … look at your fucking kid! The resolution of your kid is unbelievable!' he says, before observing that you will never 'watch videos of your kids doing shit you missed the first time it happened, these kids are dancing for no one!' Kassaei didn't use the video to make a critical observation of the way mobile devices affected our relationships with family and friends. Rather, he told the audience that CK illustrated an important lesson for advertisers. There was no longer 'any difference between online and offline'. Given this, 'everything is potentially an entry point to the digital infrastructure'. For the advertising professional, Louis CK's astute observation about social relationships in a device-saturated culture was a theory about the dramatically expanded range of moments advertisers could now access and from which they could generate value. The culture CK skewers is, in advertising-land at least, one to be celebrated as a great opportunity. Kassaei explained that advertising was now about connecting devices with people, and as such, practitioners should see digital not as 'media'—in fact, he declared that social media 'doesn't exist'—but rather as 'infrastructure'. By this he meant that advertisers must invest their energy and creativity in digital devices as tools for orchestrating a proliferating range of everyday actions and moments. Advertisers must conceptualise media as infrastructure for coordinating the relationships that produce markets. There is no separation between online and offline, no gap between brands' representations in imagery and the relationships they orchestrate in the world.

Paramount in Kassaei's narrative was a cohesive industry 'theory' of branding as a participatory and creative process, in line with the participation paradigm we outlined in Chapter 2. First, advertising is a social process that depends in part on consumer participation. Secondly, participation is open-ended, and so advertisers must cede some control to consumers to exercise choices about their expressions and actions. Thirdly, to be able to harness consumer participation brands need to be a socially meaningful part of consumers' identities. Brands therefore have to use media infrastructure to deliver 'something meaningful and useful in the life of the consumer'. Kassaei positioned this claim within industry folklore by invoking the mythology of DDB founder Bill Bernbach's 'creative revolution'. He referred to Bernbach's preserved original office at DDB in New York as a 'holy place', and described the creative revolution 60 years ago as the last great innovation in advertising. In the mid-20th century the 'solution' to the problem of the savvy consumer was advertisements that revealed their own artifice. As already mentioned, Bernbach's VW campaign is mythologised in industry history as the campaign that anointed this knowing and sceptical consumer as the primary object of advertisers' imaginations. By making this move, advertising unravelled its belief in the direct ideological purchase of its claims—consumers that believed the information advertisers gave them—and moved into a more complicated relationship with consumers, one that imagined them as empowered in a savvy sense: aware, knowing and sceptical. Advertisers began to build a mode of advertising that revealed its own mechanics to audiences. If Bernbach set down the principle that advertisers needed to focus on the solution and therefore think beyond the direct ideological purchase of their claims, Kassaei said today's practitioners need to recognise that the solution is no longer content. They need to start with a problem and end with a touchpoint. Advertising is not the content in between, but the way that devices are used to build and orchestrate experiences. It is, in other words, a combination of devices, networks and channels that articulate interactions and moments. Advertisers, Kassaei argued, therefore needed to build a machinery for stimulating consumers to 'create truth for the brand'. They could do that by giving consumers structured tools and resources to work with. Consumers needed to be understood as 'friends' not 'targets', and, with this maxim in mind, Kassaei demonstrated how DDB followed Bernbach's spirit by employing a problem-solving 'friends first' logic with several case studies.

Each of the case studies contained critical elements: the identification of a problem, the location of that problem within an everyday cultural context that makes it meaningful to consumers, the creation of a device that enables consumers to solve the problem, and the utilisation of the device as a stimulus for the consumer to connect with and communicate the brand. Importantly, sometimes the device is a media object (such as a smartphone app) whereas on other occasions the device is a material object of another kind (such as a plastic bag or a bottle). Regardless of whether it is a digital interface on a smartphone or an analogue material object, the device stimulates and orchestrates action within a media and cultural infrastructure. Our aim in this chapter is to think about how the creation of these problem-solving devices is at the heart of the imagination of a participatory mode of branding that extends beyond merely expressive forms of participation that require the consumer to create meaning or embed brands into meaningful portrayals of their own identities. The participatory mode of branding we are illustrating here is one where participation is experimental, data-driven and action-oriented.

Advertising as Infrastructure

One of the case studies Kassaei presented was a DDB campaign for Glad plastic trash bags (Alma Agency 2013). The agency conceptualised the piles of rubbish left behind in the camping grounds of popular music festivals as a problem that undermines consumers' festival experience in ethical terms. For many consumers, music festivals are an ethically meaningful and visually aesthetic experience. Festival organisers invest significant resources in making the sites appear inviting, for instance with art installations and wilderness spaces. Many festivals promote environmental or sustainability values as part of the festival experience. Festivalgoers for their part capture images of the festival site and distribute them via their social media profiles. Images of the festival grounds not only convey their experience but also their values—for art and music, but also for natural spaces and ecological sustainability. The ethics of this experience are undermined by a final morning ritual familiar to anyone who has camped out at a major music festival: Often tired, filthy and hungover after several days of partying away from home, thousands of people pile into their cars and head back to the city, leaving behind all their trash. Many festivalgoers in fact leave their entire camping set up behind: tents, sleeping bags, couches and discarded rubbish. The 'disposable' nature of the festival experience not only undermines festivals' environmental credentials, but it also leaves many festivalgoers feeling bad about the damage festivals do to the natural parklands and farms they are held on. Festivalgoers find themselves in a campground surrounded by piles of rubbish with nowhere to put it. This is a problem for the festival organisers, who have to invest significant resources in cleaning and regenerating the site each year, but also for the consumer in terms of how they 'feel' about their own practices and values.

Having conceptualised the problem in this way, Kassaei explained how DDB employed a 'friends-first' logic with Glad to offer festivalgoers a readymade solution. The agency created a plastic tent that doubled as a giant trash bag. On the way into the festival patrons were given the tents which they could sleep in for the duration of the festival, and then on the final morning they could place all their rubbish in the tent and zip it up for easy rubbish collection. The brand described this solution as a 'zero waste camping experience' (Alma Agency 2013).

The tent can be thought of as a device in several important ways. First, the tent is a device that structures participation. It generates *action* in a relatively standardised way. The tent prompts consumers to set it up, sleep in it and put rubbish in it. The tent orchestrates a predictable and repeatable activity within a given social context. But it also stimulates the production of media *content*. The tent gets incorporated into the streams of images festivalgoers create of their experience. The tent is a symbolic device in the most literal sense. It was distributed from a Glad-branded 'provisions' store on festival sites in a Glad-branded box. The stall, box and tent are 'cool' objects that festivalgoers capture images of and post online, incorporating the brand logo into their narrative about the festival. It stimulates the use of other devices (such as a smartphone to take images of it and post them on social media), and therefore prompts the production of *data* as a by-product.

Secondly, the tent is a device that enacts an ethical claim by giving the consumer something to do. Glad doesn't just express a concern for the environment in a symbolic sense, it offers the consumer a device for taking an action that they construct as ethical. In Kassaei's terminology the brand acts as a 'friend' in the sense that it enables the consumer to undertake a meaningful action. The tent doesn't actually offer any environmental benefit; it primarily enables consumers to act and feel good about caring for the environment. This affective dimension is the critical element of the device's ethical claims. The device gives consumers a basis for expressing a set of values. The solution enables the consumer to 'feel good'. The brand offers a solution that aligns with the moral economy of the music festival—hedonistic wild abandon with a spot of cleaning up before you leave. The tent appeals to the ethical consumer: an individual whose ethics are performed within the framework of consumption. As we discussed in Chapter 3, the consumer is 'responsibilised' as an actor in the market.

Thirdly, the tent is a device that enables the smooth functioning of a market. In this case, the tent structures action in a way that makes the management of the festival site more efficient. Importantly, the environmental claims of the tent are quite thin. Despite Glad's claims that the tent is a 'zero waste camping experience', the tent clearly does not offer any actual environmental benefit; it doesn't reduce waste, it just offers consumers a large enough receptacle to enclose their waste. The material benefit is to festival organisers who effectively get consumers to undertake some of the labour of collecting waste together for more efficient disposal. The tent makes cleaning up the festival site easier by 'outsourcing' some of the work to consumers. While DDB claim to create a 'simple idea from Glad that redefines the way we look after our environment', we might respond and say the device does little for the environment; it is after all just a rubbish bag big enough to sleep in! But, nonetheless, it may well be highly effective in orchestrating the smooth functioning of a brand and a market.

In each of these respects the Glad tent illustrates critical components of many of the devices advertisers now create. This conceptualisation of the tent reveals several aspects of what we mean by claiming that devices are critical to contemporary advertising practice. Objects such as the tent, and also the buoy and the beer bottles from Chapter 4, are devices in the sense of being a bespoke material object with a specific purpose *and* an invention or scheme with certain imperatives to direct or channel action. If, as Kassaei explained, a brand is the 'sum of all experiences you have with a company', then a brand is the infrastructure that coordinates that interaction. Content is only one element of that process. Advertisers are therefore moving into the business of *doing* infrastructure: orchestrating action, managing flows of content, generating insights from data that enable brand machines to be optimised.

Participation After Expression

This chapter examines how orchestrating consumer action generates brand value. What productive activities do consumers undertake in a mode of branding no longer entirely organised around the creation and circulation of particular meanings? Consumers have long been understood to be productive participants in branding and advertising via their capacity to 'watch'. That is, their ability to make sense of (predominantly broadcast) meanings and incorporate them into their everyday practices. Since the 20th century the commercialisation of successive media technologies and industries has been driven by the demands of advertisers. The emerging mode of advertising we document here is one where advertisers and media platforms imagine themselves as creating tools that organise action rather than merely distribute ideas. Media still create, store, transmit, process and disseminate information, but not only with the aim of persuading people. Media are increasingly able to use information to undertake a more calculated and controlled management of social processes. In the following, we first develop an account of how branding came to be understood as a social process, participatory and culturally embedded and, secondly, how it is now moving—in both industry and academic accounts—to be understood as more than just participatory expression. As branding and advertising become device-based and data-driven, their mode of participation extends beyond expression to encompass experimental, calculative and action-based forms of participation.

The previous chapters have illustrated a 'tension' in an advertising system that claims on the one hand to be beholden to 'empowered' consumers given the licence to participate in continuous and open-ended ways, while on the other hand advertisers promote the use of devices and data to exercise greater control over consumers at the behavioural level. The upshot is that consumers are empowered at the level of expression but malleable at the level of behaviour. The industry maxim might be, 'say whatever you want, we control what you do anyhow!'. Rather than see this impulse within contemporary advertising as a contradiction, we instead map out how it functions as a comprehensive logic—advertising is a system of control based not only on an understanding of the subject in terms of the capacity to be self-expressive, but also on their capacity to be generative by making their bodies available to the sensing and stimulation of advertising infrastructure.

Several critical histories chart the development, from the post-war counter-culture onwards, of a mode of branding embedded within cultural life (Holt 2002; Lury 2004; Frank 1997; Klein 2000; Heath and Potter 2005, to name a few). These industry and critical accounts of branding have two critically important elements in common. The first is that brands are dependent on the productive activity of consumers. The second is that this conceptualisation of the consumer as a participant rather than a passive target leads to a reimagining of the brand as an object, platform, process or device for coordinating action.

Holt (2002) articulates the historical shift from advertising as a 'cultural blueprint' to advertising as 'cultural resources'. He argues that mid-century critics understood brands as 'cultural engineers' that organised how people thought, felt and acted. Branding worked because consumers were pliable targets on the end of a vast and powerful media and marketing complex that controlled the production and schematisation of cultural life. Brands exerted control not because people were dupes, but because they were embedded in a system that had the capacity to organise the symbolic and cultural landscape of everyday life. Consumer culture worked because it was permissive and pervasive. In both industry and critical accounts of brands, the purchase of this 'cultural authority' model eroded throughout the latter part of the 20th century. This became especially evident with the emergence of the counter-culture. Bill Bernbach's appeal to savvy and cynical consumers in the 'creative revolution' is routinely pinpointed as the key moment in this shift (Frank 1997). The 'creative revolution' led not just to new modes of communicating with consumers, but also to new techniques for devising what a consumer was. Qualitative, interpretive, symbolic, psychological and psychoanalytic methods and ideas became a key part of mainstream advertising agencies, after a long incubation stretching back to the 1920s (Schwarzkopf 2009). Advertisers sought to understand the productive role consumers played in making and performing their cultural world. In the academy, more attention began to be paid to the 'culture' or 'doing' of consumer life. Holt (2002) suggests that once brands recognised consumers' creative capacities to evade, ignore or deliberately misappropriate and adapt brand meanings, marketers faced the imperative to incorporate consumer creativity into their branding strategies.

In Holt's (2002: 83) account, brands came to thrive on consumer creativity and resistance by presenting themselves 'not as cultural blueprints but as cultural resources, as useful ingredients to produce the self as one chooses'. Rather than 'prescribe' meanings, marketers offered consumers cultural resources they could use as part of their own identities and social life. Holt (2002: 83) observes that

> Journalists and academics routinely characterize the output of DDB and other renegade agencies as a creative revolution, suggesting that artistry took precedence over strategy. But it was quite the opposite. These seemingly wild-eyed creative treatments were actually a flurry of strategic experiments to locate a new branding model that would work in the shifting consumer culture. Bernbach, along with his peers (e.g., George Lois, Jerry Della Famina, Howard Gossage, and Mary Wells) cobbled together a new prototype that their progeny would perfect in later decades.

DDB were 'experimenting' with techniques for managing the open-ended and creative nature of consumer culture. What this draws our attention to is that Bernbach did not just introduce the 'savvy wink' to advertising, but perhaps even more importantly he set in motion the process of turning brands into platforms of continuous and iterative experimentation.

While during the 1950s resistant consumers would have threatened brands that relied on conformity to their informational appeals, the 'creative revolution' enabled these resistant consumers to become a productive part of the branding process. Resistant consumers are

> more accurately theorized as participants in a countercultural movement that, working in concert with innovative firms, pursued market-based solutions to the contradictions of modern consumer culture. Consumers are revolutionary only insofar as they assist entrepreneurial firms to tear down the old branding paradigm and create opportunities for companies that understand emerging new principles. Revolutionary consumers helped to create the market for Volkswagen and Nike and accelerated the demise of Sears and Oldsmobile. They never threatened the market itself. What has been termed 'consumer resistance' is actually a form of market-sanctioned cultural experimentation through which the market rejuvenates itself. (Holt 2002: 89)

Brands depend on creative and unruly consumers. Holt's (2002) claim about the reliance of brands on the open-ended creativity of consumers is echoed extensively throughout advertising, marketing and consumer culture literature (e.g. Arvidsson 2005; Frank 1997; Heath and Potter 2005; Moor 2003; Zwick et al. 2008). For example, Moor (2003) observes that brands are partially constructed by consumers who create 'unintended consequences' that contribute to the brand over time (Moor 2003: 47). And, Arvidsson (2005: 244) argues that brands work by 'enabling or empowering the freedom of consumers so that it is likely to evolve in particular directions' rather than impose a 'certain structure of tastes and desires'. The critical issue in these accounts of brands is the various ways in which brands are understood—explicitly and implicitly—to exert control. There are two basic ways of accounting for how brands control creative consumers. If we take brands to be open-ended platforms that establish certain coordinates within which they manage consumer activity and innovation, then the critical issue is the definition of 'certain coordinates'. One way of understanding them is that brands set these coordinates symbolically by choosing what 'cultural resources' are made available to consumers. That is, consumer creativity is channelled by only making ideas available to consumers that work in the brand's interests. At one level we can see the various ways in which brands, as critical actors in commercial media systems, shape the symbolic landscape within which consumer creativity unfolds. As a simple example, take a reality TV show such as *Masterchef*. One could say that consumer creativity is channelled by deploying various food and appliance brands as resources in a creative food culture. Ultimately, all the food practices enabled within the format of the show cohere with the consumption practices beneficial to sponsoring brands. We argue, however, that a strictly symbolic understanding of the 'coordinates' within which brands manage consumer activity is too narrow in some important ways.

When Lury (2004) describes brands as 'programming devices' we take the brand's capacity to program, calculate and adapt as extending beyond controlling specific symbols. While the brand's preference might be to contain consumer activity within certain symbolic coordinates, a brand is a platform that has the capacity to respond to, recuperate and incorporate consumer activity that extends beyond a set of preferred meanings. In this sense, the capacity of a brand to contain action within coordinates involves making consumer creativity available for modulation in general. Rather than attempt to discipline consumers into particular frameworks of meaning, brands are devices for coordinating meaning making and social action in general (see also, Carah 2014a, 2015). The rise and development of the marketing industry practice of 'coolhunting', which emerged in the 1990s as a way of harnessing the creative agency of trend-setting consumers, is illustrative of the emergence of attempts to coordinate creative meaning making in general. Holt's (2002) account is particularly instructive because he takes a unique intermediary position between critical and industry accounts. He is familiar with both, having worked as both a brand consultant and in the academy. This appears to lead him toward a unique proposition. Holt (2002) argues that brands need to be perceived as authentic in the sense that consumers take them to be 'invented and disseminated by parties without an instrumental economic agenda'. Brands developed techniques for embedding themselves within cultural life, and where they exposed their commercial intentions they did so in ironic and self-deprecating ways. Holt (2002) identified several problems with these strategies. First, the ironic gesture of protecting commercial intentions by exposing them only works until consumers recognise the ruse. Secondly, the effort to conceal commercial intentions by going underground using below the line, guerrilla and word-of-mouth marketing only works until sceptical consumers see through it. Thirdly, co-opting and coat-tailing on 'authentic' cultural practices and scenes only works until you run out of authentic ideas to co-opt. Fourthly, making claims to authentic values ups the stakes because consumers will go looking for the evidence that brands adhere to those claims. For example, a brand that claims to be environmentally responsible needs to demonstrate that it actually is in its business practices. Finally, if you make branding too dependent on creative consumers they are required to do too much work and may opt out altogether.

Holt's account generates some interesting problems. First, the idea that authenticity is naturally occurring appears to rest on an essentialist understanding of cultural values and practices. Authenticity, though, isn't a resource, but rather a dynamic function of social relations. Authenticity could only become extinct if humans somehow lost the capacity to have meaningful communicative relationships. Secondly, the idea that brands must materially perform their symbolic claims suggests that brands set up lifestyles that cannot be resolved within a capitalist society. Some critical autonomist Marxist accounts of the 'immanent' potential of networked sociality gesture in a similar direction (see Arvidsson 2005). It seems unlikely, however, that branding would purposefully generate subjects that overthrow its own means of production. Each of these accounts appear to intimate that brands risk ceding too much control to consumers, creating modes of consumption that undermine capitalism itself, or deplete culture of meaning to the point where it no longer functions as a tool for coordinating social life. One rejoinder to these perspectives might simply be that the history of capitalism is characterised by its ability to regenerate and use crises as a grounds for forming new and more durable relations of production. We might also respond, though, that by suggesting consumer creativity could really threaten brands these accounts miss the ways in which consumer creativity is productive in general, despite the specific meanings that are made.

The practice of 'coolhunting', the crises it generated for brands and its evolution over the past generation helps to illustrate how engagement with 'creative consumers' extends beyond the co-option and control of particular meanings. Coolhunting emerged as a marketing industry tactic in the 1990s. Coolhunters used ethnographic methods to track cultural trends and channel them into the planning decisions of major corporations. They recruited informants, went to cultural events and photographed attendees, did field interviews and set up street teams. Coolhunters relied on their human capacity to observe, form relationships, record meanings and feelings, and make judgements about cultural life. Coolhunting is historically important as part of the process of developing branding as a reflexive and malleable framework of meaning embedded within cultural life. Coolhunters didn't attempt to present 'cool' as a 'coherent philosophy' (Gladwell 1997) but rather to offer brands a live commentary on the way hip consumers and cultural intermediaries gave and gained attention from one another. However, coolhunting ran into distinctively human problems. While coolhunters responded to the recognition that brands could not control the open-ended play of meaning in cultural life, it was difficult to develop forms of knowledge that could be coded into the calculative decision-making of corporations. Coolhunting rested on qualitative judgements by individuals who claimed an authentic insider status in trend-setting cultural scenes. These judgements were not dependably scalable or actionable.

Coolhunting was an attempt to develop methods for formatting the open-ended creativity of cultural life into data that enabled routine decision-making. It involved the intrusive collection and interpretation of meaning by individuals. Since then, brands have shifted to observing and calibrating the action of consumers in less obtrusive ways. For example, think of the way smartphones and social media function as an always-on ubiquitous coolhunter or—perhaps more appropriately—affect-sensor. If 'cool' refers to a specific cultural meaning or practice, 'affect' refers to the general capacity to give and gain attention from one another. Rather than be distracted by the specific 'cool' meaning being sought, this prompts us to focus instead on the capacity to capture and calibrate relationships of attention in real time.

Coolhunting was an early attempt to assert control over reflexive frameworks of meaning. Brands attempted to follow the open-ended meaning making of consumers. While at first inspection it might appear to be the practice of co-opting consumer innovations, with a longer perspective coolhunting could be placed within an evolving effort to develop the technical capacity to manage brands as rules-based platforms. Coolhunting might productively be viewed in a similar way to Bernbach's 'creative revolution'. If the creative revolution was not only about the savvy claims in the advertisements but also the attempt to make branding an ongoing experimental platform, then coolhunting wasn't about co-opting authenticity as much as it was about developing methods for brands to make ongoing calculative responses to cultural life. The method of making and managing brands is ultimately more significant than the symbolic content of brand messages.

Considered in relation to the algorithms of social media, the history of coolhunting illustrates how marketing decisions once made by humans are now complemented by automated devices. In Chapter 1 we used the example of Pepsi Pulse as an instructive (and extreme) illustration of this process. The algorithmic turn alters the scope and capacity of media systems to orchestrate cultural action. Furthermore, it draws cultural spaces into the management of populations in new ways—not just as spaces where ideal subjects are shaped and formed, but also as spaces that orchestrate action and make it available to algorithmic forms of decision-making. Brands attune themselves to algorithms by assembling cultural spaces and sensors where target audiences generate flows of content that create affinity with the brand. The algorithms of social media recognise those connections between individuals and brands as 'affinity'. The more 'affinity' brands generate, the more visible they are in ongoing flows of content. At the present moment, algorithmic media platforms enable coolhunting to be done at scale through a combination of discursive and algorithmic rules. Following Kittler, media are in part rules-based decision-making devices (Winthrop Young 2011). The discursive part of these networks of devices involves the development of cultural spaces and practices that orchestrate action. The algorithmic component involves collecting, storing and processing data about that action. Viewed this way, the emergence of algorithmic communication can be situated in relation to the longer effort to assert control over the participatory and reflexive nature of meaning making (Striphas 2015). Brand activations and sensors are part of a trajectory of devices for standardising, orchestrating and measuring consumer action. Activations and sensors are market devices that 'standardise' the subject as a predictable and recognisable actor. These devices orchestrate the interplay between the soft human judgements of actors and the hard calculative judgements of sensors.

This brings us, then, to think of a brand not as a project of 'finding' some 'authentic' meaning 'out there' in the world, but as a platform that links together devices that sense, calculate and orchestrate consumer action. The notion of authenticity invoked here is not one that rests on identifying particular ideas, but rather on the capacity of people to affect one another in an ongoing way. Authenticity is a social relationship of recognition, not a specific catalogue of symbols. What matters is the capacity to orchestrate those relationships, rather than to find particular 'authentic' ideas and cultural expressions. We might say that Holt was writing at a historical moment that was halfway there. He correctly articulates the relational quality of brands: they do depend on the creative relationships they have with consumers. And during the 1990s and early 2000s some brands ran into trouble with their efforts to co-opt specific authentic meanings, scenes and practices. Brands, though, solved this problem in a variety of ways, and they did that by realising—whether explicitly or intuitively—that if co-opting meaning in particular was difficult, then they would need to create the brand as a platform for managing meaning making as a general social process. To account for how they did this we turn to conceptualising how brands format themselves as infrastructure.

QUALIFICATION INFRASTRUCTURE

In Chapter 4 we illustrated how advertisers' development of bespoke devices is interrelated with the larger engineering project of media platforms. So far in this chapter we have suggested that where brands manage consumer participation within certain coordinates, those coordinates need not be only symbolic. In other words, brands do not need to insist that consumers participate within a pre-established set of meanings if they are able to use media to watch and respond to the open-ended creativity of cultural life in general. The engineering of media devices and platforms brands invest in is part of this larger effort to harness the general capacities of consumers to make meaning and to judge, qualify and affect one another. The tent, buoy and beer bottles we have discussed so far are produced for a mode of branding that relies on consumer participation, but does not need to discipline consumers into co-creating particular meanings. Instead, the brand operates at the infrastructural level to provide utility, stimulate the capacity to give and gain attention, and orchestrate action. The more that advertisers are able to create an architecture for watching and responding to meaning making in general, the less they are dependent on securing and retaining the attachment of specific meanings to their products and services. The flow of meaning between cultural life and brands is ongoing and multi-directional. In one direction brands use interactive media platforms to offer consumers a specific set of cultural resources to work with. In the other direction responsive media platforms enable brands to harness the open-ended flow of meanings that consumers generate. Advertising involves the iterative calibration of a trajectory of value to the brand with the creative impulses of consumers.

To illustrate the differing roles material objects can and will play in making meaning and orchestrating action, we examine a black bathtub that was placed in the Smirnoff Double Black House in 2013 (Alfred Event Production 2013). Via the bathtub we can conduct a speculative experiment to map out how a bespoke material object can function in symbolic, participatory and algorithmic modes of action and control. To launch their new product Double Black on the Australian market in 2013, Smirnoff built an all-black venue called the Double Black House featuring brand iconography and performances by bands and DJs. Cultural intermediaries such as fashion stylists, micro-celebrities, musicians, DJs and models were invited to party in the venue along with hip consumers. At least one of the functions of the house was to act as a 'set' for the production of brand images. The brand encouraged cultural intermediaries and consumers attending the venue to use #doubleblackhouse to post images to Instagram of themselves partying in the house. An important feature was bespoke black material objects such as kettles, ironing boards and a retro claw-foot bathtub. The bathtub was filled with black and coloured balls and had the Smirnoff logo on the side (see Carah and Shaul 2015).

The bathtub can be understood as playing symbolic, stimulatory and computational roles in the production of brand value. We examine each way of looking at the bathtub in turn.

To begin with, we can speculate backwards to imagine how Smirnoff might have used a black claw-foot bathtub in a previous, 'traditional' mode of advertising involving print and TV advertisements. The tub might have been used as a prop in a photograph for a magazine advertisement. A model might have posed in the tub drinking a vodka martini. The tub, positioned in a decadent bathroom, with a conventionally attractive model consuming the vodka, would have been part of a composition that represented a context for consumption. The utility of a material object like a claw-foot bathtub in print advertising would be its symbolic capacities to convey meaning when positioned in relation to bodies, products and cultural settings.

Once the bathtub is placed in an all-black venue it takes on a different utility. The tub retains its symbolic character. It sits within the imaginary all-black bathroom of the Smirnoff Double Black House. We could imagine Smirnoff using the house to produce a print or billboard advertisement. But instead of using the house for the production of highly orchestrated media content like a print advertisement, the tub and house become a set or stage upon which consumers individually perform. In making a print advertisement, the photographer would instruct the model how to pose. The advertising agency would then control the editing of the image and its association with copy and positioning in chosen media channels. In the Smirnoff Double Black House, however, the brand did not necessarily 'instruct' attendees how to use the tub. It was simply placed in the venue. Its placement marked it out as a curious and inviting object. The tub prompted or stimulated repeated actions. As consumers enjoyed the atmosphere of the club, music performances and the Smirnoff Double Black drinks, they were drawn toward the tub, jumping into it, sitting in it with friends, throwing balls around. The tub captured attention and stimulated actions that drew the attention of others. The tub can be seen as a stimulus to act within a larger network of media devices and platforms. Like the bespoke objects we discussed in the previous chapter, the tub is quite deliberately a stimulus for using the smartphone to create images and circulate them on social media platforms. Upon entry to the Double Black House Smirnoff advised attendees to use #doubleblackhouse in any images they circulated. Several of the invitees were 'Instafamous' celebrities invited quite deliberately because of their following on Instagram (Marwick 2015). These cultural intermediaries and consumers acted like fashion models on the set of a photo shoot. Scrolling through #doubleblackhouse on Instagram on the nights the Double Black House was open revealed many images of the tub. At one level, each of the images featured different people who used their distinctive creative judgements. They each had different poses, were wearing different clothes, and had different kinds of bodies. At another level, though, the images were routinely the same: young, conventionally attractive, hip bodies drinking vodka in a retro bathtub. The bathtub is a symbolic resource that stimulated the production of the same image over and over again. By the same image we mean that the symbolic work the image did was to connect the vodka to an immersive cultural context of consumption, but those images were attached to a variety of bodies and circulated in a multiplicity of niche social networks.

The 'interaction between information machines and living organisms' that Wissinger identifies in the play between models and photography offers a useful framework for understanding how the interplay between the bathtub, consumers, smartphone and media platform acts as an 'attention capture and calibration device' (Wissinger 2007: 235). Together the smartphone and a media platform such as Instagram constitute an architecture that enables spaces such as clubs, cultural events and other locations where bodies and web-connected smartphones appear to become sites where affect is released, channelled and directed. In the case of Smirnoff's Double Black House the bathtub is an affect switch that stimulates performances that are channelled onto Instagram. The tub is part of a material coolhunting apparatus, a brand machine that stimulates users to make themselves visible, to code the performance of social relationships and generative affects into the digital protocols and databases of a media platform.

The tub stimulated the production of the same end product that it would on the set of a traditional print advertisement in terms of producing standardised images of product consumption in a meaningful cultural setting. But its means of producing this brand image are different. In the Double Black House the tub stimulates 'affective flow' (Schüll 2012) between bodies in the activation, which is then translated into the circulation of images online. While the content of the image remains the same, it is able to take on an array of meanings by virtue of the fact that the range of producers and contexts in which the image is circulated has changed. Each of these images is a unique production: different pose, different body, being distributed to a specific social network. The brand becomes embedded in a range of narratives about urban nightlife experiences but remains steady throughout these images. The participatory consumers are creative in terms of the way they deploy their bodies and their imaginations, but the brand offers the material objects that stimulate and orchestrate those performances. The tub calibrates the playful energy of the consumers, harnessing it as part of the brand imagery that is standardised enough to make the brand legible and recognisable. The tub is not only a cultural resource in a symbolic sense, but also via its capacity to stimulate cultural action. Importantly, if consumers create images they are not only representative devices but packets of digital information that can be processed by both humans and media machinery.

We can also speculate forwards and think about how objects like the tub might come to function as important affect switches in increasingly calculative media systems. If the tub presently has both symbolic and stimulatory functions, we might also think about what calculative processes it currently enables or will come to enable. At present, the forms of image production the tub stimulates not only function in a symbolic way, they also function as data. When a consumer takes an image and circulates that image on a media platform such as Facebook or Instagram they register connections between their individual profile and the location. Furthermore, they signal a co-location with other users who are also engaging with the platform in that time and space, along with any associated brands or cultural performers. For instance, by taking an image of the tub and tagging friends or using the brand hashtag, the image functions as a device that links together consumers, cultural events and brands in time and space. This might enable real-time targeting of individual users. A use of a brand hashtag might trigger a customised post from the brand or a partnering cultural intermediary. This interaction is also archived and can be leveraged later. If an individual is associated with Smirnoff Double Black House now it might indicate their taste in music or presence in urban nightlife culture, market intelligence that might be leveraged next time they check in at a nightlife venue. Additionally, at the platform level, the collective activity of consumers, cultural intermediaries and brands circulating content from the branded venue and featuring brand objects might reveal patterns and practices at the population level. Each person interacting with a brand at a given moment in time also attaches to that interaction an extensive archive of information that their previous engagements with the platform have generated. By making a connection with the brand and a specific cultural setting they are also establishing new connections between cultural archives of lived experience that may reveal new patterns or insights upon which the platform can help the brand leverage further activities. For example, the interplay between consumers and the brand may reveal that those consumers share a common interest in a specific cultural commodity or performer that the brand can associate itself with in further marketing activities.

In the possibilities considered so far the tub functions as a stimulus that prompts action which generates useful configurations of data. Objects like the tub, however, may well come to function as scannable or recognisable codes in their own right. Already the facial, landmark and logo recognition capacities of platforms such as Facebook and Google are relatively functional. Google's photo app now sorts images based not only on familiar faces and locations, but also on repeated objects (Google 2015a). If a user takes a lot of images of claw-foot bathtubs, Google's photo app will tag and catalogue those images into a collection. What this demonstrates is how an object such as a tub generates data in an algorithmic media system. Connections between consumers, brands and cultural spaces can be made legible without those consumers needing to undertake specific actions that code the image with meta-data, such as tagging friends, enabling geo-locative data to be associated with the image or using a brand hashtag. Instead, brands such as Smirnoff could work with platforms such as Facebook to use image recognition algorithms to locate any images of the bathtubs. Links between consumers, the brand and the location could then be generated and leveraged.

It is simple enough to consider how this logic could be expanded. In the case considered here the tub is one object in a purpose-built venue. But imagine if Smirnoff produced a number of bathtubs which they placed in urban nightlife venues throughout a city or country. Each tub would have a unique code embossed on it together with the brand logo. They could function as a stimulus for image production, and those images—when uploaded to platforms such as Facebook or Instagram—could be apprehended by image recognition algorithms. The productive activity of clubgoers would not just generate a flow of standardised images that embed the brand within their cultural narratives. The images would also generate data that made those individuals visible and available. Visible in the sense that their location in space and time, together with their archive of information on the platform, could be rendered viewable and actionable for the brand; and therefore available in the sense that the brand could respond to them immediately or set up future actions as triggers. The bathtub and trashbag tent can both be understood as components of a larger brand machine. They are material objects situated in specific contexts of consumption—a nightlife venue or a music festival. They orchestrate cultural action, switching or channelling it onto media platforms. The capacity of a brand to make cultural life available to computation is grounded in a machinery that consists of material objects, cultural spaces, living bodies, hardware and software. Coolhunting is no longer undertaken only by discerning humans who interpret cultural life, but by building infrastructure that makes cultural life computable. In this configuration, the bathtub, venue, smartphones and cultural intermediaries together form the brand's coolhunting and sensing machine.

STIMULATING QUALIFICATION

In the above sequence we considered how a participatory algorithmic media system makes use of a material object such as a bathtub as symbolic object, stimulus to create content and data, and potentially scannable code. We can observe a shift in the way that advertising seeks to manage the process of qualification. When advertisers select an object to place in a purposefully curated image, they are attempting to apprehend the object's capacity to invoke a specific quality and attach it to the brand. If the object is a bathtub and the product is vodka, the image may be one where the tub is part of a bathroom scene that evokes decadence and pleasure. In an interactive media system that bathtub can attain a functionality beyond its specific symbolic qualities. The bathtub can stimulate the production of content and enable data to be registered and leveraged on media platforms. It comes to function as part of a process of calibrating qualification in general.

In their sociology of markets Callon et al. (2002) theorise consumer participation as 'qualification'. What kind of qualification work is a consumer doing when they pose in a branded bathtub and post images to Instagram? At one level they are making specific attachments between their own bodies, symbolic props, brand imagery and a product. More broadly, though, the scene illustrates how a media platform can harness the capacity of consumers to qualify in general, their open-ended capacity to attach and reattach feelings, affects, and meanings to their bodies and objects. Callon et al.'s (2002) account offers a useful extension to the argument developed already about coolhunting. Coolhunting can be understood as one historical tactic in the ongoing effort of brands to optimise qualification. Coolhunting began as a process of apprehending, cataloguing and directing the specific attachments consumers made. Coolhunting gradually moved toward the creation of brand machinery that harnesses the general capacity *to qualify*.

In Callon et al.'s (2002) account, consumers are active participants in the 'process of qualifying' products. Advertisers and their brands cannot impose specific qualities on consumers, but depend on consumers making their own judgements and attachments. Consumers' capacity to qualify and requalify does not disrupt the smooth functioning of markets. The economy of qualities is a highly reflective ensemble where actors continually interact to qualify goods. Advertisers who attempt to narrate or fix a particular quality to a product or service face the risk of those attachments breaking down; advertisers that build an infrastructure for managing qualification in general mitigate those risks. If consumers change, their infrastructure of qualification can adapt around them.

In a participatory mode of branding, a consumer needs to be sensitised to a living relationship with a brand as much as the brand needs to invite consumer creativity. Callon et al. (2002: 212) argue that it is preferable for marketers to deal with a 'calculating consumer' by constantly stimulating new negotiations and adjustments. Rather than assume that marketers are responding to consumers who somehow or accidentally became active, creative and savvy, Callon et al. (2002) suggest that it is in marketers' interests to *create* calculating consumers. Calculating consumers stimulate more flexible, malleable, and therefore durable, relationships of exchange. Brands that operate at the level of media as infrastructure for calibrating the ongoing judgements of consumers create value by modulating a way of life (Clough 2008: 16). If brands are a continuous social process, then they work by adapting, adjusting and responding to cultural practices and identities. Within this process people give meaning to commodities but on platforms and within protocols they do not control (Andrejevic 2010; Foster 2008). This mode of branding is part of a shift that Clough (2008: 16) has described as media moving from an ideological infrastructure to one of 'continuous modulation and variation of affective response in real time'.

Brands do attempt to attach specific qualities to products and maintain those attachments over time, while undergirding these activities by embedding consumers within an *infrastructure of qualification*. That is, brand value is not only preserved by protecting the attachment of specific qualities to products and services, but also by seeking to make the general process of attaching and reattaching qualities visible and available to continuous modulation. By doing so, if the attachment between specific qualities and products erodes, brands can harness the shift as a productive and generative moment in the ongoing management of consumer life. If a brand manages the broader cultural and media infrastructure within which qualification happens then all kinds of consumer actions, even those that are resistive in nature, are potentially generative for the brand (Zwick et al. 2008). Consumers' capacity to change is not a threat to brand value but a valuable source of energy in the brand machinery. In this account, marketers do not attempt to teach specific qualities that a consumer will then hold as an unchanging schema for categorisation, but rather to sensitise consumers to being one component in the brand's body–machine interface. This relationship between marketer and consumer requires a media infrastructure that can monitor actors and modulate their action over time. If the economy of qualities is one where continuous requalification is the norm, then advertisers incrementally create devices and infrastructure that stimulate, monitor and calibrate the ongoing productive capacities of the calculating consumer.

The media platforms and devices that consumers use to make themselves visible to each other, to affect one another, to live out their relationships in the social world, *double* as devices that make those relationships and capacities more available to marketers for monitoring and modulation. The particular qualities a brand becomes attached to at a particular time and place are contingent, pragmatically deduced as the best qualities for securing action and attention at that moment. For Lury a brand is 'a way not of representing but of modelling markets in many dimensions'. The media infrastructure brands create manage populations where heterogeneity is the norm (Lury 2009: 71). Rather than target masses where the institutionalisation of common tastes and practices is necessary, brands use media infrastructure to act as 'devices for the reflexive organisation of a set of multi-dimensional relationships between products and services, subject to statistical testing and the rapidly changing processes of mediation, stylisation and practices of commercial calculation' (Lury 2009: 78). Brands are 'computational loops' within participatory calculative media platforms. On these media platforms brands manage qualification trials as ongoing and iterative processes.

While there is a long history of marketers attempting to use media such as television to structure routines of consumption within the home, broadcast media imposed technical limits on the capacity to monitor and modulate qualification in the home or intimate space in real time. Broadcast media were largely confined to structuring daily life in routine or pedagogical ways. By routine we mean that media consumption became part of the daily habits of consumers and therefore provided dependable and repetitive opportunities to provide qualifying information; by pedagogical we mean that the key technical capacity of media was its ability to offer consumers instructions on *how to qualify*. Media platforms extend the range of spaces and corresponding practices that are visible and available to advertisers. The bedroom, the club, the bar, the kitchen or the jog in the local park are now potentially added as spaces, activities and moments that can be incorporated into an ongoing process of orchestrated qualification, in addition to recognisable spaces of designed consumption such as the supermarket and the mall. As we argued in Chapter 4, media platforms such as Google, Facebook and Instagram need to be understood in part as the iterative product of investments and design decisions made in response to the real and anticipated imperatives of advertisers. They are projects to engineer qualification infrastructure.

THE WORK OF SENSING AND TUNING

So far we have argued that brands rely on consumer creativity by operating as computational platforms that orchestrate action and calibrate attention. Consumers matter in this mode of branding because their capacity to affect one another, using sensing and stimulating devices to give and gain attention, is critical to making culture visible and computable. To conclude this chapter, we consider how the form of productivity demanded of consumers in a computational mode of branding can be situated in relation to accounts of audience labour. The productive activity of consumers that unfolds around devices such as the buoy, beer bottle, garbage bag tent and bathtub functions as more than the symbolic labour of watching, interpreting and circulating meaning. Audience labour was originally understood as the work of watching (Jhally 1990; Smythe 1981). In a mass media system the work required of audiences is primarily symbolic. They watch content, make sense of it and use the meanings to shape their identities and practices. The work of watching forms ideological subjects who learn how to desire and enact a consumer lifestyle. With the emergence of interactive technologies the work of being watched becomes an intrinsic part of the media system (Andrejevic 2002). The work of being watched involves engaging with interactive media platforms that both provide opportunities for self-expression and capture those expressions as data. Audience members are being watched both by other audience members and by the databases that log their participation as information. Of course, interactive media enable the extension and automation of forms of being watched that already existed. The work of watching always incorporated the aspect of audiences making their consumer identities visible to others, and collecting data about consumers precedes interactive media via the history of marketing research. Making oneself available to 'be watched' is a productive activity because it generates data that enables the work of watching to be rationalised. Interactive media platforms sell a more customised audience product to advertisers, using data to target particular individuals at particular times and places.

Alongside both the development of an account of branding as a social process reliant on consumer productivity and interactive media platforms that harnessed audience activity in more extensive ways emerged the conceptualisation of consumers as immaterial labourers. Arvidsson (2005: 242) argues that the 'value' consumers produce is the social connections, feelings, practices and ideas around brands. Consumers produce the 'social relation ... within which goods make sense'. This conceptualisation of immaterial labour can be placed within the already existing account of the work of watching and being watched. By engaging with the symbolic content of brand messages, consumers form the capacity to incorporate those brands into their own identity. They do the work of watching where they view and make sense of brand messages, and the work of being watched when they make their brand-informed identities visible to others.

In a mode of branding built on computational media platforms, audience productivity extends beyond watching and being watched. If in Chapter 4 we used the vomit problem as a metaphor for ironing out friction between living bodies and media platforms, then the associated labour these devices harness is the capacity of individuals to tune their bodily and social capacities into platforms. They do the productive work of being the living organism attached to the affect switch, of harmonising the connection between living body and brand machine. The affect switch is a combination of the living capacity of the user who 'switches' it and the technical hardware that captures the sensation. The switch relies on the human capacity to *sense* and *tune*. Sensing and tuning open up a way of thinking about the specific characteristics of audience labour in an increasingly calculative digital media system.

The affective labour of *sensing* involves those moments where consumers use devices within everyday life to observe, capture and circulate content or data about events, people or relationships. Sensing here is similar to Durham-Peters' (2001: 707) notion of witnessing as the 'intricate' entanglement of 'truth and experience, presence and absence, death and pain, seeing and saying, and the trustworthiness of perception'. To witness is to make claim to a lived relationship to the events being apprehended, documented and circulated. We suggest the term sensing as one of the forms witnessing takes in a digital media system. Sensing is not confined to the realm of vision; it can encompass any of the body's capacities for registering the affects of stimuli. In our particular application here, we mean sensing as witnessing or apprehending human experience with a media device. Sensing takes place when consumers use their human capacities to translate some aspect of their world or experience into digital information. In a society where networked mobile media devices are ubiquitous, sensing is a distributed everyday activity. To sense is to use the living body to deploy devices that translate lived experience into digital information. We raise our device, capture and circulate content that affects others. In doing so, we generate data about ourselves and our social relationships as much as we directly represent the event. The media device itself captures and records in ways that store events, enabling them to be replayed and revisited. Sensing is a 'live' activity, in that processes of reflective meaning making are displaced by a continuous stream of 'first-person' apprehension of events that generate attention on computational media platforms. Sensing is also a mode of reconnaissance that involves discerning appropriate events to capture and circulate because they will be of interest to others in a network.

Sensing involves the capacity to curate. Consumers judge the appropriate moments to witness. They determine how to capture social moments and relationships in ways that their peers consent to and find appropriate. They mobilise frameworks of knowledge, like a sense of taste, to capture and frame social life in ways that will capture the right attention. Curation highlights the capacity to deploy frameworks of taste to frame objects, moments and individuals in ways that others want to pay attention to. This involves the capacity to judge and choose the right objects to capture, which platforms to circulate content on, which filters and devices to apply (like hashtags or tags), the right time of day to circulate an image, the right position in a live flow of content to insert the content into. The computational and calculative capacities of media platforms depend in the first instance on this capacity of users to discern appropriate ways of generating attention on media platforms.

Consumers undertake the affective labour of *tuning* themselves into the calculative decision making of media platforms. They not only seek to capture the attention of other human actors on a platform, they also seek to address the algorithmic decision-making of the platform itself. Here, users tune into the intersection between the forms of human attention they seek and their understanding of how the platform will play a role in structuring those flows of visibility and attention. Users are agents in a flow of brokered attention. Calculative media depend on the constant interplay with users who move about urban space and everyday life with sensory devices such as smartphones and wearables attached to their bodies, seeking ways to tune their experiences and desires into the computational rhythms of the media platforms they use to make themselves visible. As much as affect switches are one part material device, they are also one part human body. A switch needs to *be switched* somehow by someone in the appropriate time and place. In a sensor society the work of simply participating in everyday life generates traces on media platforms. Individual users tune when they use their devices to code social life in computable ways. This involves, for instance, knowing that tagging a friend in an image will make that image more visible in particular feeds of information on a platform. In these moments they harmonise and tune their action to the platform's protocols and algorithms. They address the platform's algorithms as much as they do other users (Hallinan and Striphas 2014).

This schema of sensing and tuning may prove useful in thinking about the productive activity of the consumer in a computational mode of branding. Users are, at a basic level, productive when they make themselves visible to the computational capacities of media devices and platforms. The work of watching and being watched speaks to the capacity of users to make sense of flows of symbols. The work of watching is the work of decoding the meaning in media content and incorporating it into lived identities and narratives. The work of being watched involves users generating both content and data. Users do the work of being watched when they make use of media platforms to narrate their lives and when they make themselves available to surveillance. In most accounts of social media, this surveillance is understood as a corollary to the effort to optimise watching. The more data platforms have about users, the more they can tailor the flow of symbols they are immersed in. Watching and being watched are still productive activities in the media system, but they do not account for the full span of audience labour. The work of sensing and tuning draws attention to the work of coding lived experience, of registering everyday life on databases, of harmonising social life with the decision-making of media platforms. When users sense and tune they optimise and harmonise the interface between their living bodies and lived experience and the technical decision making of platforms. Sensing and tuning is the work of knitting media devices into our lived experiences. When we dance in the club with a flashing beer bottle or jump into a black tub full of balls, we sense the moment to frame and capture an image, to upload that image to a media platform, to code it with appropriate meta data such as filters, tags and comments. The brand might arrange objects that stimulate and nudge us, but our capacity to sense and tune the performance of our lives into the flows of information on media platforms undergirds the process by which they become prostheses for everyday life.

BRANDS AS COMPUTATIONAL APPS

Brands are a series of experiments with media that are explicitly 'open-ended, question-generating, in process and requiring completion' (Lury 2004: 42). Brands are not developing more sophisticated ways to appropriate meaning from cultural life or insinuate themselves into our identities, as much as they are experimenting with media as an infrastructure for using culture as a field for calibrating action and attention. They operate as computational loops that calibrate meaning and action over time (Lury 2004: 8). Brands are important innovators and investors in the development of algorithmic and computational media. Lury (2004: 8) illustrates how brands operate as an iterative 'loop' that calibrates meaning and action over time. In her account brands are 'open-ended objects', platforms for 'the patterning of activity, a mode of organising activities in times and space' and devices for structuring or calibrating markets. While her account is situated in a similar history to Holt's and others, one where brands transition from prescriptive informational claims to more open-ended lifestyle processes, Lury sets a conceptual foundation that enables us to consider how brands become calculative platforms not entirely dependent on controlling specific meanings. In this framework, rather than to see brands as becoming caught in the 'contradictions' of co-opting specific meanings they don't 'believe' in, they can be understood as computational loops that incorporate the consumers in the process of branding. Brands watch and respond to consumers, entangling them in the ongoing loop of consumer life. By describing this process as a loop we intend to draw attention to the process by which human experience is coded into the computational capacities of media infrastructure, to which humans than respond in creative ways, prompting further adjustments and tuning in the infrastructure, and so on. The critical difference here is understanding media as primarily computational rather than symbolic. Or, at least at a minimum, understanding media as having both computational and symbolic functions.

Rather than only disseminate information, brands mediate 'the supply and demand of products through the organisation, coordination and integration of the use of information' (Lury 2004: 6). A brand is a 'medium' in the sense that a medium is a platform for action (Lury 2004). Media devices collect, store and process information that enable platforms to calculate, respond and calibrate. Once the brand is a multi-dimensional platform, then all sorts of material objects and social processes are programmed into the process of branding: retail stores, cultural events, smartphone apps, plastic bags, bottles and so on. In a fundamental sense a brand is not symbolic content but a series of experiments with media infrastructure and the assembly of culture (Lury 2009).

If we follow Lury's (2004, 2009) lead in understanding brands as primarily computational media devices, platforms and processes, then we must revisit the relationships between brands and culture. In a symbolic account of branding, culture provides authentic meanings. In a computational account culture is a resource for calibrating attention. The important point here is that brands are not developing more sophisticated ways to appropriate meaning from cultural life or insinuate themselves into our identities, as much as they are experimenting with media as an infrastructure for using culture as a field for calibrating attention. While these computational devices may well have evolved from their efforts to become 'authentically' embedded in cultural life, in the process it has taken them beyond attempting to co-opt specific 'authentic' meanings.

Banet-Weiser (2012: 8) observes that brands do not encroach on authentic culture but rather 'transform and shift' cultural practices into market formations. Following her account, we argue that we should examine how brands use culture as an infrastructure for organising attention and action. Brands are critical players in the imagination of, and investment in, the 'primary cultural form(s)' (Banet-Weiser 2012: 8) and media infrastructure that undergird public life. Media platforms and the forms of social and cultural life they afford need to be understood as partly the product of the impulses and experiments of brands over a long period of time. The capital brands invest (or that others invest in an effort to generate revenue from brands) employs the creative and technical professionals who imagine, instigate and manage the process by which media become social, mobile and algorithmic.

To this end, we argue that brands are a 'primary cultural form' (Banet-Weiser 2012) in an increasingly 'algorithmic' and 'computational' media system (Hallinan and Striphas 2014; Lury 2004). Banet-Weiser's (2012), Lury's (2004) and Hallinan and Striphas' (2014) concepts can be brought into a useful exchange with each other. Hallinan and Striphas (2013) argue that algorithms do not only respond to culture—they also shape cultural content. If, however, we follow Banet-Weiser (2012) and examine the 'form' brands take in an 'algorithmic culture' in terms of the experiments they conduct, then we can observe how their actions indirectly shape the form and infrastructure of culture. The media platforms that brands invest in, or that respond to brands' imperatives, seek to make culture available as a zone for generating extensive and ongoing flows of attention and action. The form culture takes is not one that aims to shape coherent subjects with specific meanings, as much as it is one that intends to engage individuals in uninterrupted flows of attention and data sharing. Media depend on subjects who can sense and tune everyday life into digital code.

In the platform and device-based account of branding we offer here, Banet-Weiser's (2012) account of ambivalence is particularly helpful. In an account of brands as experiments with devices, brands can be understood as ambivalent not just in a symbolic sense but also in a material sense. They are at one level 'found' objects we incorporate into our everyday lives. I'm at a festival and someone hands me a tent that is also a garbage bag, I enjoy myself at the festival and take photos of me and my friends of which the tent is a part. The tent has a code on it that makes it algorithmically identifiable within the media architecture of Facebook that the brand can access because it is a partner. This relationship with brands is one which is based on the 'unavoidableness' and their 'embeddedness' within our lives: we can't help but 'handle' them as part of moving through cultural space and interacting with one another. Branding works on this logic, needing culture not as a domain where people invest in brands as essentially meaningful, but as a space within which—via our daily interactions—we must handle brands in symbolic and material ways to get things done in the world.

From this we might follow Lury (2004) where she employs Žižek's logic of interpassivity to argue that brands no longer present a disciplinary command as in 'you must!' but rather a softer invitational command, as in, 'you may!'. Implicit in Žižek's argument is that subjects *must* participate in an interactive system on the terms which that system establishes. As Lury (2004: 132) notes, 'the user of an interactive machine allows the machine to be active on the user's behalf ... the activity of the machine is a projection of the user's activity, but is largely predictable, pre-selected and highly circumscribed'. All we might add here is that as time goes on and the computational capacity of branding machines escalates, the range of activities that brands can calibrate are likely to proliferate and become less circumscribed, at least from the vantage point of participants. The invitational 'you may!' is still a command to 'login'. Once you are in you can do 'whatever you want'. You *may* say whatever you like, but you *must* participate. You must make yourself available to the capacity of media devices and platforms to compute and calculate. If 'you must' is an ideological claim, then 'you may' is the experimental participatory imperative. If brands become open-ended computational experiments, then what they require is not consumers that adhere to ideological frameworks, but rather consumers that make themselves available to a continuous process of experimentation. Brands are a 'primary cultural form' in a culture that is increasingly organised by and performed in part for calculative media platforms.

References

Alfred Event Production (2013). 'Smirnoff Double Black House', *Alfred Event Production*. Accessed December 12, 2015. Available at: http://alfred.com.au/projects/smirnoff-double-black-house/
Alma Agency. (2013) 'Glad Tent Case Study', *You Tube*, 2 May. Accessed December 12, 2015.Available at: https://www.youtube.com/watch?v=FWafX3cgV30

Andrejevic, M. (2002). The work of being watched: Interactive media and the exploitation of self-disclosure. *Critical studies in media communication*, 19(2), 230–248.

Arvidsson, A. (2005). Brands a critical perspective. *Journal of Consumer Culture*, 5(2), 235–258.

Banet-Weiser S. (2012) *Authentic TM: The Politics of Ambivalence in a Brand Culture*. New York: New York University Press.

Callon, M., Méadel, C., & Rabeharisoa, V. (2002). The economy of qualities. *Economy and society*, 31(2), pp. 194–217.

Carah, N. (2014a). Brand value: how affective labour helps create brands. *Consumption Markets & Culture*, 17(4), pp. 346–366.

Carah, N. (2015). Algorithmic brands: A decade of brand experiments with mobile and social media. *New Media & Society*. Published online before print September 17, 2015, doi: 10.1177/1461444815605463

Carah, N., & Shaul, M. (2015). Brands and Instagram: Point, tap, swipe, glance. *Mobile Media & Communication*. Published online before print August 12, 2015, doi: 10.1177/2050157915598180

Durham-Peters, J. (2001). Witnessing. *Media, Culture & Society*, 23(6), pp. 707–723.

Foster, R. (2008). *Coca-globalisation: Following soft drinks from New York to New Guinea*. New York: Palgrave-Macmillan.

Frank, T. (1997). *The Conquest of Cool*. Chicago: Chicago University Press.

Gladwell, M. (1997). 'The Coolhunt', *The New Yorker*. Accessed December 12, 2015. Available at: http://gladwell.com/the-coolhunt/

Hallinan, B. and Striphas, T. (2014). Recommended for you: the Netflix Prize and the production of algorithmic culture. *New Media & Society*. Published online before print. June 23, 2014, doi: 10.1177/1461444814538646

Heath, J., & Potter, A. (2005). *The rebel sell: Why the culture can't be jammed*. Capstone: Chichester.

Holt, D. (2002). Why Do Brands Cause Trouble? A Dialectical Theory of Consumer Culture and Branding. *Journal of Consumer Research*, 29(1), pp. 70–90.

Jhally, S. (1990). *The codes of advertising: fetishism and the political economy of meaning in the consumer society*. Routledge: New York.

Klein, N. (2000). *No logo*. London: Flamingo.

Lury, C. (2009). Brand as assemblage: Assembling culture. *Journal of Cultural Economy*, 2 (1–2), pp. 67–82.

Marwick, A. (2015). Instafame: Luxury selfies in the attention economy. *Public Culture*, 27(1 75), pp. 137–160.

Moor, L. (2003). "Branded Spaces: The Scope of New Marketing." *Journal of Consumer Culture*, 3(1), pp. 39–60.

Schüll, ND. (2012). *Addiction by Design: Machine Gambling in Las Vegas.* Princeton: Princeton University Press.

Schwarzkopf, S. (2009). What was Advertising? The Invention, Rise, Demise, and Disappearance of Advertising Concepts in Nineteenth- and Twentieth-Century Europe and America. Accessed December 12, 2015. Available at: http://www.thebhe.org/publications/BEHonline/2009/schwarzkopf.pdf.

Smythe, D. W. (1981). *Dependency road: Communications, capitalism, consciousness, and Canada.* Ablex Publishing Corporation.

Striphas, T. (2015). Algorithmic culture. *European Journal of Cultural Studies,* 18 (4–5), pp. 395–412.

Winthrop-Young, G. (2011). *Kittler and the Media.* Polity: Cambridge.

Wissinger, E. (2007). Modelling a way of life: Immaterial and affective labour in the fashion modelling industry. *Ephemera: Theory and Politics in Organization,* 7(1), pp. 250–269.

Zwick, D., Bonsu S. and Darmody A. (2008). Putting Consumers to Work: 'Co-creation' and new marketing govern-mentality. *Journal of Consumer Culture,* 8(2), pp. 163–197.

CHAPTER 6

Interventions: Reimagining Advertising

In this book we have argued that brands' efforts to manage consumer participation do not operate only by prescribing fixed symbolic coordinates. They do not require consumers to circulate pre-set meanings. Rather, brands profit from the generative and open-ended nature of consumer creativity as long as devices and platforms are in place to capture, modulate and channel their capacity to affect one another. In this chapter we consider the implications of a mode of branding that is open-ended, calculative and participatory to policy-makers, regulators, activists, critics and so-called ethical consumers who each have a stake in advertising's societal effects. The purchase of critical accounts of advertising depends in the first instance on appropriately defining what advertising is and how it works. In part, this chapter aims to respond to some of the shortcomings of critical perspectives and regulatory frameworks that imagine advertising as a practice of persuasion based on the manipulation of signs. We use a campaign of the Australian beer brand XXXX (pronounced 'four-ex') to develop this account. Alcohol brands offer a particularly instructive case because, as we have already seen in this book, they actively experiment with emerging media technologies. Furthermore, alcohol brands and their promotional experimentation are the subject of extensive public debate in Australia and elsewhere. Alcohol generates a range of social and individual harms to health, well-being and quality of life. In Australia, the regulation of alcohol advertising is managed by an industry framework that is predominantly focused on the content of advertising messages. This enables a range of alcohol advertising strategies to thrive outside the pur-

© The Author(s) 2016   157
S. Brodmerkel, N. Carah, *Brand Machines, Sensory Media and Calculative Culture*, DOI 10.1057/978-1-137-49656-0_6

view of the regulatory framework and often also 'below the line' of public scrutiny (see Brodmerkel and Carah 2013; Carah 2014c).

The interplay between public health advocates, the alcohol industry and governments is a complicated and longstanding one. Recent policy debates in Australia about alcohol advertising revolved around policy development undertaken by the Australian National Preventative Health Agency examining the self-regulatory framework of the industry. As the agency was nearing the publication of its report it was disbanded by the conservative coalition government. The report was subsequently acquired under Freedom of Information legislation by the Foundation for Alcohol Research and Education (FARE) and published on their website in 2015 (Foundation for Alcohol Research and Education 2015). The report calls for an extensive revision of the regulatory codes. A pragmatic assessment of the relationships between the major political parties and the alcohol industry would suggest, however, that legislative change is unlikely. While this political inertia continues, the alcohol industry is developing new devices for intervening in and inhabiting the social world. The increasing sophistication of alcohol marketing, however, is most definitely not located in more persuasive symbolic appeals. In some respects, the symbolic appeals brands make to savvy consumers have not changed all that much since the 1960s (Frank 1997). Instead, the innovation happens at the interface between the living body of consumers and calculative media platforms. Consequently, we require a politics for the sensory touchpoints between brands and consumers. If brands are creative, participatory and calculative devices that seek to modulate our actions in the world, then we need to reflect on how we account for their capacity to control the infrastructure of our social and communicative lives. From individual activists and consumers seeking modes of everyday resistance through to society-level policy frameworks, we require mechanisms for appropriating, circumventing, critiquing and controlling brand interventions in our social world. We begin this chapter by examining the case of the XXXX Island campaign and use this illustration as a challenge to think about how to situate ourselves in relation to a mode of branding that operates as the communicative infrastructure for our identities and social lives.

Resisting and Regulating Brand Infrastructure: The Case of XXXX Island

From 2012 to 2015 the iconic Australian beer XXXX leased Pumpkin Island on the Great Barrier Reef in Queensland. As part of what was potentially 'the biggest marketing campaign ever initiated by a beer brand in Australian history' (Atkinson 2012), the island was renamed XXXX Island and leveraged as a platform for a range of promotional activities: television advertising, branded content, social media engagement and sales promotions. Before the island was officially opened, the campaign invited fans to imagine and design the island as an Aussie 'bloke's paradise'. XXXX fans on social media suggested a number of innovations, including a pulley system to deliver beer to the island bar and a 'loo with a view' (an outdoor toilet hut placed on an exposed cliff overlooking the ocean). Most importantly, as a key feature of the campaign, fans could win weekend getaways onto the island, and during its three-year existence as a 'branded' island destination more than 3000 XXXX fans won exclusive trips (*The Chronicle* 2015).

XXXX Island illustrates how complicated brands become when they operate as cultural and media infrastructure. At one level the campaign worked within the symbolic register well established by beer brands in Australia. Like many of its main competitors XXXX Island situated beer in relation to traditional, hegemonic masculine identities (Kirkby 2003; Wenner and Jackson 2009; Rowe and Gilmour 2009; McKay et al. 2009). But additionally, the island also incorporated much of the brand machinery we have described in this book. The island served as material infrastructure or hardware designed to leverage and orchestrate participation in a calculative media system. As we have argued in the previous chapters, a calculative mode of participation is one where devices stimulate, orchestrate and transfer action between the living bodies and lived experience of consumers and a data-driven media infrastructure. Following this claim, we can examine the XXXX Island campaign not only as a symbolic representation of the brand's desired image, but more fundamentally as an infrastructure for cultivating the generative affective capacities of consumers. The campaign paradigmatically illustrates a mode of branding in which the brand provides the symbolic coordinates and the infrastructural elements that prompt and enable its fans to perform the brand in ways that can be leveraged for subsequent promotional activities, ranging from niche targeting to the utilisation of networked sociality in terms of content elicitation and authentication to the ongoing modulation of affect circulating around the brand.

By focusing on the calculative dimension of participation, we open up necessary provocations to a reimagining of a critical response to brands in the era of media infrastructure. XXXX Island offers useful examples at the individual and societal level. At the individual level, XXXX Island prompts us to consider what might constitute productive forms of resistance to the symbolic hegemonic power of brands, especially in this case where a brand explicitly leverages gender violence *and* the critical responses to it as valuable affective resonances around the brand. At the societal level, the island requires us to consider how policy frameworks might contend with a mode of branding that involves not just the circulation of symbols, but the configuration of a tropical island, purpose-built resort, digital media platforms and infrastructure as well as audience participation alongside the already established content-focused aspects of advertising.

XXXX Island began with a real-world intervention. By leasing and appropriating the island, the brand created a bespoke material object that operated as the touchpoint between the cultural lives of consumers and calculative marketing devices. XXXX Island is not unlike Durex's Fundawear, Heineken's Ignite bottle or Smirnoff's bathtub. Each of these campaigns take an ordinary material object—underwear, a bottle, a bathtub, an island—and engineer it as a device within a calculative media infrastructure. XXXX Island served simultaneously as a natural wilderness and as a pre-configured stage for consumers to enact the brand upon. The island was engineered with prompts and nudges that directed consumers toward certain behavioural responses and symbolic performances. The nature of this participation generated symbolically rich narratives that incorporated the brand within consumers' identities. As much as XXXX Island stimulates the production of meaningful brand narratives, it also makes consumers more visible to the data-driven decision-making of media platforms on which those narratives are engaged with and performed.

By approaching XXXX Island as a device within a mode of calculative participation, we can identify three mechanisms through which it functioned as an infrastructure for modulating consumer action to generate brand value.

First, XXXX Island illustrates how brands operate as powerful symbolic frameworks. As we illustrate in more detail below, the real-world tropical island served as a set for staging a narrative of hegemonic masculinity. But, importantly, the island worked as a catalyst for the open-ended generation of fantasies and affects around the brand. While the brand provided the cultural resources for many of these fantasies, the affective labour of consumers was significantly expanded as they incorporated the brand into their own life narratives. Of particular concern related to this mode of branding is the capacity for the brand to become incorporated into consumer narratives in a way that the brand itself could never explicitly endorse if it wanted to adhere to the existing regulatory regimes for alcohol marketing. In Australia the ABAC and AANA self-regulatory codes govern what alcohol brands can and cannot do (Australian Association of National Advertisers 2015; The ABAC Scheme Limited 2015). For example, these codes prohibit the association of alcohol consumption with positive changes in mood and professional or sexual prowess. They preclude representations that appear to promote the excessive consumption of alcohol or feature people under the age of 25; and they ban the production and distribution of vilifying and discriminatory content. With participatory modes of branding, however, as we will illustrate in the following, comes the capacity for the brand to profit from the symbolic violence of others. Fans can say things and articulate the brand with fantasies that a brand can only ever wink at. Furthermore, if the brand only provides a stage that orchestrates the production of media content by consumers, that brand content—while purposively stimulated—is not open to public scrutiny even though it might generate harms that carry broader public consequences. To illustrate, if a campaign like XXXX Island stimulates a fan to embed the brand within hyper-masculine jokes about violence against women, that expression by the fan is likely to only be seen in his peer network. In fact, alcohol brands have explicitly used this as a defence in complaints to the regulatory authorities. The Australian beer brand Victoria Bitter, for example, argued in response to a complaint about misogynistic and homophobic material on its Facebook page that this should be considered to be like a bonding ritual among males in a pub or bar, rather than a public expression, precisely because Facebook's algorithmic architecture channelled content to like-minded users (Brodmerkel and Carah 2013).

Secondly, while the island acted as a set for the performance of symbolic narratives that embedded the brand within lived identities, it also served as a device that stimulated the registering of social life in databases. The island generated affects that drew consumers into engagement with the narratives and images that this kind of participation elicited. As the island stimulated and generated these digital narratives, they registered as data on media platforms that enabled the brand to operate in a more calculative fashion over time.

Thirdly, while the brand became associated with narratives of excessive consumption and symbolic violence, it also simultaneously used the island to present itself as a meaningful actor in the social, cultural and political world. For example, XXXX's custodianship of the island was marketed as an important valuing of the natural environment and investment in environmental sustainability. XXXX promoted the lightweight architecture of island facilities as well as the recycling programmes, promising a low impact approach to the island's pristine environment. When the Island was disbanded in 2015 the brand auctioned off the brand memorabilia at the island to raise money for not-for-profit organisations looking after the Great Barrier Reef. Here the brand operated as an important part of the infrastructure of public life. In doing so, XXXX Island illustrates how brands undertake a diverse range of activities and investments in public life, ranging from sales promotion to offering a stage for the performance of hegemonic identities to making material investments in wilderness environments. Each of these activities taken on their own can be judged on their merits, but taken together as interrelated components of a brand infrastructure, judging the implications of branding for public life becomes more intricate.

The XXXX Island campaign is an example of brands becoming more participatory, more culturally-embedded, and more calculative in their engagements with and management of culture. The complexity of brand machines such as XXXX Island has consequences not only in terms of the theoretical conceptualisation of branding, but also with regard to strategies for regulating and resisting this mode of branding. In the following sections we take up the consequences of understanding brands as brand machines by examining the modes of everyday resistance and regulation that emerge in relation to this brand infrastructure. In some instances, these modes of resistance become part of the productive affect- and data-generating efforts of the brand, while in others they suggest openings for more productive modes of critique and regulation.

Programming Narratives of Sexism and Excessive Consumption in Media Infrastructure

Advertising contributes to how we think about and perform gender relations, it structures the possibilities of masculine and feminine consumption (Schroeder and Zwick 2004). In this context, beer brands in particular have drawn on and perpetuated notions of hegemonic masculinity based on normative, time- and place-bound ideals that legitimise men's dominance over women (Connell 1995). In Australia, hegemonic masculinity is associated with sporting prowess, manual labour, heterosexuality, the objectification of women, as well as alcohol consumption and mateship (Buchbinder 1994;

Coad 2002; Connell 1995, 2005; Pease 2001; Coles 2008). The depiction of this hegemonic masculinity is an enduring feature of Australian beer advertisements (Kirkby 2003; Rowe and Gilmour 2009). The XXXX Island campaign was no exception in this regard. In the participatory mode of branding that characterised this campaign, however, the ideals of hegemonic masculinity were defined, circulated and authenticated not exclusively by the brand, but in close collaboration with consumers.

In March 2012, after XXXX secured the lease of Pumpkin Island, the brand used its Facebook page to share the news with its fans. In a video where exclusively male actors participated in typical male pastimes, a voice-over explained:

> Men have sought out places to call their own. The cave. The shed. In a car. Under a car. On the playing field. In the garden … the beer garden, that is. But no man is an island. (XXXX Gold 2012a)

The video goes on to describe the island as a place where mates 'can get away and fish, dream about beer as they fish, daydream about the fish that got away over a beer'. Importantly, the 'rules' of the island are then set out: 'Thongs are in, sarongs are out. Barbeques yes, buffets no. Footie matches on TV, but no foot massages to be seen. It's nothing fancy, and that's just fine.'

When XXXX Island was officially opened in October 2012, the brand supported the promotional campaign with a set of four television spots that portrayed life on the island according to the brand. Similar to the initial promotional video for the island competition, each TV commercial featured 'Aussie blokes' enforcing the 'rules' for living on the island. A spot named 'Etiquette', for instance, shows 'mates' being punished for bragging after successful golf putts or for enjoying alone time (XXXX Channel 2014a). It also declares that toilet seats have to stay up. The spot 'Equality' frames the island as a place 'where everyone is equal and democracy rules' (XXXX Channel 2014b). It is, for example, unacceptable to have a longer fishing rod than one's mates, and decisions are made by vote (in the ad it regards the dumping of salad in favour of grilled sausages). The performance of democracy here is one that fits the Australian cultural value of egalitarianism, or 'tall poppy syndrome'; no person is allowed to be conspicuously better than another. Another spot clarified that on XXXX Island one is 'free from 5 Star treatment' and should not expect chocolates on the pillow, no heated pool and no fancy towels (XXXX Channel

2014c). Mates on XXXX Island will be given a hard time for 'unmanly' behaviour such as personal grooming, wearing tight shorts or taking long walks on the beach (Pash 2012).

The video and the television spots invited the viewer to associate the island and its 'culture' exclusively with male pastimes, masculine ruggedness, heterosexual ideals of Australian 'mateship' and the conspicuous absence of women. In the case of the XXXX Island campaign, hegemonic masculinity still worked in the symbolic register. Symbolic extensions were then made by consumers who took the brand narrative far beyond the confines for the brand. This, at least to a certain degree, insulates the brand from public scrutiny and the impact of regulatory regimes in two ways: by getting fans to express brand narratives on behalf of the brand; and by using the technical capacity of a platforms to amplify and mute these expressions in specific flows of content.

For example, shortly after the official opening of XXXX Island, the brand posted the following question on the campaign's Facebook page (XXXX Gold 2012b): 'If you were setting foot on XXXX Island, what's the first thing you'd do?' Many of the replies from the brand's Facebook fans depicted women as servile sexualised objects. Fans suggested they would 'head straight to the bar hunting a hot chick' (Peter, 5 November 2012),[1] 'look for the bar and the strippers and atm' (Andrew, 8 October 2012), 'let one of the XXXX Angels [a group of conventionally attractive female XXXX promoters] rub some sunscreen on' (Tony, 10 October 2012) or 'crack a Gold and explore for the Angels' (Stuart, 8 October 2012). The objectification of women is coupled with celebrations of excessive alcohol consumption expressed in colloquial expressions such as 'hit it hard', 'neck oil' and 'can on like a mongrel'. While XXXX official branding and advertising always depicts male-only bonding rituals, it could never explicitly link these values to this kind of aggressive and excessive alcohol consumption. Operating as media and cultural infrastructure, though, the island, together with a platform such as Facebook, prompted fans to undertake these brand extensions. XXXX routinely stimulated these expressions from their target market by asking them to discuss their ideal identities and ways of life.

Drinking was often presented as a primarily male ritual which women were either excluded from or only welcome as sexual objects or servants. For instance, on 21 September 2012, XXXX posted (XXXX Gold 2012c), 'We all know thou shall NEVER wear budgie smugglers on XXXX Island, what else do you reckon is an Island no-go?', and fans responded that wives, girlfriends and 'fat chicks' were not welcome on the island. If women were present they ought to be 'topless'. Men were not allowed to make phone calls unless they were organising strippers. XXXX fans used the Facebook page to incorporate drinking beer into hyper-masculine identities that the brand itself could only ever nudge at. Furthermore, the fans expressed the brand within their own vernacular and posted it to a network where it was expressed via their own identity. These colloquial and at times confronting contributions remained largely uncensored by the brand's page moderators.

The particularly aggressive, misogynistic and excessive brand extensions contributed by fans can be understood at the symbolic level as authentic performances of the masculine identities the brand gestures toward. But they should also be conceptualised as generative activities within a calculative media infrastructure. Where brands offer cultural resources that stimulate resonant affective engagement with consumers, that engagement generates both content and data. The data can be used to configure relations between the brand and consumers over time. At least one consequence of this is the growing technical capacity of brands to shift this activity below the line and out of reach of public scrutiny. While there is no hard evidence in the public domain that alcohol brands are engaged in this strategy, we argue it is worth considering some of the technical possibilities of these platforms. What follows is a brief thought experiment about these possibilities. Consider a brand such as XXXX identified resonant performances of excessive consumption and misogyny within segments or networks of consumers. It could then use Facebook's custom audience features to produce lookalike audiences more broadly on the platform. This would for instance enable the brand to identify male consumers who would find content promoting excessive consumption or misogyny resonant and engaging. Then the brand could deploy the platform's targeting and gating devices to ensure that content was targeted directly at those consumers and gated so that it could not be seen by anyone outside the target market. This would enable the brand to stimulate modes of engagement that generated larger public effects, but prevented those modes of engagement being visible to anyone outside target groups who—according to the platform's judgement—would find this form of engagement acceptable. As a consequence, these representations and modes of participation would be rendered impervious to public scrutiny. If these practices are not already happening, the technical tools certainly exist, and the trajectory of platforms toward more customised and gated engagements with custom audiences is explicitly clear. Alcohol brands already gate for location and age, and gating for other features makes strategic sense from their perspective (The ABAC Scheme Limited 2012). Importantly, a platform may automatically amplify the most excessive statements simply because they generate the most engagement.

Another scenario we might consider here is that the brand might choose to present the island differently to consumers based on their gender, cultural background or other characteristics, using targeting and gating. It is technically possible to imagine how a platform might present content and discussions that feature women more prominently to female users, or it might make a distinction based on cultural capital that leads the brand to favour the environmental and wilderness narrative of the island over the 'bloke's paradise' one. The important point here is that the island is not a pre-determined set of stable cultural meanings, but a material part of a media infrastructure that can be reconfigured as necessary in a variety of ways. The island is a potentially endlessly reconfigurable set of cultural symbols that can be deployed to generate affects.

The lesson from each of these somewhat speculative scenarios is that a critical understanding of the role of a brand in promoting harmful behaviours and attitudes cannot be developed without a thorough account of the technical capacities of the underlying media infrastructure. Calculative media enable brands to program, code and engineer the affective relationships that cultural narratives generate beyond merely providing symbolic resources.

The Limits of Symbolic Resistance in Calculative Media Infrastructure

Some consumers explicitly resisted the hegemonic masculine narrative of XXXX Island evident on Facebook. Several women posted comments that they 'love fishing and beer' as much as 'blokes'. XXXX did reply to explain the island was for males and females, but only after a male enquired whether he could get married on the island. A female fan used her husband's account (Robert, 19 March 2012) to post that 'As a beer loving female I find this rather sexist! I will make sure I only buy beer that wants my female business (and urge all my other women-type beer drinkers to do the same).' This prompted Vance (19 March 2012) to respond 'Hey cynbob, how about you go post ya femanazi shit on ya coffee club page ...' The brand responded a little later, repeating that 'XXXX island is for women as well. It's the perfect place for mates' trips away—males and females alike'. The brand did not deem it necessary to comment on Vance's derogatory comment, however.

Critically important here is that where women resist the hegemonic masculinity of the brand, they do so by arguing that women too can adhere to these masculine norms. These performances reflect Dobson's (2014) argument that displays of feminine power on digital media platforms draw on, and even amplify, masculine norms. What we might add to this post-feminist critique is the need to conceptualise the potential feedback loop between platform architecture and critical interventions by platform users. The critical interventions by many female consumers on the XXXX page take the form of arguing that women are 'more masculine' than the men—equally able to consume beer excessively, fish, camp and so on. In doing so, these post-feminist interventions resonate more than others because they affirm hegemonic masculinity by positioning themselves as a part of it, and therefore, at least within the architecture of the platform, produce relationships of affinity in databases of the platform between the brand, masculine identities and their own forms of everyday resistance.

The ambiguity about whether women were allowed to visit the island was a recurring issue in the fan discussions on Facebook. Women saw themselves as being excluded, despite XXXX's half-hearted attempts to correct this impression, and men predominantly reacted negatively towards women's encroachment on this 'sacred preserve' for men provided by the brand.

This controversy was particularly evident when XXXX posted photos of women on the island (XXXX Gold 2012d). Male fans responded by asking why there were women on the island. Tony (25 October 2012) commented 'So much 4 Man Island, Forgot how country was run ...' and Paul (25 October 2012) announced that 'if females can go to XXXX Island (Mans Island) I'm joining Fernwood Gym (Female only gym)!' Roger (25 October 2012) posted 'Someone call security there blokes on XXXX Island dressed like women' and Jeff (27 October 2012) said 'Why are women doing on the island ... I thought it was a man cave?'

Only a few men came to the defence of women. Dale (27 October 2012) posted 'Not sure why a lot of blokes are whinging about women being on the island ... does it really affect you in any way whatsoever? remember fellas, it's 2012 not 1912'. Then he added in a second post 'If you really want a boys club I'm sure there's a gay brothel somewhere in the city/valley for you'. In a similar vein Stu (25 October 2012) commented 'now now boys ... its all good, if there was no chicks there thay probly call it gay island ... lol ...'. In these posts the presence of women is regarded as acceptable because it protects men's hetero-normative notions of masculinity. Women were also welcome on the island if they were conventionally attractive. Daryl (25 October 2012) commented 'Beer drinking babes, awesome' and Guido (1 November 2012) said 'nothin' better than good lookin' chicks with a beer in hand'.

A similar discussion ensued when a set of photos of life on XXXX Island was posted by the brand on 20 November 2012 (XXXX Gold 2012e). Brian (20 November 2012) asked in response 'I thought the island was a blokes retreat! Why are there women there?' Richard (20 November 2012) wondered 'I didn't think Sheilas were allowed?' Evan (20 November 2012) said 'Come on, no fun if the Sheilas are allowed in, it should be blokes only'. Simon (20 November 2012) sarcastically remarked 'Advertise it as a mens island and put pics up of women there … great work xxxx'. Ciaran (6 December 2012) complained 'It's crazy that xxxx invites women … I mean please, thank god for men who are men … this is xxxx island'. And Robert (8 December 2012) concluded 'Now we need another Island. Shit!!!'

In typical hyper-masculine fashion, these comments represent women as a threat to the enjoyment of masculine pastimes and sociability. This time, the responses by women were varied. Many only expressed their disappointment about being excluded. For instance, Annette (20 November 2012) wondered 'Do you have to be a bloke. I like xxxx, get me there'. And Sonia (22 March 2013) asked 'Why never any women in photos? I drink xxxx gold'. Some women, however, directly challenged the attitude of dominance and exclusion expressed by the men. Jocene (22 March 2013) commented 'To the gentlemen commenting on women on the island, I say this … It is the year 2013, we drink, we fish, we vote and often we are better at it!' Sylvia (20 November 2012) posted 'Look out Fellas, I'm winning the XXXX Comp, and the Girls and I are taking over', and Melissa (20 November 2012) said 'the women are there cos the blokes know what's good for them *wink wink nudge nudge*'. Other female members of the brand community were disgusted by the tone and direction of the discussion. Rachel (20 November 2012) asked 'seriously, why would a women want to go there, u boys can have it' and Lynne (20 November 2012) posted 'Sexist pricks'. The brand only intervened twice in the discussion between fans (21 November and 6 December 2012), both times simply stating that 'XXXX Island is for all mates—sheilas and blokes—alike!' At no time did XXXX Gold respond in a more detailed way. However, a post by Simon (20 November 2012) saying 'love how everyone that commented about women being there had there post deleted ... nice one, jerks' indicates that the brand moderated the discussion by deleting some posts that were deemed inappropriate. This, in turn, suggests that the brand considered the posts quoted above to be acceptable.

Worth consideration here, particularly in the context of an ethical assessment of these 'branded' conversations, is how these male fantasies and women's responses might prove to be particularly slippery and malleable within the calculative architecture of a social media platform. It is possible to read both the interventions of women on the page and the rejoinders of men in both ironic and sincere ways. The women complaining about sexism on the page might really be engaging in what they see as a deliberate political intervention or, alternatively, they might just as well see themselves as throwing a good-hearted jab at the 'yobbos' on the page. Just as the blokes performing particularly aggressive forms of masculinity might be simply getting off on playing the part of the 'bawdy yob', or they might really be taking it seriously as a space to perform their 'real' masculinity. From the perspective of the brand, the seriousness or truthfulness of consumers' expressed opinions in each instance of participation is not of high importance, though. On the contrary, the capacity of those performances to have different meanings is valuable for the brand. They make the brand more impervious to critique and enable it to be appropriated in a wider array of cultural performances. As a result of Facebook's algorithmic gatekeeping, most people who see this content would not have sought it out on the brand's Facebook page, but it would have appeared automatically in their Facebook news feed as a post pushed to them on the basis of a friend having commented or interacted with it. They would be reading the content via their perceptions of their friends' personality. And so, via that lens, the content is never likely to be offensive, but rather to always be read in the context of users' personal relationship with each other and the specific cultural associations and experiences they share. In assessing this likelihood, we also need to take account of the fact that Facebook's news feed tends to favour content from friends we already share high affinity with. If you do have a friend in your Facebook network who posts content you find offensive, you are less likely to interact with them, or using Facebook's protocols may even have switched their posts 'off' so they don't appear in your feed. Therefore, regarding individual pieces of content posted on social media sites such as Facebook as individual, self-contained 'advertising texts'—as current regulatory codes tend to do—fails to account for the algorithmic nature of content distribution on these platforms. Content appears in as many different contexts as there are users into whose news feed it has been inserted. This, while posing problems for regulators, benefits brands. It 'authenticates' them within the various networks of users that assemble around these particular pieces of content circulating on social media. As a consequence, the content becomes even more culturally embedded and relevant for the individual users.

One reading of these frequent exchanges on the XXXX Island Facebook page might see women who posted in to resist the hegemonic masculinity of the island as an important symbolic critique of the brand. However, in a mode of branding that works on a participatory and calculative logic, we might argue that where women resist the male-led dominant reading and extension of the brand's meaning, they open up opportunities for male fans to perform the brand even more aggressively. And, most problematically, these forms of symbolic resistance are not so much co-opted by the brand, into say a politically correct ethics, but used in themselves as generative affects. The symbolic resistance that unfolded on the XXXX Island Facebook page actually worked to generate engagement around the brand and served as a stimulus for the performance of more generatively affective brand narratives. Although the brand only ever prompted or stimulated these exchanges, it rarely sought to regulate them. Furthermore, these exchanges, because they elicited rich forms of engagement, no doubt generated value for the brand. In places, the exchanges that unfolded on the page evidence performances of the brand that fall outside what the brand could say itself under its own self-regulatory guidelines.

Calculative media either disarm or redeploy symbolic forms of resistance. They disarm symbolic resistance where it is a minority view that algorithms can easily discern and filter out of the conversation or where platform protocols can easily marginalise it. For instance, in recent years a significant change to brand pages on Facebook is that consumers cannot post directly to the brand page. Any consumer-initiated comments are not published on the brand's 'wall' but rather in a side box that other page users are unlikely to visit. This gives brands greater control over the narrative on their page. Symbolic resistance is also redeployed where it stimulates charged affective exchanges. If a female consumer posts a critique of the hyper-masculinity of the brand, this might serve as a stimulus for more performances of hyper-masculinity from other consumers. In doing so, critique generates engagement that, again using the algorithmic architecture and protocols of the platform, can be calibrated in productive ways. If that exchange is only seen by the hyper-masculine consumers of the brand, then the critic is a productive part of the performance of the brand—offering a clear 'other' for consumers to position themselves against. On the flipside, the architecture of the platform would be unlikely to display the exchange to those who may be sympathetic to the critic's point of view because the algorithms would very likely determine those users to have a low affinity with the brand. Where affinity with the brand is what generates the platform's choices about who sees content, then critical interventions become little more than opportunities for more vilification.

GENERATIVE AMBIVALENCE IN THE AGE OF MEDIA INFRASTRUCTURE

Critics, activists and policy-makers need to develop frameworks for understanding and engaging with brands whose sensory and calculative capacities have taken them beyond the realm of the symbolic. The XXXX Island campaign illustrates some of the limitations of regulatory frameworks and everyday resistance based on a symbolic conceptualisation of brands. For example, where women resisted the hegemonic masculinity on the page, they stimulated the performance of more masculine performances of identity under the moniker of the brand. Rather than simply promote specific product qualities, the brand here acted as a platform for enacting culture and identity.

Beyond their symbolic character, brands operate as computational media infrastructures that orchestrate cultural life and consumption. The computational infrastructure brands use to structure social action is not open to public scrutiny, however. The opacity of computational infrastructure can be seen as a matter of public concern in other domains too. This is a feature that applies equally to media platforms and industries that rely on computational devices. As an example, in 2015 activists in Australia went to court to argue that poker machines are illegal since their algorithmic routines deliberately and systematically deceived players. They weren't 'games of chance' because they were programmed to ultimately always generate profits for the 'house'. The action illustrates one of many dimensions of everyday consumption where the invisibility and inaccessibility of computational infrastructure is an object of concern. Another facet of the way brands are entangled in the world can be observed in the interplay between their calculative devices and public infrastructure. When a brand appropriates a public or wilderness space, such as an island or a public square, and uses it as a stage or stimulus to generate user engagement and data within a calculative media infrastructure, that investment is routinely presented as an investment in the quality of public life. XXXX Island is an investment in a wilderness space as much as it is in the creation of a valuable beer brand. When examining the interplay between cultural life and computational media, Banet-Weiser's (2012: 41) account of ambivalence is highly productive. The notion of ambivalence gets us productively beyond overly simplistic separations between 'authentic' and 'commercial' or 'exploitative' and 'altruistic' accounts of brands. Brands promise political empowerment and public investment within the logic of market exchange. They are entangled in our lives and world, and as a consequence, our efforts to navigate our lives in relation to them produce ambivalent affects.

Reflecting on the media experiments of advertisers in this book, we propose that the concept of ambivalence can be developed in relation to the calculative media infrastructure within which brands function. To do this we will critically reflect on and extend Banet-Weiser's (2012) notion of ambivalence in brand culture. Banet-Weiser's (2012) notion of ambivalence takes the brand to function as a symbolic device. Brands and brand culture are conceptualised as discursive performances produced via the efforts of individuals and institutions to make meaning in the world and to use those meanings to structure relationships of exchange. As we participate in these relationships in ways that both give our own identities meaning but also alert us to the strategic motives of brands, we form ambivalent entanglements with them. As we have argued in this book, brands' capacity to organise the social world and relationships of exchange extends beyond the symbolic. We need an account of ambivalence, or any political–ethical stance in relation to brand culture, that functions in the context of media platforms, brand machines and their sensory touchpoints with living bodies and lived experience.

Banet-Weiser (2012: 92–93) argues that 'critique and commentary on branding in advanced capitalism do not lessen the value of the brand but rather expand it as something that is ambivalent, a recognisable part of culture, indeed, a recognisable part of ourselves'. The advertising industry's participation paradigm is testament to the way brands 'nurture a politics of ambivalence' (Banet-Weiser 2012: 219). As we described in Chapter 2, 'utility' now serves as the central 'persuasive appeal' characterising the applications, tools and devices advertisers develop under the moniker of the brands they work for. This 'usefulness' not only ensures that brands become ever more deeply embedded in the performance of everyday activities and practices, but it is also likely to reinforce the ambivalence consumers experience when interacting with these applications and devices. Brands are not only 'useful' as creators of 'intimate publics' (Banet-Weiser 2012: 218) that bring consumers together by means of shared symbolic meanings and histories, but also by just providing the gadgets that decrease the frictions of everyday life. For instance, Westpac's Impulse Saver application discussed in Chapter 3 represents ethical awareness on part of the bank in its most 'practical' form. Instead of developing narratives about the social responsibility of the brand or evidencing the brand's ethical commitments by supporting 'macro-initiatives' in third-world countries, the bank directly 'solves' one of the everyday 'problems' many of its customers are likely to experience. At the same time, applications such as the Impulse Saver are invitations to develop an ambivalent relationship to ourselves. On the one hand we are addressed as 'empowered' consumers who confidently navigate the world, smartly recruiting all the tools on offer for managing our daily affairs, but on the other hand we supposedly need these tools for countering our innate irrational and flawed nature. Here we see one of the ways in which ambivalence does not harm brands, but actually is productive and 'useful'.

We live in an era where brands *can be* ambivalent precisely because they have the calculative tools to manage an open-ended relationship with consumers. As we discussed in Chapter 5, brands have developed the infrastructure to harness consumer resistance, irony and ambivalence. Where brands of previous eras were not sufficiently reflexive or calculative enough they demanded consumer conformity (Holt 2002). In the era of participatory and calculative media, ambivalence is an extremely productive configuration for a brand to adopt. Ambivalence is one of many affects that generate play, expression and articulation that make users available to the computational capacities of media.

The gesture of ambivalence can be situated in the wider 'decline of symbolic efficiency' associated with savvy, ironic and cynical stances toward media representation. Banet-Weiser's (2012) aim is to avoid a pessimistic account of critique as politically inert in a climate of reflexive doubt and savvy cynicism (see, Dean 2010; Andrejevic 2013; Žižek 1999). Her account productively presses on the all too easy and deflating argument that brands completely colonise culture. Instead, she argues for the 'generative power' of ambivalence. Brands are ambivalent in the sense that they simultaneously enable and exploit consumer creativity. Here, Banet-Weiser's (2012) account reflects accounts of audience labour in the interactive era (see Terranova 2000; Andrejevic 2002; Zwick et al. 2008). Rather than work against the unpredictability of consumers, attempting to make them conform to pre-set ideological frameworks, brands build an infrastructure for thriving on consumer creativity as a generative affect. Banet-Weiser's (2012) contention, though, is that in doing so brands generate a 'failed relation' that leaves a remainder, surplus or potential political capacity. To some degree ambivalence protects the autonomy of the consumer as an actor. Here her account echoes in some important ways the autonomist Marxist accounts of creative labour in the post-industrial society that also argue for its immanent political capacities, such as Arvidsson's (2005) notion of ethical surplus.

In response to this call we argue that where ambivalence takes shape as a savvy attitude or strategy of symbolic distance and debunkery it is hard to see it as anything other than politically inert. Ambivalence as nothing other than a cultivated performance of what Sloterdijk (2013) terms 'chronic elegance', which results only in the discerning consumer expressing ever more fine-grained distinctions in their everyday habits and preferences. Cultural consumption is replete with these elegant rituals surrounding the consumption of coffee, craft beer, wine and food in particular. Where consumers invest their identities and affective capacities in making 'elegant' distinctions between the qualities of products and brands as part of the social performances of their savviness, they still participate thoroughly in modes of production and life that produce brand value. In some respects, they become particularly valuable consumers because they incubate, innovate and generate new modes of product distinctions and rituals of consumption that can be industrialised more broadly. Think here of the explosion of product categories like craft beer in Anglo societies such Australia, New Zealand and the USA. This kind of performative ambivalence is generative for the brand. It has been astutely skewered by Slavoj Žižek in his critique of cultural capitalism, a situation characterised by acts of consumption where the ethical duty of the consumer is built into the act of consumption: the purchase of fair trade coffee at Starbucks, or a pair of Tom's Shoes where another pair is donated to the developing world for each pair you purchase (Žižek 2010). As Chouliaraki (2013) has explicated, this kind of branding and consumption appears to offer opportunities for the consumer and brand to present themselves as particular kinds of ethical actors, rather than being about addressing the lived experience of others. At worst, this kind of ambivalence displaces the possibility of meaningful forms of political intervention.

Where ambivalence is generative, however, is where it stimulates consumers, activists, critics and policy-makers toward devising ways of reshaping the relationships between our lived experience and the calculative media and market systems we inhabit. We might understand ambivalence as elevating our own capacities to recode our engagement with calculative media. Ambivalence takes on a productive character if we imagine it as opening up space to refuse to use the designated protocols and interfaces as directed; to hack, reset and redeploy databases; to explicate and even rewrite algorithms. Here, van Dijck's (2013) lexicon for media platforms—data, algorithm, protocol, interface, default—gives us the objects that our ambivalent attitude should be directed at. This would lead us toward modes of activism, regulation and everyday resistance targeted at media infrastructure and its participatory, sensory and calculative capacities. For example, in the case of an alcohol brand on a social media platform, what matters is not just what the brand has to say and what consumers say back, but also how the brand uses the algorithmic architecture of the platform to ensure some engagements are only visible to the target market and not open to wider forms of public scrutiny. Or where the media platform and brands use databases to determine and manage audience engagement, those databases should be equally available to the public or to regulators to assess individual and social harms.

MEDIA AS BODY-MACHINE INFRASTRUCTURE

Part of what we have charted in this book is the technical experimentation and implementation with devices for managing the body–machine interface. We have focused selectively on the touchpoints between the living generative body of consumers and the calculative infrastructure of media. Where brands are invested in the emergence of media platforms such as Facebook, Instagram or Snapchat, it is not only because those platforms offer protocols and algorithms for managing content in more customised ways. When viewed in relation to the broader experimentation of brands with bespoke hardware such as baths, bottles, underwear, buoys and islands that orchestrate and engineer the playfulness of social life, we can see that brand investments in media platforms are part of managing the generative exchange between creativity and calculation.

Brand applications built on a calculative media stack are a technical hack to the irreducibly ambivalent, contrary and open-ended nature of human life. They are a way of configuring brands so that they depend on humans making their lives and bodies available to brand infrastructure. Brands don't require humans to enter into enduring authentic relationships built on stable frameworks of meaning, but rather to plug into body–machine configurations that are open to calculation. The critical issue is not just that media platforms are saturated with brand content, but rather that the protocols, interfaces and algorithms of these platforms are designed to manage brand value. In this context, authenticity and ambivalence are each *lived* social relations that depend on continual performance and therefore drive us toward sustained engagement with communication infrastructure. Self-branding is not just the labour of self-disclosure, but also of making the body available to a calculative media platform. As we discussed in relation to the black Smirnoff bathtub in Chapter 5, the brand is not aiming to stimulate only the production of a symbolic narrative in Instagram images, but to link the body, brand and other cultural contexts in ways that open up vectors in databases. Placing the body in the bathtub is not just an identity narrative—about conspicuous consumption, post-feminist empowerment, savvy hipsterdom—it is making the body available as a code in a larger system of computation.

In today's 'communicative capitalism' (Dean 2010), participation makes us available to regimes of computation. An account of authenticity, ambivalence or any other generative affects within the contemporary operation of brands must account for how they operate as media and cultural infrastructure. To demonstrate the distinction, where Banet-Weiser (2012: 70) argues that 'self-branding is fraught with tensions between empowering oneself as a producer and occupying this empowered position within the terms and definitions set up by broader brand and commercial culture', the reference to 'terms and definitions' prefigures a primarily symbolic conception of brands. But, if we changed this expression to 'protocols and interfaces' of brand culture, we could critically examine how self-branding is the act of plugging the living body into the calculative infrastructure of the brand.

Instead of seeing ambivalence as just the possibilities opened up by dissatisfaction, we might instead look to Durham-Peters when he argues that media are 'delicate systems of contingent conditions for the organisms that live in them' (Durham-Peters 2015: 45). There may be some value in taking the fact that media platforms rely on our living bodies as an impetus for thinking about how we might recode our body–infrastructure relationships. As such, a critical approach to branding must account for it as a process of engineering and experimenting with media as infrastructure.

Durham-Peters (2015: 32–33) makes a persuasive argument for conceptualising media as infrastructure. He defines media as:

> infrastructures that regulate traffic between nature and culture. They play logistical roles in providing order and containing chaos. [...] Once communication is understood not only as sending signals—which is certainly an essential function—but as altering existence, media cease to be only studios and stations, messages and channels, and become infrastructures, habitats, and forms of life. Media are not only important for scholars and citizens who care about news and entertainment, education and public opinion, art and ideology, but for everyone who breathes, stands on two feed, or navigates the ocean of memory. Media are our environments, our infrastructures of being, the habitats and materials through which we act and are.

Infrastructure orchestrates the interplay between nature and culture, living bodies and human capacity for calculation and intervention in the world. While digital media might seem like a 'historical rupture', Durham-Peters (2015: 36) demonstrates how ancient media such as 'registers, indexes, census, calendars, catalogues have always been in the business of recording, transmitting, and processing culture [...] or organising time, space and power'. The symbolic understanding of media as audio-visual 'entertainment machines' which undergirds most accounts of advertising and society is something of an historical exception; 'digital media return us to the norm of media as data-processing devices'. For Durham-Peters (2015a: 38) media are logistical infrastructures before they are content-delivery or management systems. As such, media are infrastructures that open and close possibilities of action. As much as they encode meanings, they also encode standards and protocols that govern practice. Durham-Peters' (2015: 45) invocation is to take the media 'apparatus' as an 'entanglement of human and nonhuman beings' seriously. Following the understanding of media from the life sciences as 'containers in which organisms can grow', he regards media as 'enabling environments'. By following this lead, we can begin to understand media not only as institutions that tell us what to think, but as infrastructures that sustain, enable, stimulate and govern our bodies and the ways of life we construct. What is at stake in this turn to infrastructure for a critical account of advertising is that it emphasises the need to develop ways of directing our ambivalence at infrastructure.

Reimagining and Reengineering Advertising

The recent fascination policy-makers exhibit for behavioural interventions based on the idea of 'libertarian paternalism' appears to indicate a shift away from the rational actor presupposed by neoclassical economics. Instead, by drawing attention to the impact of choice architectures on human decision making the proponents and followers of behavioural economics seemingly take the notion of 'enabling environments' seriously. Consequently, human subjectivity and agency then needs to be understood as a much more complex faculty than assumed by proponents of rational choice. It would need to be redefined as property distributed across human as well as non-human actors and therefore as sensitive to varying contexts emerging from situated actions. As Hayles (2011: 25) argues, ethical considerations would then need to concern themselves with social implications 'that emerge from complex contexts in which information is being processed both consciously and unconsciously to create a rich picture of embodied, emplaced and enacted interactions'.

With their focus on choice architectures libertarian paternalists appear to account for these more complicated ethics. However, as we outlined in Chapter 3, their nudges predominantly tend to be utilised for initiatives of self-responsibilisation, which—in an effort to 'preserve' people's liberty—de-contextualise and individualise the harmful environmental effects they seek to counter. We used the example of gaming—and poker machines in particular—for illustrating the paradoxes of a libertarian paternalism that attempts to counterbalance nudges deliberately designed by commercial interests with even more nudges. At this point we might at least briefly question the efficacy and logical consistency of such efforts. If the 'predictable irrationality' of humans now serves as an accepted ontological model of human nature, and policy-makers task advertising agencies with designing social marketing campaigns based on this model, shouldn't regulators also pay attention to cases of deliberate exploitation of consumers' cognitive impairments by commercial interests? For instance, similar to the gaming industry, the alcohol industry reportedly invests intellectual effort and financial resources into research programmes that tinker with the choice architecture of venues and the mechanics and functionality of devices. Even more than a decade ago the leading drinks company Diageo experimented with the design of bar 'environments', bottle display techniques and gadgets for increasing alcohol consumption, or at least for ensuring that consumers are upsold to more expensive products (Beck

2001). At the same time, research exists that outlines the environmental effects that contribute to increased alcohol consumption and, in turn, how these nudges could be mitigated (Wood 2012). Thus, if policy-makers now accept the unconscious impact choice architectures have on human decision-making, the regulation of alcohol promotion (and we take alcohol here just as an example for the reasons outlined below) should not only focus on advertising content, but also include the physical environment, branded activations and mechanics of consumer participation.

Critics of a more stringent incorporation of the findings of behavioural economics into laws and regulations (as well as critics of libertarian paternalism in general) point out, however, that while certain mental biases might appear in carefully controlled experimental settings, this does not necessarily mean that these 'irrationalities' surface reliably and consistently when humans act in the complexity of real-life situations (McQuillin and Sugden 2012; Field 2008; Yeung 2012). But if these critics question the efficacy of regulatory regimes based on behavioural economics, they simultaneously call into questions the efficacy of nudging interventions that are meant to mitigate social ills. This aspect has, for example, come to the fore in a report by the UK House of Lords' report on Behaviour Change (2011: 33; 34). It concludes:

> We were given no examples of significant change in the behaviour of a population having been achieved by non-regulatory measures alone, confirming the view of some witnesses that non-regulatory measures in isolation could have little or no effect and that the most effective means of changing behaviour at the population level was a package of different types of interventions. [...] Several witnesses told us that, though some nudges reflect experimental evidence about what influences behaviour, they would be unlikely to have a significant effect if used in isolation. (Science and Technology Committee, House of Lords: 2012)

Thus, according to the findings of this inquiry, in many instances libertarian paternalist interventions alone will not be sufficient for tackling more ingrained social and behavioural issues effectively. What both the critics as well as the inquiry do not really consider is that in the digital enclosure the efficacy of nudges is, first, much easier to ascertain, and, secondly, does not need to be generalisable on the level of larger populations. Digitally mediated environments allow for what legal scholar Ryan Calo (2014) calls the 'systematization of the personal'. Big data analysis now allows advertisers to test on a large scale whether consumers are indeed susceptible to certain mental biases and in what contexts these biases occur. And, even more importantly, data analysis enables marketers and advertisers to not only identify certain general biases and their context-dependency within particular populations or target audience segments, but also to infer the specific, context-dependent biases of *individual* consumers. Based on big data analysis of consumer interactions and transactions, marketers are now able to surface the specific nature of individual consumers' deviation from making rational choices and the individual level of susceptibility to particular nudges. Marketers can develop models of individual consumers and record the circumstances under which consumers behaved unexpectedly and to the marketers' commercial benefit. Importantly, marketers neither need to know why the consumer behaved in unexpected ways nor the identity of the particular consumer. It is only important that personalisation technologies respond to the identified cognitive weaknesses by targeting the consumer at the right time and with the right pitch. As Calo (2014: 9) notes, the 'availability of data about people, coupled with the power to make sense of this data and apply the insights in real time, will lend the behavioural turn an even greater relevance to law and daily life'. These technologies are well advanced and are likely to become even more prevalent in a media environment that connects everyday items to the Internet. The Internet of Things creates an ambient intelligence that allows for the utilisation of persuasive technologies that are 'almost unavoidable and subtly and intrinsically bound to the material environment in which one is located' (Verbeek 2009: 237). Thus, as Calo (2014: 22; emphasis in original) writes, 'firms will increasingly be in the position to *create* suckers, rather than waiting for one to be born every minute'.

The tendency of behavioural economics to displace attention to questions of manipulation with claims about paternal liberalism is echoed to some extent in Turow's (2012) account of the emergence of online advertising strategies. He argues that the advertising system has embarked on a systematic process of social discrimination. The process he documents is the use of an expanding array of data to target and customise advertising appeals. In this story advertising takes advantage of the data-driven capacities of the emerging media platforms. In this book we have argued that advertising is a media infrastructure project that extends beyond the targeting of content to include the design and engineering of bespoke hardware, investment in the development of the calculative and sensory capacities of media platforms, and the design of choice architectures that operate across material and media environments. Given this, a critical account of advertising must centre the computational capacities of brands and their capacity to calibrate lived experience and living bodies. Turow (2012) centres the computational elements of advertising as an object of public concern and debate. In proposing constructive ways forward, Turow (2012: 198) reflects:

> In 2008 I suggested to *New York Times* technology reporter Saul Hansell that the industry ought to post an icon on every tailored advertisement that when clicked would lead to a 'privacy dashboard'. The dashboard would show you the various levels of information that the advertising company used about you to create the specific ad. The information disclosed would not only show behavioural targeting but would include knowledge collected from any sources, including third-party data providers, the U.S. Census, and online discussions. The dashboard would reveal precisely which companies provided that information, how certain data were mixed with other data, and what conclusions were drawn from this mixing. It would also allow you to suggest specific deletions or changes in various companies' understanding of you.

Turow's suggestion is a compelling one. It is immediately apparent how this proposal would serve both the interests of individuals by granting them more control but also advertisers where it helped to improve the accuracy of their targeting. The ad industry would perhaps resist such a technology roll out because it would instantly reveal the infrastructure of their advertising system that is built to look like natural flows of content. But the 'politics of the button' gesture in the right direction, in that they point to the calculations taking place in this media infrastructure and the capacity of users to recode the relationship between that infrastructure and their lived experience.

Leading on from our claims about generative forms of ambivalence, such an interactive icon or button would enable people not just to be aware and cynical about the uses of their data, but to give them a way of being *involved* with their data and the way it was being configured, processed and leveraged by the media infrastructure they used. Significantly, Turow also points to how tools of individual control need to be complemented by regulation of media infrastructure at the societal level.

To illustrate, we can return to our consideration of alcohol branding in this chapter. Alcohol consumption is a matter of public concern, generating both individual and social harms. For the purposes of this conceptual exercise, though, we will remain agnostic about whether or not we think alcohol advertising ought to be regulated. Rather, we are working on the evidence that public debate and indeed industry creation of a self-regulatory framework indicates widespread acceptance that it should be. Our point is that if there is a commonly accepted view that alcohol advertising ought to be regulated somehow, any regulatory framework must adequately describe how advertising works, which means addressing how advertisers use media infrastructure, not just the content they create. If we follow Turow's icon suggestion, then we could imagine a regulatory code insisting that any item of alcohol brand content on a media platform contains an icon that marks it out as advertising content and gives the user control over how information about them is used to target that content. The icon ought also to give users 'one-click' capacity to report content to an advertising regulatory body. That is, notifying the regulator of content that breaches the code ought to be possible from within the everyday use of a media platform. Nothing of what we are suggesting here is technically impossible. In fact, most platforms already have 'reporting' options attached to each item of content on their platform, including advertisements; and platforms already have these protocols and interfaces for other kinds of content. As we have discussed in this book, we envisage that this would reveal to users an expanding sensory interface between their everyday lives and brands, that brands were not just targeting them based on their demographic characteristics or even cultural interests, but also their movements and bodily affects. The illustration gets more complex still. Something that Turow did not have to contend with so much in his account was the increasing prevalence of 'native' content models on media platforms. Native content refers to paid promotional content from brands that flows in the same interface and format as other content on the platform. For example, on Facebook most advertising takes the form of ordinary posts in the news feed that have been promoted, and on Instagram paid ads appear like any other item of content in the home feed. So it is likely that both advertisers and platforms would strongly resist such a revelation of the computational backbone of these platforms, because to reveal how an advertisement was targeted would be to reveal the full array of information used to shape engagement on the platform in general. If a user can see how an advertisement is targeted, then why not reveal how a user's news feed is compiled? Of course, platforms such as Facebook and Google would steadfastly resist any such regulatory oversight because it would, so they would argue, erode their competitive advantage by revealing the algorithms that are the basis of their platforms' commercial value.

Efforts to give users greater individual control over the use and application of the data that their bodies and lives generate immediately come up against larger questions about the politics of media infrastructure. In the case of alcohol branding, gating and customisation enable content that might be vilifying or promote excessive consumption to be confined to audiences where those sentiments are an accepted cultural norm, even though they may generate wider public harms. Advertising on these platforms is not open to public scrutiny in the way that advertising in a broadcast media system is. If members of the public, activists or policy-makers want to scrutinise how alcohol advertisers are using television or magazines they can easily access the content, and be assured that the content they see is the same that each audience member sees. On computational media platforms, though, this is not the case. It is not possible for any member of the public—activist, researcher or policy-maker—even to see what kind of content is being produced let alone who is seeing it. A regulatory framework that took the media infrastructure of alcohol brands seriously might determine that brands reveal what data they collect and use, how they use it to customise, target and gate content, and what kind of engagement they generate with users. In broader public health terms, platforms probably hold data that enable better understanding of how promotion is interrelated with excessive forms of consumption and associated harms in specific locations such as nightlife precincts and at specific times of the day relative to factors such as trading hours and venue density. The industry uses this information as market intelligence, so the public might well ask why it should not also inform public oversight of these commodities and the harms they generate. As this information is readily available to brands via insights dashboards that platforms provide, there is technically no reason why it could not be made available to a regulatory process of some kind. Except, of course, that to do so would be to erode the market advantage of brands' innovative use of these computational forms of media. At least in Australia, the proposals being imagined here would be politically unpalatable.

Where this discussion might be generative, though, is where it turns critical attention away from the endless deciphering of symbolic exploitation and instead toward the infrastructure: how it works, how it is expanding, who controls it and to what ends. Media platforms use data, algorithms, protocols and interfaces to calibrate social action. Our experiences and bodies generate flows of data that enable brands to fulfil their imperatives (Andrejevic 2010). This is what should occupy our critical imaginations and actions. For the critical, ethical or informed consumer we need to argue for a recoding of the interface of media platforms along the lines Turow advocates: giving consumers access to a dashboard that expands their capacity to intervene in and recalibrate the algorithms that organise their communicative lives. For policy-makers and regulators, this would mean to shift the emphasis away from seeking to set rules about content to setting frameworks for scrutinising and governing algorithms, data and protocols of platforms. A regulatory framework is now of little consequence if it does not define and address the infrastructural dimensions and computational capacities of media. Regulatory frameworks must grapple with data architectures, algorithms, protocols and interfaces of media platforms. For activists the challenge is to invent modes of culture jamming that jam the infrastructure rather than the symbolic content of brands. Consumer activism has to learn how to hack and code to reveal and reshape the computational capacities of media. At every level, an analysis of the brand—if it is to be politically charged as regulation, activism or everyday resistance—must grapple with the interface between our bodies and their lived experience and the computational infrastructure of media. In a lecture on Sloterdijk, Latour (Latour 2011: 158) argues that to 'define humans is to define the envelopes, the life support systems ... that make it possible for them to breathe'. In the age of media infrastructure, policy-makers, resisting consumers, activists and critics need to concern themselves with the way brands affect human experience. To engage productively with these questions we need to develop ways of understanding and intervening in the infrastructural support systems humans and their everyday experiences are entangled with. Brands are not just content that travels via media, they are the media infrastructure itself. They are not just woven into our identities, they are the devices and platforms we use to navigate everyday life.

Note

1. User comments are quoted as close as possible to the original post in terms of grammar, spelling and punctuation. However, at times minor corrections are made to allow for better readability, mostly by adding punctuation.

REFERENCES

The ABAC Scheme Limited (2012). 'Best Practice for the Responsible Marketing of Alcohol Beverages in Digital Marketing', *ABAC*. Accessed December 12, 2015. Available at: http://www.abac.org.au/wp-content/uploads/2013/11/Best-Practice-in-Digital-and-Social-Media-November-2013.pdf

Andrejevic, M. (2002). The work of being watched: Interactive media and the exploitation of self-disclosure. *Critical studies in media communication*, 19(2), 230–248.

Andrejevic M. (2013). *Infoglut: How Too Much Information Is Changing the Way We Think and Know*. New York: Routledge.

Arvidsson, A. (2005). Brands a critical perspective. *Journal of Consumer Culture*, 5(2), 235–258.

Atkinson, J. (2012). 'XXXX Island: The biggest beer campaign ever?', Accessed December 12, 2015. Available at: http://www.theshout.com.au/2012/03/16/article/XXXX-Island-The-biggest-beer-campaign-ever/ADQYEKPBCA.html

The Australian Association of National Advertisers. (2015). 'The Australian Association of National Advertisers code', *AANA*. Accessed December 12, 2015. Available at: http://aana.com.au/self-regulation/codes/.

Banet-Weiser S. (2012) *Authentic TM: The Politics of Ambivalence in a Brand Culture*. New York: New York University Press.

Beck, E. (2001). 'Diageo Attempts to Reinvent the Bar in an Effort to Increase Spirits Sales, *Wall Street Journal*. Accessed December 12, 2015. Available at: http://www.wsj.com/articles/SB982887473913839492

Brodmerkel, S., & Carah, N. (2013). Alcohol brands on Facebook: the challenges of regulating brands on social media. *Journal of Public Affairs*, 13(3), pp. 272–281.

Buchbinder, D. (1994). *Masculinities and Identities*. Melbourne: Melbourne University Press.

Calo, R. (2014). Digital Market Manipulation. *82. Geo. Wash. L. Rev.*, pp. 995–1051.

Carah, N. (2014c). *Like, Comment, Share: Alcohol brand activity on Facebook*. Foundation for Alcohol Research and Education: Canberra.

Chouliaraki, L. (2013). *The ironic spectator: Solidarity in the age of post-humanitarianism*. Polity: Cambridge.

The Chronicle (2015) 'XXXX Island auction offering paradise for charity', *The Chronicle*. Accessed December 12, 2015. Available at: http://www.thechronicle.com.au/news/xxxx-island-auction-offering-paradise-charity/2801280/

Coad, D. (2002). *Gender Trouble Down Under: Australian Masculinities*. Valenciennes: Presses Universitaires de Valenciennes.

Coles, T. (2008). Finding space in the field of masculinity: Lived experiences of men's masculinities. *Journal of Sociology*, 44(3), pp. 233–248.

Connell, R. W. (1995). *Masculinities*. Cambridge, UK: Polity Press.

Connell, R. W. and Messerschmidt, J. W. (2005). Hegemonic Masculinity: Rethinking the Concept. *Gender & Society*, 19(6), pp. 829–859.

Dean, W. (2010). 'Mad Men: season one, episode 13', *The Guardian*. Accessed December 12, 2015. Available at: http://www.theguardian.com/tv-and-radio/tvandradioblog/2010/jun/17/mad-men-season-one-episode-13-finale

van Dijck, J. (2013). *The culture of connectivity: A critical history of social media*. Oxford: Oxford University Press.

Dobson, A. S. (2014). Laddishness online: The possible significations and significance of 'performative shamelessness' for young women in the post-feminist context. *Cultural Studies*, 28(1), pp. 142–164.

Field, C. (2008). Having one's cake and eating it too – an analysis of behavioural economics from a consumer policy perspective. In *Australian Government Productivity Commission: Behavioural Economics and Public Policy. Roundtable Proceedings. Productivity Commission*, Canberra, pp. 89–102.

Foundation for Alcohol Research and Education. (2015). 'Buried government report calls for overdue reform of alcohol advertising', Foundation for Alcohol Research and Education: Canberra. Accessed December 12, 2015. Available at: http://www.fare.org.au/2015/10/buried-government-report-calls-for-overdue-reform-of-alcohol-advertising/

Frank, T. (1997). *The Conquest of Cool*. Chicago: Chicago University Press.

Holt, D. (2002). Why Do Brands Cause Trouble? A Dialectical Theory of Consumer Culture and Branding. *Journal of Consumer Research*, 29(1), pp. 70–90.

Kirkby, D. (2003) Beer, glorious beer: Gender politics and Australian popular culture. *The Journal of Popular Culture*, 37(2), pp. 244–256.

Latour, B. (2011). A Cauutios Prometheus? A Few Steps Toward a Philosophy of Design with Special Attention to Peter Sloterdijk. In Schinkel, W. and Nordegraaf-Eelens, L. (eds.), *In Media Res: Peter Sloterdiks's Spherological Poetics of Being*. Amsterdam: Amsterdam University Press, pp. 151–164.

McKay, J., Emmison, M. and Mikosza, J. (2009). *Lads, Larrikins and Mates: Hegemonic Masculinities in Australian Beer Advertisements*. In Wenner, L. A. and Jackson, S. J. (eds.), *Sport, Beer and Gender. Promotional Culture and Contemporary Social Life*. New York: Peter Lang, pp. 163–179.

McQuillin, B. and Sugden, R. (2012). Reconciling normative and behavioural economics: the problems to be solved. *Soc Choice Welf 38*, pp. 553–567.

Pash, J. (2012). 'Rules are Rules', *Vimeo* 2012. Accessed December 12, 2015. Available at: http://vimeo.com/51103345

Pease, B. (2001). Moving beyond mateship: Reconstructing Australian men's practices. In Pease, B. and Pringle, K. (eds.), *A man's world: Changing men's practices in a globalized world*. London: Zed., pp. 191–204.

Rowe, D. and Gimour, C. (2009). Lubrication and Domination. Beer, Sport, Masculinity and the Australian Gender Order. In Wenner, L. A. and Jackson, S. J. (eds.), Sport, Beer and Gender. Promotional Culture and Contemporary Social Life. New York: Peter Lang, pp. 203–224.

Schroeder, J. E. and Zwick, D. (2004). Mirrors of Masculinity: Representation and Identity in Advertising Images. *Consumption, Markets and Culture*, 7(1), pp. 21–52.

Sloterdijk, P. (2013). You Must Change Your Life. trans. *Wieland Hoban. Cambridge: Polity.*

Terranova, T. (2000). Free labor: Producing culture for the digital economy. *Social text*, 18(2), pp. 33–58.

Verbeek, P. (2009). Ambient Intelligence and Persuasive Technology: The Blurring Boundaries Between Human and Technology. *Nanoethics*, (3), pp. 231–242.

Wenner, L. A. and Jackson, S. J. (2009). *Sport, Beer, and Gender in Promotional Culture: On the Dynamics of a Holy Trinity.* In Wenner, L. A. and Jackson, S. J. (eds.), *Sport, Beer and Gender. Promotional Culture and Contemporary Social Life.* New York: Peter Lang, pp. 1–34.

Wood, O. (2012). 'Calling Time on Drinking', *MRS Annual Conference.* Accessed December 12, 2015. Available at: https://mrresource.files.wordpress.com/2012/07/8.pdf

XXXX Gold (2012a). 'XXXX Island, it's the ultimate destination for mates' trips away.' Facebook post from March 19, 2012. Accessed December 12, 2015. Available at: https://www.facebook.com/XXXXGOLD/

XXXX Gold (2012b). 'If you were setting foot on XXXX Island, what's the first thing you'd do?' Facebook post from October 8, 2012. Accessed December 12, 2015. Available at: https://www.facebook.com/XXXXGOLD/

XXXX Gold (2012c). 'We all know thou shall NEVER wear budgie smugglers on XXXX Island, what else do you reckon is an Island no-go?' Facebook post from September 21, 2012. Accessed December 12, 2015. Available at: https://www.facebook.com/XXXXGOLD/

XXXX Gold (2012d). 'Brooke, we love your work!' Facebook post from October 25, 2012. Accessed December 12, 2015. Available at: https://www.facebook.com/XXXXGOLD/

XXXX Gold (2012e). 'Mates living the good life on XXXX Island'. Facebook post from November 20, 2012. Accessed December 12, 2015. Available at: https://www.facebook.com/XXXXGOLD/

Yeung, K. (2012). Nudge as Fudge. *The Modern Law Review,* 75(1), pp. 122–148.

Žižek, S. (1999). *The Ticklish Subject.* London:Verso.

Žižek, S. (2010). First as Tragedy, Then as Farce, *YouTube,* 28 July. Accessed December 12, 2015. Available at: https://www.youtube.com/watch?v=hpAMbpQ8J7g

Zwick, D., Bonsu S. and Darmody A. (2008). Putting Consumers to Work: 'Co-creation' and new marketing govern-mentality. *Journal of Consumer Culture,* 8(2), pp. 163–197.

CHAPTER 7

Conclusion

Brand machines are infrastructure, sensory apparatus and calculator. Since the creative revolution of the 1960s brands have been a 'primary cultural form' (Banet-Weiser 2012), woven into our everyday practices, imaginations and politics. They came to shape not only the symbolic environment of our experience, but more fundamentally the infrastructure through which we act in the world and affect one another. Brands make symbolic appeals, attach specific qualities to products and set out to shape the cultural resources we use to animate our lives. Even so, a critical account of brands can no longer aim at their symbolic register. Culture jamming the symbolic landscape of brands is little use. Symbolic critique is politically meaningless to savvy consumers. It becomes just another productive way of generating valuable forms of attention and dispositions in brand culture. In this book we have documented the turn of advertisers toward the infrastructural, architectural, sensory and calculative dimensions of branding. We argue that to account for how brands are embedded in the world scholars, critics, activists, policy-makers and consumers need to ask what it means to address the infrastructural, sensory and calculative components of brand machines.

The current moment is characterised by large-scale media engineering projects (McStay 2013; van Dijck 2013). Platforms such as Google and Facebook are historically distinctive as advertising-funded media institutions because rather than producing original content they produce platforms that engineer connectivity (van Dijck 2013). As we have observed, if the 'rivers of gold' that once flowed through print and broadcast media

© The Author(s) 2016   189
S. Brodmerkel, N. Carah, *Brand Machines, Sensory Media
and Calculative Culture*, DOI 10.1057/978-1-137-49656-0_7

organisations funded quality content for much of the 20th century, they now flow through media platforms where they fund research and development projects in machine learning, robotics and augmented reality. In some important respects this is a unique event in media history, where investment is made not in the production of content but in the sensory and calculative capacities of the medium. Platforms such as Google and Facebook first formed productive relationships with advertisers by offering tools to target customised audiences at scale. In their current incarnations platforms are dissolving the boundaries between advertising and other forms of content or stimuli. We argue that this effort ought to be understood as part of the drive of platforms to resolve points of friction or dysmorphia between the lived experience and living bodies of users and the calculative and sensory capacities of media technologies. Advertisers and platforms work together to incorporate brands into the infrastructure of platforms. Platforms offer advertisers the infrastructure to sense and stimulate bodies in specified times and places. Media platforms, and the mode of branding they trigger, are productively understood as engineering projects in the sense that first and foremost they create technologies for experimenting with reality. Media platforms do not enable brands to make somehow more sophisticated ideological appeals. They experiment with reality by creating devices that stimulate bodies and orchestrate social action. This system does not depend on persuading individual actors with meanings as much as it aims to observe and calibrate their action. It depends less on exerting control at the symbolic level and more on governing the infrastructure that opens and closes possibilities to specific users at certain times and places.

Advertisers are the generative energy in the platform ecosystem. The experiments and innovations of media platforms address the demands of the advertisers whose investments fund them. Google, Facebook and Instagram are media platforms whose existence depends on generating advertising revenue. The effort to experiment with platforms that intervene in reality responds to the imagined desires of advertisers. The more sophisticated a platform's capacity to orchestrate the affects and actions of users the more they can sell that capacity to advertisers. Platforms and advertisers form partnerships where they experiment with infrastructure, interfaces, protocols and algorithms. They iteratively work together to configure new ways of identifying bodies, spaces and moments that media infrastructure can sense and stimulate.

Dynamic experimentation changes the relationship between advertisers and media institutions in critical ways. No longer are advertisers just seeking to purchase units of attention or exposure from media; rather, they treat media as platforms for orchestrating ongoing loops of stimulus, adaptation and response with consumers (Lury 2004; Schüll 2012). Advertisers are also active experimenters within platform ecosystems. We have observed advertisers developing bespoke I/O devices that act as switches or transfer points between the living capacities of consumers and the calculative capacities of platforms. If the smartphone and related devices such as the wearable are the generic or backbone transfer point between living body and media platforms, then advertisers are one part of a larger effort to diffuse these transfer points into urban, natural and intimate locations. In this logic everyday objects such as underwear, bathtubs, T-shirts, bottles and islands become devices that are connected to, or address, the calculative logic of media platforms. The imperative is for us to see brands as not only the producers of symbolic mediascapes within which we *make sense* of our lives, but also as critical actors in the creation of the material infrastructure we use to *do* our everyday lives.

Brand machines depend on active participants. In this respect they follow the longer sequence of brands becoming a recognisable and durable part of culture. Brands are something that we need to handle and engage with as part of our everyday lives. Brand machines, though, change the quality and utility of participation in significant ways. Participants are not only required to incorporate pre-determined brand narratives into their life-casting, they more generally make their lives and bodies visible and available to the sensory and calculative capacities of media infrastructure. They 'plug' their bodies and living capacities into the brand machine. The participant is productive in general once they are available to be observed, sensed and affected, and prompted to stimulate, affect and act. Participation as a general availability to be sensed and stimulated is evident in both the behavioural turn of advertisers and the creation of open-ended and reflexive brands. Both strategies depend less on persuading a consumer to find a specific quality credible or authentic, and instead look to harness the productive capacity of the consumer to act, create, sense or stimulate.

Within this media system participation is not only the expression of particular ideas, but more generally the making available of the living body to experiments, calibration and modulation. Advertisers' behavioural turn illustrates their effort to bypass the faulty or inefficient meaning making of consumers in order to modulate their behaviour directly. The advertiser creates choice architecture that nudges the consumer toward intended actions, rather than attempting to persuade the consumer as a rational actor. Where brands set out to ask consumers to incorporate them into their everyday practices, narratives and identities they create infrastructure that harnesses the capacity of consumers to qualify in general. If brands can harness the capacity of consumers to qualify in general, then they are able to manage qualification as a heterogeneous and ongoing process. Meaning matters, but not in a monolithic sense. It matters because it stimulates and affects, and it prompts action that makes social life visible to the calculative capacities of media.

Brand machines comprise a human and non-human sensory apparatus. Brands depend on the creative capacities of human users to witness, apprehend, curate and publicise their lives and environment. This activity can be understood as the performance of body–machine relationships. Sensing involves both the human capacity to affect and judge and the technical capacity to convert human experience into digital information. Participation is productive as the activity of sensing and tuning living bodies and everyday life into the calculative apparatus of media. The engineering projects of media platforms are focused on expanding the sensory and calculative frontier of media. On this frontier media infrastructures are interwoven with our habitat and bodies; and our bodies are drones that weave the sensory tentacles of media into urban, social and intimate locations and moments (Andrejevic 2015). We need to develop an account of participation that allows for the expanding capacity of media to sense and calibrate the full range of physiological, discursive and affective sensations our bodies excrete and express.

The expanding capacity of media to sense and stimulate is interdependent with the escalation of its ability to calculate. Over the past decade Google and Facebook dominated the media platform ecosystem in part because of their capacity to collect, organise and process data. They developed algorithms that customised content for users and advertisers. Media platforms such as Google increasingly direct investment toward machine learning projects. The collection and storage of information unfolds in a loop with the capacity to process information. More information requires more processing power, more processing power generates the incentive for more information collection and so on. Calculation enables brand machines to manage consumer participation as an open-ended generative stimulus. The more a machine can make real-time calculation and responses, the more capable it is of harnessing a heterogeneous array of actions and impulses from participants.

Calculation is the critical element of products such as custom audiences, context-aware advertising and programmatic buying. But the calculative capacity of media platforms extends beyond targeting advertisements. Calculative media establishes the imperative that bodies and relationships be rendered visible and available as digital information. Recursive loops form between the sensory-calculative elements of media infrastructure and the bodies and locations they are entangled with. Users begin to shape their practices, bodies and material spaces in response to the calculations that media platforms make. We have argued that material objects address not only human users but also the algorithmic decisions of platforms. Material objects are created and placed in social spaces because of the ways in which configurations of data are produced for algorithms: linking users, brands and contexts of consumption together in space and time, enabling the platform to detect, categorise and respond in ongoing ways. Users, for their part, adapt their bodies and behaviour to this logic. They choose particular types of content and times of day to post it to be most visible. They sculpt, style and edit both images of the bodies and the corporeal body itself in ways that will attract desirable forms of attention. They learn to code their lived experience as data that algorithms can process. The complicated interplay between human judgement and machinic calculation that is unfolding goes beyond the targeting of advertisements. The sensory and calculative devices of media infrastructure not only serve advertisers' interests, they also reshape our social practices, spaces and even bodies.

Critical responses to brands—from policy-makers, consumers or scholars—need to train their attention on the capacity of brand machines and media infrastructure to sense, calculate and stimulate. Advertising is morphing into the process of programming the interface between living bodies and calculative machines. A contemporary theory of branding and advertising must offer a critical account of the interplay between the body in all its sensory capacities, the cultural practices of everyday life and the calculative and technical elements of media infrastructure. The sensory and calculative infrastructures of brand machines deserve our full attention.

REFERENCES

Andrejevic, M. (2015). 'Becoming Drones: Smartphone Probes and Distributed Sensing' (pp. 193–207) in Wilken, R. and Goggin, G. (eds.), *Locative Media*. Routledge: London.

Banet-Weiser S. (2012) *Authentic TM: The Politics of Ambivalence in a Brand Culture*. New York: New York University Press.

van Dijck, J. (2013). *The culture of connectivity: A critical history of social media.* Oxford: Oxford University Press.

McStay, A. (2013). *Creativity and Advertising.* Affect, Events and Process. London: Routledge.

Schüll, ND. (2012). *Addiction by Design: Machine Gambling in Las Vegas.* Princeton: Princeton University Press.

Index[1]

[1] **Note**: Page number followed by "n" denotes

© The Author(s) 2016
S. Brodmerkel, N. Carah, *Brand Machines, Sensory Media and Calculative Culture*, DOI 10.1057/978-1-137-49656-0

GPSR Compliance
The European Union's (EU) General Product Safety Regulation (GPSR) is a set
of rules that requires consumer products to be safe and our obligations to
ensure this.

If you have any concerns about our products, you can contact us on

ProductSafety@springernature.com

In case Publisher is established outside the EU, the EU authorized
representative is:

Springer Nature Customer Service Center GmbH
Europaplatz 3
69115 Heidelberg, Germany